The Apostolic Fathers

The Apostolic Fathers

A New Translation

Translated and Edited by

Rick Brannan

LEXHAM PRESS

The Apostolic Fathers: A New Translation
Translated and edited by Rick Brannan
Copyright 2017 Lexham Press

Lexham Press, 1313 Commercial St., Bellingham, WA 98225

LexhamPress.com

ISBN 9781683590644

Cover Art: Benedetto di Bindo, *Madonna of Humility and St. Jerome*, 1400–1405. Public domain.

For Amy, Ella, Lucas, and Josiah

Contents

− Introduction

Several translations of the writings of the Apostolic Fathers have been published over the past 150 years. The major translations available today are those of Michael W. Holmes and Bart D. Ehrman. These both are excellent translations, available in print (and, in the case of Holmes, electronically), with excellent editions of the Greek. Holmes' edition in particular has a concise and useful textual apparatus.

ABOUT THE TRANSLATION

This translation is not meant to replace either Holmes' or Ehrman's editions in print. Instead, my goal in creating a new English translation was to create a tighter and more transparent relationship with the underlying Greek text. As this translation has its genesis with my *Apostolic Fathers Greek-English Interlinear*, it began with a direct relationship with every word and phrase of the underlying Greek. From here, the English translation was reviewed and edited to become more readable yet still retain its relationship with the Greek text. Finally, using tools provided by Logos Bible Software, the English text was completely re-aligned with the Greek text, word by word, phrase by phrase. When the English text is read with the reverse interlinearized Greek text displayed in Logos Bible Software, the result is an English translation that shows exactly where each word and phrase has its origin.

This level of alignment becomes more useful in reading and particularly when studying how words and structures found in the New Testament are used in contemporary literature. And this, to my mind, can help the writings of the Apostolic Fathers play a larger role in one's study of the New Testament and Septuagint, which is my larger goal.

NOTES IN THE TRANSLATION

Notes in the translation offer cross-references, deal with matters of translation, note text-critical issues, and discuss word meanings. Further, where available English commentaries or editions of the Apostolic Fathers include material deemed helpful, notes include brief quotations. Unless otherwise noted, these notes are from material by the mentioned author (e.g. Lightfoot, Meecham, Holmes, Ehrman, Kraft) on the verse in question.

GREEK TEXT UNDERLYING THE TRANSLATION

The Greek text underlying this translation is Kirsopp Lake's edition, originally published in the Loeb Classical Library:

Lake, Kirsopp. *The Apostolic Fathers*. 2 vols. Loeb Classical Library 24–25.
    Cambridge, MA: Harvard University Press, 1912–13.

Most areas where there are serious differences between Lake and the other available Greek editions (those of Holmes, Lightfoot, and Ehrman) are discussed in notes.

LATIN TEXT UNDERLYING THE TRANSLATION

The Latin text underlying portions of this translation extant only in Latin is also that of Kirsopp Lake. In these areas (some portions of *Polycarp to the Philippians* and the *Shepherd of Hermas*) the translation and notes are also largely those of Lake, with some modifications.

ABOUT THE WRITINGS

The writings in the corpus now referred to as the "Apostolic Fathers" are diverse and, among many today, relatively unfamiliar. The below descriptions are brief and altogether inadequate to paint a full picture of the details of each writing, but should serve as brief introductions to their contents and import. This material is taken from my article "Apostolic Fathers" in the *Lexham Bible Dictionary* and used with permission. Most citations are to introductions (Jefford, Pratscher) or editions (Holmes) as these will be easiest to locate and obtain for further study into these documents of the early church.

FIRST CLEMENT

What is known as "First Clement" is actually a letter (epistle) written from the Roman church to the church in Corinth. Tradition views Clement, who was either the second or third bishop of Rome, as the author. It was likely written during the reign of the emperor Domitian, between 81–96 AD (Jefford, *Reading*, 98). The letter was written due to the Corinthians' seemingly unwarranted expulsion of their leaders. The letter from Rome advocates reinstitution of the leaders and restoration of peace within the body. To make the case, the letter uses extensive quotations from the Septuagint (Job, Genesis and Isaiah are popular sources) and possible quotations and allusions from the New Testament (Gospel tradition and Hebrews).

SECOND CLEMENT

In recent history, the writing known as "Second Clement" has been distanced from Clement himself and titled "An Ancient Christian Homily." There is no internal evidence for associating this writing with the same Clement likely responsible for First Clement; this is likely a happenstance of transmission as all known manuscripts including Second Clement place it immediately following First Clement. The author is unknown, and the homily is typically dated between 120–140 AD (Jefford, *Reading*, 117) though some date it earlier, perhaps even contemporary with First Clement, between 98–100 AD (Donfried, *Setting*, 1–48).

The homily, likely based on Isaiah 54, includes reference to Scripture, interpretation, and exhortation. It is the earliest known example of a homily outside of the New Testament, and as such is a valuable example of how early Christians used Scripture in their preaching and teaching.

THE IGNATIAN LETTERS

This collection of letters was written by Ignatius, bishop of Antioch, while he was being transported from Antioch to Rome to stand trial for being a Christian. He would become a martyr in Rome. These letters are mentioned by Polycarp and date from the earliest of times. Eusebius places Ignatius' martyrdom in the middle to end of the reign of Trajan, between 110–117 AD. Six letters are to churches (Ephesians, Magnesians, Trallians, Romans, Philadelphians and Smyrnaeans) and one is to a person, Polycarp, the bishop of Smyrna.

The letters are known in three different forms, commonly called the "long recension," the "middle recension" and the "short recension." Most today hold the middle recension (the corpus of seven letters described above) to be the most accurate representation of Ignatius' letters. The long recension has witnesses in Greek and Latin. It includes expanded forms of the seven letters of the middle recension as well as six additional letters: one each to Tarsus, to Antioch, to Philippi, to the bishop Hero who succeeded Ignatius at Antioch; and two letters associated with Mary of Cassobola (Jefford, *Reading*, 54). The short recension is an edited collection of only three letters: to Polycarp, to Ephesus, and to Rome; it is typically held to be an abridgment of either the middle or longer recension (Jefford, *Reading*, 54). Some hold that all forms of the Ignatian corpus are forgeries; R.M. Hübner and T. Lechner are representative of this position (Pratscher, *Apostolic Fathers*, 94).

Ignatius frequently references Pauline epistles. He encourages churches he was able to visit while being transported as a prisoner, argues against Docetism, advocates for a strong bishop, and implores the church of Rome to not intervene in his martyrdom.

POLYCARP TO THE PHILIPPIANS

Polycarp is unique among those whose writings are included in the Apostolic Fathers because there are multiple testimonies from multiple sources concerning him and his life. His letter to the Philippians is included, the letter from Ignatius to Polycarp is included, and the account of his death, the Martyrdom of Polycarp, is included. Polycarp also has connections with the previous and succeeding generations of Christians. By tradition he is considered to be a disciple of the Apostle John, and as a child Ireneaus met with Polycarp and records some of his teaching (Hill, *Lost Teaching*, 12).

The composition history of Polycarp's letter to the Philippians is cloudy. Two primary theories exist. One holds that the letter was composed around the time of Ignatius' death, between 110–113 AD. The other holds that most of what is known as Polycarp's letter (chapters 1–12 or, in some theories, 1–12 and 14) was written in 135 AD while a smaller portion (chapters 13–14 or, in some theories, 13) was written closer to the time of Ignatius' death. The problem involves Polycarp's reference to Ignatius in §9 as a martyr, but in

§13 he requests further information about Ignatius from the Philippians. Those who hold the two letter view (Harrison, *Polycarp's Two Epistles*, 15–20) see this as a chronological conflict. Those who hold the one letter view, however, are able to reconcile the differences between §9 and §13 (Pratscher, *Apostolic Fathers*, 120–121).

Polycarp's letter to the Philippians is remarkable for its use of the New Testament. Polycarp's language is infused with the language of the New Testament and replete with quotations and allusions to several New Testament sources.

MARTYRDOM OF POLYCARP

The Martyrdom of Polycarp is formally a letter from the church at Philomelium to the church at Smyrna, but it functions as one of the earliest known martryologies, telling the story of the death of Polycarp, bishop of Smyrna.

The day and time of Polycarp's martyrdom is recorded as on "the second day of the first part of the month of Xanthicus, the seventh day before the calends of March, a great sabbath at the eighth hour" (MPoly 21). This converts to February 23, at around 2:00 in the afternoon. The year of Polycarp's death is not provided, but MPoly 21 also notes that Statius Quadratus was proconsul at this time, and his proconsulship can be reliably dated to 154–155 AD (Jefford, *Reading*, 87–88). As a result, most date Polycarp's death to February 23, 155. Because the internal testimony of the Martyrdom of Polycarp leads the reader to believe that it was composed by eyewitnesses, the date of composition is likely between 155–160 AD.

The Martyrdom of Polycarp tells the story of Polycarp's arrest and subsequent death in a stadium. The telling of the story contains many miraculous elements, several of which appear to be parallels with gospel images from the arrest, crucifixion and death of Christ (Jefford, *Reading*, 93–95).

DIDACHE

The formal title is "The Teaching of the Twelve Apostles" but it is commonly known as the Didache, from the Greek word διδαχή (*didache*), which means "teaching." It was only known from fragments and brief citations until 1873, when a manuscript (dated to 1056 AD) was recovered that contained the whole of the text (Kraft 1992, 2:198).

The Didache is a handbook for Christians, giving instructions on how to act (§§1–6) and how to worship (§§7–15), ending with a section on eschatology (§16). Intertextual relations abound. Many see similarities between the Didache and Matthew (Jefford, *Reading*, 47–49), but other documents (e.g. Epistle of Barnabas 18–20) share the "Two Ways" material of Didache 1–6.

Because of the intertextual relationships and the uncertainty of which writings are dependent on each other, dating the Didache is tricky. It is safest to establish a range of 80–120 AD (Jefford, *Reading*, 32).

EPISTLE OF BARNABAS

The title claims Barnabas as author, but the text itself is silent on the question of authorship. Either the text is pseudepigraphal, written by someone claiming to be Barnabas in an attempt to gain authority, or later tradition associated Barnabas with the text. The time of composition is as mysterious as the authorship. Jefford gives a range from 70–135 AD and prefers the smaller range of 96–100 AD (Jefford, *Reading*, 11). The contents are fascinating as they preserve an allegorical investigation of scripture for posterity.

EPISTLE TO DIOGNETUS

Unique amongst the Apostolic Fathers due to its apologetic nature, this document provides a glimpse into how Greek pagans and Hellenistic Jews viewed Christianity, and how Christians portrayed themselves to Greek pagans and Hellenistic Jews curious about the new religion of Christianity. The author is unknown, though some have suggested Quadratus (Andreissen 1947, 129–136). Recently, Polycarp has been suggested as well (Hill, *Lost Teaching*, 128–160). Diognetus is commonly dated between 150–180, though this is by no means universally accepted. A date range of 117–310 AD is more appropriate (Jefford, *Reading*, 159).

Like Polycarp's letter to the Philippians, there are questions as to the composition history of Diognetus. There are strong reasons to consider it a combination of two different documents (§§1–10 and §§11–12). A lacunae exists between §10 and §11, and some recognize the first section as an apology and the second as a homily; with requisite differences in vocabulary and style (Pratscher, *Apostolic Fathers*, 199). However, Hill has recently argued that Diognetus is to be seen as a unified document (Hill,

Lost Teaching, 106–126), addressing various concerns about differences in style and vocabulary.

The Epistle to Diognetus is a fascinating peek at arguments for Christianity in opposition to paganism and Judaism in the early centuries of Christianity.

SHEPHERD OF HERMAS

With 114 chapters distributed among three major sections (Visions, Mandates, and Parables), the Shepherd of Hermas is a long and complex text with a long and complex history. But it was popular in the second and third centuries (Holmes, *Apostolic Fathers*, 442) and has been preserved in various editions, likely because it wrestled with real questions that real people had, such as the problem of sin after baptism.

Hermas is commonly considered to have been composed in two major parts. The first part, consisting of Visions 1–4 (§§1–24), is routinely dated at the end of the first century (90–100 AD). The remaining portion, consisting of Vision 5–Similitude 10 (§§25–114) in the early to middle second century (100–154 AD) (Jefford, *Reading*, 134).

There are two different numbering systems used by editions of the Shepherd of Hermas. The first, usually seen in older editions of the text, divides the text into its three major components or parts (Visions, Mandates, and Parables). Each of these are divided into sections, subsections, and verses. In this edition, the sections and subsections of the classic numbering system are represented in the section headings. A simplified chapter and verse numbering system also exists. The part, section, and subsection numbering of the classic system map to the chapter of the simplified system, with both systems treating verse units similarly. In this edition, the simplified system is represented by the in-text numbering. As an example, the heading "3.5 About the Stones in the Tower" in the Visions section (Vis. 3.5) maps directly to the simplified system's chapter 13. Both Vis. 3.5.1 and Hermas 13.1 point to the same material.

— Bibliography

Andriessen, P. 1947. "The Authorship of the Epistula ad Diognetum." *Vigiliae Christianae* 1:129–136.

Arndt, William, Frederick W. Danker, and Walter Bauer. *A Greek-English Lexicon of the New Testament and Other Early Christian Literature.* 3rd ed. Chicago: University of Chicago Press, 2000.

Bird, Michael F. "The Reception of Paul in the Epistle to Diognetus," in *Paul and the Second Century: The Legacy of Paul's Life, Letters, and Teaching*, edited by Michael F. Bird and Joseph R. Dodson. LNTS; London: T&T Clark, 2011.

Brannan, Rick. "Apostolic Fathers," in *Lexham Bible Dictionary*, edited by John D. Barry and Lazarus Wentz. Bellingham, WA: Lexham Press, 2016.

Donfried, Karl P. *The Setting of Second Clement in Early Christianity*, Leiden: E.J. Brill, 1974.

Edgecomb, Kevin P. "1 Clement" Online: http://www.bombaxo.com/1clement.html. Accessed September 25, 2011.

Ehrman, Bart D. *The Apostolic Fathers.* 2 vols. Loeb Classical Library 24–25. Cambridge, MA: Harvard University Press, 2003.

Holmes, Michael W. *The Apostolic Fathers: Greek Texts and English Translations.* Third Edition. Grand Rapids, MI: Baker Academic, 2007.

Grant, Robert M., and H.H. Graham. *First and Second Clement.* Vol 2 of *The Apostolic Fathers*, edited by R.M. Grant. New York: Nelson, 1965.

Gregory, Andrew, and Christopher Tuckett, eds. *The New Testament and the Apostolic Fathers: The Reception of the New Testament in the Apostolic Fathers.* London: Oxford University Press, 2005.

Gregory, Andrew, and Christopher Tuckett, eds. *The New Testament and the Apostolic Fathers: Trajectories through the New Testament and the*

Apostolic Fathers. London: Oxford University Press, 2005.

Harrison, P.N. *Polycarp's Two Epistles to the Philippians*. Cambridge: Cambridge University Press, 1936.

Hill, Charles E. *From the Lost Teaching of Polycarp: Identifying Irenaeus' Apostolic Presbyter and the Author of Ad Diognetum*. WUNT I 186. Tübingen: Mohr Siebeck, 2006.

Jefford, Clayton N., ed. *Reading the Apostolic Fathers: An Introduction*. Peabody, MA: Hendrickson, 1994.

Kraft, Robert A. *Barnabas and the Didache*. Vol 3 of *The Apostolic Fathers*, edited by R.M. Grant. New York: Nelson, 1965.

Kraft, Robert A. 1992. "Didache." Pages 197-198 in vol. 2 of *Anchor Yale Bible Dictionary*. Edited by David Noel Friedman. 6 vols. New York: Doubleday, 1992.

Lake, Kirsopp. *The Apostolic Fathers*. 2 vols. Loeb Classical Library 24-25. Cambridge, MA: Harvard University Press, 1912-1913.

Liddell, Henry George, Robert Scott, Henry Stuart Jones, and Roderick McKenzie. *A Greek-English Lexicon*. Rev. and augm. throughout. Oxford; New York: Clarendon Press; Oxford University Press, 1996.

Lightfoot, J.B. *The Apostolic Fathers*. Part 1, *S. Clement of Rome*. 2nd ed. 2 vols London: Macmillan, 1890.

Lightfoot, J.B. *The Apostolic Fathers*. Part 2, *S. Ignatius; S. Polycarp*. 2nd ed. 3 vols. London: Macmillan, 1889.

Louw, Johannes P., and Eugene Albert Nida. *Greek-English Lexicon of the New Testament: Based on Semantic Domains*. 2nd edition. New York: United Bible Societies, 1989.

Meecham, Henry G. *The Epistle to Diognetus: The Greek Text with Introduction, Translation and Notes*. Manchester: Manchester University Press, 1949.

Niederwimmer, Kurt, and Harold W. Attridge. *The Didache : A Commentary*. Hermeneia—a critical and historical commentary on the Bible. Minneapolis: Fortress Press, 1998.

Osiek, Carolyn, and Helmut Koester. *Shepherd of Hermas : A Commentary*. Hermeneia—a critical and historical commentary on the Bible. Minneapolis: Fortress Press, 1999.

Pratscher, Wilhelm, ed. *The Apostolic Fathers: An Introduction*. Waco: Baylor University Press, 2010.

Schoedel, William R., and Helmut Koester. *Ignatius of Antioch : A Commentary on the Letters of Ignatius of Antioch*. Hermeneia—a critical and historical commentary on the Bible. Philadelphia: Fortress Press, 1985.

Spicq, Ceslas, and James D. Ernest. *Theological Lexicon of the New Testament*. Peabody, MA.: Hendrickson, 1994.

Varner, William. *The Way of the Didache: The First Christian Handbook*. Lanham, MD: University Press of America. 2007.

— *The First Letter of Clement to the Corinthians*

SALUTATION

The church of God which temporarily resides in Rome, to the church of God which temporarily resides in Corinth, those who are called *and* sanctified by the will of God through our Lord Jesus Christ. Grace and peace from Almighty God through Jesus Christ be multiplied to you.

CORINTH'S PAST

1.1 Because of the sudden[a] and repeated misfortunes and calamities that have happened to us, we realize that *we have been* somewhat slow to pay attention to the events disputed among you, beloved, the abominable and unholy rebellion, both foreign and strange to the elect of God, which a few reckless and arrogant people[b] have kindled to such a state of frenzy that your name, honorable and well known and ₗworthy of everyone's loveₗ[c] has been greatly slandered. 2 For who, having stayed with you, has not approved your most excellent and reliable faith? Who has not admired your prudent[d] and gentle piety in Christ? And who has not proclaimed your magnificent custom of hospitality? And who has not blessed your

---

a. Of these "sudden and repeated misfortunes and calamities," Lightfoot comments: "This language accurately describes the persecution which the Roman Christians endured under Domitian. Their treatment by this emperor was capricious, and the attacks upon them were repeated. While the persecution of Nero was one fierce and wholesale onslaught in which the passions of the multitude were enlisted on the emperor's side, Domitian on the other hand made use of legal forms and arraigned the Christians from time to time on various paltry charges."

b. On the rendering of this word, Lightfoot notes: "Not simply 'persons' but 'ringleaders.'" He points to other usage in 1 Cl 47 and also Ign *Magn* 6 that show Clement's use of πρόσωπον could be pejorative.

c. Literally "worthy of love of all people"

d. 1 Tim 3:2; Titus 1:8; 2:2, 5

perfect and certain knowledge? [3] For you did all things impartially,[a] and you walked in the lawful ways[b] of God, being obedient to your rulers and rendering appropriate honor to the older ones among you. You instructed the younger ones to think both moderate and honorable *thoughts*. You commanded the women to accomplish all things with a blameless, honorable, and pure conscience, ₁feeling appropriate affection for₁[c] their own husbands, and you taught *them* being in the rule[d] of obedience to manage the things of the household[e] honorably, with all sensibility.

THE SPIRIT POURED ON CORINTH

[2.1] And you were all humble-minded, in no way being boastful, being submissive rather than forcing submission, giving more gladly than receiving, being satisfied[f] with the provisions of Christ,[g] and paying attention to his words you have carefully stored away in your innermost being, and his sufferings were before your eyes. [2] Thus a deep and luxurious peace[h] was given to all, and an insatiable desire for good deeds,[i] and a full outpouring of the Holy Spirit was upon all of you. [3] And filled with holy plans, in great eagerness with pious confidence, you stretched out your hands to the Almighty God, imploring him to be merciful if ₁you inadvertently committed any sin₁.[j] [4] It was your struggle,[k] both day and night, on behalf of the whole fellowship of believers,[l] to save the total number of his elect with mercy and conscientiousness. [5] You were sincere and innocent and bore no malice for one another. [6] All rebellion and all division were detestable to you. You mourned about the sin of your neighbor. You considered his

---

a. 1 Pet 1:17

b. Lev 18:3; 20:23; Jer 24:4; Ezek 5:6, 7; 20:18

c. Literally "feeling affection for appropriately"

d. Lightfoot notes that the thought here is "not overstepping the line, not transgressing the limits, of obedience."

e. Lightfoot glosses as "to ply their work in the house."

f. Acts 20:35

g. Χριστοῦ Lake, Ehrman] Θεοῦ Lightfoot, Holmes. The difference is between "the provisions of Christ" and "the provisions of God."

h. 4 Macc 3:20

i. 1 Pet 4:19

j. Literally "if you committed any sin unwillingly"

k. Col 2:1

l. 1 Pet 2:17; 5:9

shortcomings *to be* your own. [7] You were without regret in every good deed, ready[a] for every good work. [8] Having been adorned with a most excellent and honorable citizenship, you accomplished all things in the fear of him.[b] The commandments and the regulations of the Lord were written on the tablets of your heart.[c]

THE DEGRADATION OF CORINTH

[3.1] All glory and growth were given to you, and that which was written was fulfilled: "My beloved ate and drank and became large and grew fat and kicked."[d] [2] From this *came* jealousy[e] and envy[f] and strife and rebellion, persecution and insurrection,[g] war and captivity. [3] So the dishonorable were stirred up against the honorable,[h] the disreputable against the reputable, the foolish against the wise, the young against the old.[i] [4] Because of this, righteousness and peace are far removed *from you;*[j] each of you has left behind the fear of God and become dim-sighted in faith in him, and neither walks in the lawful ways of his commandments nor lives life according to what is fitting in Christ.[k] Instead each of you walks according to the desires of his wicked heart, having taken up unjust and ungodly jealousy, through which also death has entered into the world.[l]

---

a. Titus 3:1

b. Here Lake supplies "of God" based on the Latin. While this may be the sense, the Greek editions only witness the pronoun here.

c. Prov 7:3; also 2 Cor 3:3

d. Deut 32:15

e. On the progression of terminology, Lightfoot notes: "The words occur in an ascending scale: firstly, the inward sentiment of division (ζῆλος developing into φθόνος); next, the outward demonstration of this (ἔρις developing into στάσις); lastly, the direct conflict and its results (διωγός, ἀκαταστασία, πόλεμος, αἰχμαλωσία)."

f. Gal 5:20, 21

g. Luke 21:9; 2 Cor 12:20; Jas 3:16.

h. Isa 3:5

i. Isa 3:5

j. Isa 59:14

k. Phil 1:27

l. Wis 2:24

EXAMPLES OF JEALOUSY
FROM ANCIENT TIMES

4.1 For thus it is written,[a] "And it came about after some days Cain offered a sacrifice to God of the fruit of the soil, and Abel himself also offered of the firstborn of the sheep and of their fat. **2** And God looked with favor upon Abel and upon his gifts, but upon Cain and upon his sacrifices, he had no concern. **3** And Cain was greatly distressed and ˌwas downcast,[b] **4** And God said to Cain, 'Why are you deeply grieved, and why ˌare you downcast,?[c] If you offered rightly but did not divide rightly,[d] did you not sin? **5** Remain quiet; he will turn to you and you will rule over him.' **6** And Cain said to Abel his brother, 'Let us go to the field.' And it came about when they were in the field, Cain rose up against Abel his brother and killed him."[e] **7** You see, brothers, jealousy and envy brought about a brother's murder. **8** Because of jealousy our father Jacob ran away from the presence of Esau, his brother.[f] **9** Jealousy caused Joseph to be persecuted to the point of death, and to come into slavery.[g] **10** Jealousy compelled Moses to flee from the presence of Pharaoh, king of Egypt, when he heard from his fellow countryman, "Who appointed you a judge or a ruler over us? Do you want to kill me ˌin the same way,[h] you killed the Egyptian yesterday?"[i] **11** Because of jealousy Aaron and Miriam had to stay outside of the camp.[j] **12** Jealousy brought down Dathan and Abiram to Hades while still alive because they rebelled against the servant of God, Moses.[k] **13** Because of jealousy David did not only incur envy from foreigners but also was persecuted by Saul king of Israel.[l]

---

a. Gen 4:3–8
b. Literally, "his face fell"
c. Literally, "is your face fallen"
d. 2 Tim 2:15
e. Gen 4:3–8
f. Gen 27:41–28:5
g. Gen 37
h. Literally, "in which manner"
i. Exod 2:14
j. Num 12
k. Num 16
l. 1 Sam 18

MORE RECENT EXAMPLES: PETER AND PAUL

5.1 But that we may cease from the ancient examples, let us come to those who became athletes near *to our own time*;[a] let us take the noble examples from our generation. **2** Because of jealousy and envy, the greatest and most righteous pillars of the church[b] were persecuted and they competed until death. **3** Let us set before our eyes the good apostles: **4** Peter, who because of unrighteous jealousy, not once or twice but many times endured hardship, and thus having given his testimony[c] he went to the place of glory he deserved. **5** Because of jealousy and strife, Paul pointed the way to[d] the prize of endurance. **6** Having borne chains seven times,[e] having been exiled, having been stoned,[f] having been a preacher[g] in both the east and in the west, he received the noble fame of his faith. **7** Having taught righteousness to the whole world and having come to the limits of the west and having given his testimony before the rulers, thus he was set free from the world and was taken up to the holy place, having become the greatest example of endurance.

THE EFFECT OF JEALOUSY

6.1 To these men who live devoutly a great multitude of the elect was gathered, who, having suffered many mistreatments and tortures because of jealousy, have become the best example among us. **2** Because of jealousy women were being persecuted as Danaids and Dirce,[h] suffering severe and

---

a. This "near" is of a temporal nature, given the contrast between ancient times and "our generation."

b. Gal 2:9; 1 Tim 3:15; Rev 3:12

c. Lightfoot has an extensive note on the use of μαρτυρέω, and how in early times it cannot be automatically assumed to represent what became known as "martyrdom." The best translation here is more conservative, implying that Peter was eventually killed as a result of persecution but not using "martyr" or "martyrdom" in a technical sense.

d. Lightfoot also explains this as "taught by his example."

e. 2 Cor 11:23–24

f. Acts 14:19; 2 Cor 11:25

g. 2 Tim 1:11

h. The phrase Δαναΐδες καὶ Δίρκαι is problematic and the source of endless speculation and conjecture. Greek editions testify to it uniformly, but its interpretation is the realm of guesswork. Holmes' summary is perhaps the most concise and informative: "In ancient mythology, the daughters of Danaus were given as prizes to the winners of a race; thus it is likely that Danaids is a reference to Christian women being raped prior to being martyred. Dirce died by being tied to the horns of a bull and dragged to death." Whatever the exact intent of the

unholy mistreatments; they finished steadfastly the race of faith, and the weak[a] in body received a noble prize. [3] Jealousy has estranged wives from husbands and has nullified what was spoken by our father Adam, "This is now bone of my bones and flesh of my flesh."[b] [4] Jealousy and strife[c] have overthrown great cities and have uprooted great nations.

REPENT FROM JEALOUSY

[7.1] We write these things, beloved, not only admonishing you but also reminding ourselves, for we are in the same arena and the same struggle[d] confronts us. [2] Therefore let us leave behind vain and futile[e] thoughts and let us come to the renowned and honorable rule of our tradition, [3] and let us see what is good and what is pleasing and what is acceptable before our maker. [4] Let us look intently at the blood of Christ, and let us know that it is precious to his Father, because, being poured out for our salvation, it brought[f] the grace of repentance to all the world. [5] Let us review all the generations and let us learn that from generation to generation[g] the Master[h] gives a place of repentance[i] to those who intend to turn to him. [6] Noah[j] preached repentance, and those who obeyed were saved. [7] Jonah[k] preached

---

author, referring to women being persecuted "as Danaids and Dirce" was severe, describing some horrible aspect of the persecution of Christian women.

a. 1 Pet 3:7

b. Gen 2:23

c. Rom 13:13; 2 Cor 12:20; Gal 5:20

d. Phil 1:30

e. Isa 30:7; Hos 12:1; Job 20:18

f. The sense of "to bring" is not witnessed in the NT. BDAG notes it is to bring or to bear "something in imagery of one who is under a burden" and further explains of this instance in 1 Cl that: "Here the blood of Christ is viewed as capable of bearing a monumental burden of χάρις that benefits the entire world."

g. Esth 9:27; Ps 48:11; 89:1

h. On the use of δεσπότης applied to the Father, Lightfoot notes: "Very rarely applied to the Father in the New Testament (Luke 2:29; Acts 4:24; Rev 6:10; and one or two doubtful passages) but occurring in this one epistle some twenty times or more. The idea of subjection to God is thus very prominent in Clement, while the idea of sonship, on which the Apostolic writers dwell so emphatically, is kept in the background. ... This fact is perhaps due in part to the subject of the epistle, which required Clement to emphasize the duty of submission; but it must be ascribed in some degree to the spirit of the writer himself."

i. Wis 12:10

j. Gen 7; 2 Pet 2:5; 1 Pet 3:20

k. Jonah 3; Matt 12:41

destruction to the Ninevites, but those who repented made appeasement for their sin to God through supplication and received salvation, although being aliens[a] from God.

THE CALL OF ISRAEL TO REPENT

8.1 The ministers of the grace of God spoke through the Holy Spirit about repentance. 2 And even the Master of everything himself spoke about repentance with an oath: "For as I live, says the Lord, I do not desire the death of the sinner so much as his repentance,"[b] also adding a generous opinion, 3 "Repent, people of Israel, from your lawlessness. Say to the sons of my people, 'If your sins stretch from the earth up to the heaven, and if they are redder than scarlet[c] and blacker than sackcloth, and you turn to me with your whole heart, and say, "Father, I will listen to you as a holy people."'"[d] 4 And in another place he says as follows: "Wash, and be clean. Put away wickedness from your souls before my eyes. Cease from your wicked deeds. Learn to do good. Seek out justice. Rescue the mistreated. Render a decision for the orphan and vindicate widows. And come and let us reason together, says the Lord. And if your sins are as crimson, I will make them white as snow. And if they are as scarlet, I will make them white as wool. And if you are willing and you listen to me, you will eat the good things of the land. But if you are not willing and you do not listen to me, a sword will destroy you, for the mouth of the Lord has spoken these things."[e] 5 Therefore intending all his beloved to have a share in repentance, he established it by his almighty will.

THE EXAMPLES OF ENOCH AND NOAH

9.1 Therefore let us obey his magnificent and glorious will and, having become suppliants of his mercy and goodness, let us fall down before *him*

---

a. Eph 2:12

b. Ezek 33:11

c. On the use of κόκκος ("seed") to indicate a reddish color, BDAG comments: "Formerly thought to be a berry, the kermes, a female scale insect (similar to the cochineal), clings to the leaves of an oak tree. The dried bodies of these insects were used by the ancients to prepare a purplish-red dye."

d. On the source of this quotation, Holmes notes, "Possibly a loose paraphrase of Ezekiel 33, or from an apocryphal work attributed to Ezekiel."

e. Isa 1:16-20

and let us turn to his compassion, abandoning the fruitless toil and the strife and the jealousy that leads to death. ² Let us look intently at those who perfectly served his magnificent glory.ᵃ ³ Let us consider Enoch who, being found righteous in obedience, was changedᵇ and death did not find him.ᶜ ⁴ Noah, being found faithful, proclaimed renewal to the world byᵈ his service, and through him the Master saved the living beings which entered in harmonyᵉ into the ark.ᶠ

THE EXAMPLE OF ABRAHAM

10.1 Abraham, being called "the friend,"ᵍ was found to be faithful in his obedience to the words of God. ² This one, he went out by obedience from his country and from his relatives and from the house of his father so that, leaving behind a little country and weak relatives and a small house, he might inherit the promises of God. For he says to him: ³ "Depart from your country and from your relatives and from the house of your father into the country which I will show you, and I will make you into a great nation and I will bless you and I will magnify your name and you will be blessed. And I will bless those who bless you and I will curse those who curse you, and in you all the nations of the earth will be blessed."ʰ ⁴ And again, when he was separated from Lot, God said to him, "Lift up your eyes, look from the place where you are now to the north and the south and the east and to the sea; for all the land that you see, I will give it to you and to your seed forever.ⁱ ⁵ And I will make your seed like the dust of the earth. If anyone

---

a. 2 Pet 1:17

b. Editions translate this various ways. Lake has "was translated"; Holmes has "was taken up"; and Ehrman has "was transported to another place." As far as what Clement intends, all that can be said is that Enoch changed in some way, and he eluded death.

c. Gen 5:24; Heb 11:5

d. Editions translate this verse differently as the attachment of the prepositional phrase is ambiguous. It could be either "Noah, being found faithful by his service" or "Noah, being found faithful, proclaimed renewal to the world by his service."

e. Lightfoot notes that this is "An indirect reference to the feuds at Corinth. Even the dumb animals set an example of concord."

f. Gen 6–9; Heb 11:7

g. Jas 2:23; 2 Chr 20:7; Isa 41:8

h. Gen 12:1–3

i. Literally "as far as the age"

is able to number the dust of the earth, then your seed will be numbered."[a]
[6] And again it says, "God led out Abraham and said to him, 'Look up to heaven and count the stars. If you are able to count them, so ‖will your seed be numbered‖.'[b] And Abraham believed God and it was credited to him as righteousness."[c] [7] Because of faith and hospitality a son was given to him in his old age, and in obedience he offered him as a sacrifice to God on the mountain which he showed to him.[d]

THE EXAMPLE OF LOT AND HIS WIFE

[11.1] Because of hospitality and godliness Lot was rescued from Sodom when the entire neighboring region was judged through fire[e] and brimstone; the Master made clear that he does not forsake those who hope upon him. But he will deliver those ‖who have another allegiance‖[fg] to punishment and torture. [2] For having gone away with him, his wife ‖changed her mind‖[h] and *was* not in harmony; a sign was made to this *end* so that she became a pillar of salt even to this day[i] to make known to all that the double-minded[j] and those who doubt concerning the power of God will be for judgment and for a warning to all generations.

THE EXAMPLE OF RAHAB

[12.1] Because of faith and hospitality Rahab the prostitute was rescued.[k] [2] For the spies were sent out by Joshua ‖the son of Nun‖[lm] to Jericho, the king of

---

a. Gen 13:14–16

b. Literally "will be your seed"

c. Gen 15:5–6; Rom 4:3

d. Gen 22

e. Isa 66:16

f. Literally "who have turned aside"

g. This word literally has to do with "being inclined away from the perpendicular," used "of buildings 'leaning to one side'" (BDAG). Lightfoot glosses as "swerving aside" and notes it was usually used in a bad sense, as here.

h. Literally "held a different opinion"

i. Gen 19:26; Wis 10:7

j. Jas 1:8; 4:8

k. Josh 2; cf. Heb 11:31; Jam 2:25

l. Literally "of the Nun"

m. The phrase "Joshua, son of Nun" is used in the OT (cf. Num 32:12; Deut 32:44; Josh 6:6). Note that the Greek for "Joshua" and "Jesus" is equivalent; the specification of "Joshua, son of Nun" could also be here to disambiguate from Jesus.

the land knew that they had come to spy out their land, and he sent out men who were to seize them, so that having seized them, they might put them to death. ³ Therefore the hospitable Rahab, having welcomed[a] them, hid *them* in the upper level, under the stalks of flax.[b] ⁴ And the men from the king came and said, "The spies of our land came in to you; lead them out, for the king has so ordered." She answered, "Indeed, the men whom you seek came to me, but they immediately departed and went on their way," ₎pointing them in the wrong direction₎.[c] ⁵ And she said to the men, "₎I certainly know₎[d] that the Lord God is handing over this land to you, for fear and trembling[e] of you have fallen upon those who dwell in it. Therefore, when it happens that you take it, rescue me and the house of my father." ⁶ And they said to her, "It will be thus as you have spoken to us; therefore when you come to know of our appearing, gather together all ₎your people₎[f] under your roof and they shall be rescued; for as many as shall be found outside of the house will be destroyed." ⁷ And they proceeded to give her a sign so that she should hang from her house something scarlet, ₎making it clear₎[g] that, through the blood of the Lord, redemption will come to all who believe and hope on God. ⁸ You see, beloved, that not only faith but also prophecy is found in the woman.[h]

REMEMBER THE WORDS OF JESUS

13.1 Therefore let us be humble-minded, brothers, putting away all arrogance and delusion and foolishness and anger, and let us do what is written, for the Holy Spirit says, "Let not the wise man boast in his wisdom, nor the strong man in his strength, nor the rich in his riches, but the one who boasts, let him boast in the Lord, to seek him out and to do judgment

---

a. The word εἰσδέχομαι can be translated "to receive," "to welcome," or "to take in." Many editions translate this "to take in", but given the emphasis on Rahab's hospitality, "to welcome" seems bettter.

b. Josh 2:6

c. Literally "explaining to them falsely"

d. Literally "Knowing, I know"

e. Gen 9:2; Deut 2:25; 11:25

f. Literally "yours"

g. Literally "making clear"

h. Gen 3:14-15

and righteousness,"[a] especially remembering the words of the Lord Jesus, which he spoke when he taught gentleness and patience. [2] For he spoke as follows: "Show mercy, that you may be shown mercy; forgive, that it may be forgiven you; as you do so will it be done to you; as you give so will it be given to you; as you judge so will you be judged; as you are kind so will kindness be shown to you; with which measure you measure, with it will be measured to you."[b] [3] With this commandment and with these instructions let us strengthen ourselves to walk, being obedient to his saintly words, being humble-minded. For the holy word says, [4] "Upon whom shall I look, but upon the gentle and quiet and the one who trembles at my words?"[c]

BE OBEDIENT TO GOD AND KIND TO OTHERS

[14.1] Therefore it is right and holy, men and brothers, for us to be obedient to God rather than to follow those instigators of loathsome jealousy in arrogance and insurrection. [2] For it is not common harm but rather great danger we will endure if we recklessly[d] surrender ourselves to the purposes of the people who plunge[e] into strife and rebellion in order to estrange us from what is good. [3] Let us be kind to them, according to the tenderheartedness and sweetness[f] of the one who made us. [4] For it is written, "The kind shall be inhabitants of the land, and the innocent shall be left upon it, but those who break the law shall be utterly destroyed from it."[g] [5] And again it says, "I saw the ungodly being exalted and lifted up [as high as][h] the cedars of Lebanon. And I passed by and behold, he was no more; and I sought out his place, and I did not find it. Guard innocence and pay attention to uprightness, for there is a remnant for a peaceful person."[i]

---

a. Jer 9:23–24; 1 Sam 2:10; 1 Cor 31; 2 Cor 10:17

b. Matt 5:7; 6:14–15; 7:1–2, 12; Luke 6:31, 36–38

c. Isa 66:2

d. Lightfoot glosses as "in a foolhardy spirit."

e. The literal sense is "to hurl out," but BDAG notes that when no object is present (as here) it may convey "to aim (at)" or "to plunge (into)." Lightfoot notes that when it occurs metaphorically (as here) λόγους (words) or γλώσσας (tongues) would be understood, if not expressed."

f. Josephus uses this word to describe the sweetness of honey (Jos Ant 3, 28); Hermas also uses it (Mandates 5:1.5).

g. Prov 2:21–22; Ps 37:9, 38

h. Literally "as"

i. Ps 37:35–37

HOLINESS, NOT HYPOCRISY

15.1 Therefore we should join with those who practice peace with piety and not with those who desire peace with hypocrisy. 2 For it says somewhere, "These people honor me with their lips, but their hearts are far from me."[a] 3 And again, "They blessed with their mouth, but they cursed in their heart."[b] 4 And again it says, "They loved him with their mouth and with their tongue they lied to him; and their heart ₁was not upright₁[c] with him and they did not show themselves faithful in his covenant."[d] 5 Because of this, "May the deceitful lips be mute, those which speak lawlessness against the righteous."[e] And again, "May the Lord utterly destroy all the deceitful lips, the boastful tongues, those who say, 'We will exalt our tongue, our lips are ₁our own,₁[f] who is lord over us?' 6 Because of the misery of the poor and the groaning of the needy, I will now arise, says the Lord. I will place *him* in safety. 7 I will deal boldly with him."[g]

CHRIST AS AN EXAMPLE OF HUMILITY

16.1 For Christ is of those who are humble-minded, not of those who exalt themselves over his flock. 2 The scepter of the majesty of God, the Lord Jesus Christ, did not come with the pomp of arrogance or pride[h] (although he could have) but with humble-mindedness, just as the Holy Spirit spoke concerning him. For it says, 3 "O Lord,[i] who has believed our report and who has revealed the arm of the Lord? We announced before him as a child, as a root in parched ground; there is no form or glory in him, and we saw him and he had neither form nor beauty, but his form *was* dishonored, inferior[j] to the form of people, being a person among wounds and pain, and knowing how to bear weakness, for his face was turned away, he was dishonored

---

a. Isa 29:13; Matt 15:8; Mark 7:6

b. Ps 62:4

c. Literally "not [was] right"

d. Ps 78:36–37

e. Ps 31:18

f. Literally "for us"

g. Ps 12:3–5

h. Rom 1:30; 2 Tim 3:2

i. Isa 53:1–12

j. The sense of "to be inferior" is that used by the LXX in Isa 53:3, which is quoted here. This sense does not occur in the NT.

and not credited. ⁴ This one bears our sins and suffers pain for us, and we regarded him as being in pain and in torment and in affliction, ⁵ but he was wounded for our sins and was made to suffer for our transgressions. The punishment of our peace *was* upon him, by his wounds we were healed. ⁶ We all wandered about like sheep, each one wandered about in his own way ⁷ and the Lord delivered him up for our sins, and he, due to his affliction, ⌊remains silent⌋.ᵃ Like a sheep he was brought to slaughter, and like a lamb silent before his shearers, so ⌊he remains silent⌋.ᵇ In his humiliation, his justice was denied. ⁸ Who shall describe his generation? For his life is taken away from the earth. ⁹ For the transgressions of my people he entered into death. ¹⁰ And I will give the wicked for his burial, and the wealthy for his death; for he did not commit any transgression and deceit was not found in his speech. And the Lord desires to purify him from his wounds. ¹¹ If you make an offering for sin, your soul will see a long-lived posterity. ¹² And the Lord desires to take away from the pain of his soul, to show him light and to form with understanding, to justify a righteous one who serves many well, and he himself will bear their sins. ¹³ Because of this he will inherit many, and he will share the spoils of the strong, ⌊because⌋ᶜ his soul was delivered to death, and he was counted among the lawless. ¹⁴ And he himself bore the sins of many, and because of their sins, he was delivered up."ᵈ ¹⁵ And again he himself says, "But I myself am a worm and not a man, a reproach of people, and despised of the people. ¹⁶ All who saw me ridiculed me; they spoke with *their* lips, they shook *their* heads; 'He hoped upon the Lord, let *the Lord* deliver him; let *the Lord* save him, for *the Lord* takes pleasure in him.'"ᵉ ¹⁷ You see, beloved people, what *is* the example which is given to us; for if the Lord was thus humble-minded, what shall we do, who through him have come under the yokeᶠ of his grace?

---

a. Literally "does not open his mouth"
b. Literally "he does not open his mouth"
c. Literally "for which"
d. Isa 53:1–12
e. Ps 22:6–8
f. Matt 11:29, 30

MORE EXAMPLES OF HUMILITY

17.1 Let us also be imitators of those who walk around in the skins of goats and in sheepskins,[a] preaching the coming of the Christ. And we speak of Elijah and Elisha, and in addition also Ezekiel, the prophets, and in addition to these[b] the famous men of old.[c] **2** Abraham was very well spoken of and was called the friend of God. And he says, looking intently at the glory of God, being humble-minded, "But I am dust and ashes."[d] **3** And in addition, it is also thus written about Job, "And Job was righteous and blameless, true, God-fearing, *and* refrained from all evil."[e] **4** But he accuses himself, saying, "No one is clean from dirt, not even if[f] his life is one day."[g] **5** Moses was called "faithful in all his house,"[h] and through his service God condemned Egypt through their suffering and torment, but even he, though greatly glorified, did not boast but from the bush he said, when an oracle was given to him, "Who am I that you send me? But I am weak-voiced and slow of tongue."[i] **6** And again he says, "But I am steam from a pot."[j]

DAVID AS AN EXAMPLE OF HUMILITY

18.1 But what shall we say about David, who is well spoken of? About whom God said, "I have found a man according to my heart, David, the *son* of Jesse, I have anointed him with eternal mercy."[k] **2** But even he said to God,[l] "Have mercy on me, God, according to your great mercy, and according to the abundance of your compassion blot out my iniquity. **3** Wash me thoroughly[m] from my transgressions, and from my sin, cleanse me; for I know my transgression and my sin is always before me. **4** I sinned against you

---

a. Heb 11:37; cf. Zech 13:4
b. Literally "with these also"
c. Literally "those who are well spoken of"
d. Gen 18:27
e. Job 1:1
f. Literally "not if"
g. Job 14:4–5
h. Num 12:7; Heb 3:2
i. Exod 4:10
j. The source is unknown; the intent is to reinforce Moses' humility.
k. 1 Sam 13:14; Ps 89:20; Acts 13:22
l. Ps 51:1–17
m. Literally "even more"

alone, and I did evil ₍in your presence₎,ᵃ that you might be justified in your words and you may overcome when you are judged. ⁵ For behold, I was conceived in lawlessness, and in sin my mother carriedᵇ me. ⁶ For behold, you have loved truth; the unseen and secret things of your wisdom you have revealed to me. ⁷ Sprinkle me with hyssop and I will be cleansed; wash me and ₍I will be made whiter than snow₎,ᶜ ⁸ You will make me hear joy and gladness; the bones will rejoice greatly, having been made humble. ⁹ Turn your face away from my sins, and blot out all my transgressions. ¹⁰ Create a clean heart in me, God, and renew an upright spirit in my inmost parts. ¹¹ Do not drive me away from your presence, and do not take away your Holy Spirit from me. ¹² Restore to me the joy of your salvation and establish me with a guiding spirit. ¹³ I will teach the lawless your ways and the ungodly will turn back to you. ¹⁴ Deliver me from blood-guilt, O God, the God of my salvation. ¹⁵ My tongue will rejoice greatly in your righteousness. O Lord, you will open my mouth and my lips will proclaim your praise. ¹⁶ Because if you had desired sacrifice, I would have given it; you will not delight in whole burnt offering. ¹⁷ The sacrifice to God is a shattered spirit; a shattered and humbled heart God will not disdain."ᵈ

FOLLOW THE EXAMPLES

¹⁹·¹ Therefore the humility and subservienceᵉ by obedience of so manyᶠ and of such a kind who are so well-spoken of have made better not only us but also the generations before us, who received his sayings in fear and truth. ² Therefore having a share in many and great and glorious deeds, let us run ahead toward what was given to us from the beginning, the goal of peace, and let us look intently on the Father and Creator of the whole world and let us cling to his magnificent and excellent gifts of peace and kindnesses. ³ Let us observe him with *our* mind and let us look intently with the eyes of

---

a. Literally "in the presence of you"

b. This word is infrequent and is used by Aristotle to denote "the cravings of pregnant women for strange food" (BDAG).

c. Literally "I will be made more white than snow"

d. Ps 51:1-17

e. Lightfoot glosses as "submissiveness" or "subordination."

f. Heb 12:1

the soul into his even-tempered intention. Let us consider how free from anger he is to all of his creation.

EXAMPLES FROM NATURE

20.1 The heavens move about,[a] at his direction they are subject to him in peace. **2** Both day and night they follow the course appointed by him ₁without hindering one another₁.[b] **3** Both sun and moon and the company of stars, according to his ordinance, in harmony, ₁without any deviation₁,[c] roll along in their appointed, fixed courses. **4** The earth, bearing fruit according to his purpose, at the proper season, in full abundance, both for humans and beasts and all the living beings that exist upon it, puts forth food without dissent and without changing any of the things decreed by him. **5** Both the fathomless *places of the* abyss[d] and the indescribable regions[e] of the underworld are restrained by the same commandments. **6** The hollow of the boundless sea, gathered together according to his creative act into its assembly, does not overstep the barriers placed around it, but just as it has been commanded, so it does. **7** For he said, "₁Thus far₁[f] shall you come, and your waves will be broken in you."[g] **8** The ocean (endless to humans) and the worlds beyond it are governed by the same commands of the Master. **9** The seasons of spring and of summer and of autumn and of winter succeed one another in peace. **10** The stations of the winds complete their service without stumbling according to their own season. And the ever-flowing springs created for enjoyment and health supply ₁sustenance₁[h] for human life without fail. And the smallest of the animals accomplish

---

a. While the common NT sense of σαλεύω is that of "to shake," here it likely has the sense of orderly movement, as noted in BDAG: "Also of the heavens moving in orderly fashion at God's command, probably in reference to the variety of motions exhibited in the heavens."

b. Literally "no one hindering one another"

c. Literally "apart from all deviation"

d. As ἀβύσσων is plural, "places of the" was added.

e. κλίματα Lake, Ehrman] κρίματα Lightfoot, Holmes. The difference is "the indescribable regions of the underworld" vs. "the indescribable judgments of the underworld." Editions are unified in their testimony to κρίματα (judgments); the reading of Lake/Ehrman is an emendation that happens to make more sense. Lightfoot notes his preference is to remove the world altogether; Holmes notes that there is no reason to emend the text given the unity of the reading in the editions, and this is surely the better course.

f. Literally "unto here"

g. Job 38:11

h. Literally "the breast"

their intercourse[a] in harmony and peace. [11] The great Creator and Master of everything ordained all these things to exist in peace and harmony, doing good to all things, and beyond all measure to us who have fled for refuge to his mercies, through our Lord Jesus Christ, [12] to whom be the glory and the majesty ₍forever₎,[b] amen.

HOW WE SHOULD LIVE

[21.1] Beloved, take care that his many kindnesses may not come to judgment on us if, leading a life not worthy of him, we should do good and pleasing things before him in harmony. [2] For he says somewhere, "The Spirit of the Lord is a lamp searching the innermost parts."[c] [3] Let us observe how near he is, and that nothing escapes his notice, either of our thoughts or of the considerations that we make. [4] Therefore it is right that we not turn away from his will. [5] Instead, let us offend foolish and dull-witted people, and those who are arrogant and those who boast in the false pride of their words rather than in God. [6] Let us hold the Lord Jesus Christ in reverence, whose blood was given on behalf of us. Let us respect those presiding over[d] us. Let us honor the aged. Let us teach the young[e] the instruction of the fear of God. Let us set our wives on the straight path, toward the good. [7] Let them demonstrate[f] the habit of purity worthy of love. Let them display the innocent will of their gentleness. Let them make evident the gentleness of their speech by their silence. Let them give their love devoutly, not according to partiality[g] but equally to all who fear God. [8] Our children, let them have a share in the instruction that is in Christ. Let them learn what humility has strength to do before God; what pure love is able to do before God; how the fear of him is beautiful and great, saving all of those in it,

---

a. Some have the far more general "come together" (Lake, Ehrman, Holmes) for "accomplish their intercourse" (Grant and Graham), but the focus on the support of the creation for life seems to indicate preference for the more specific translation here.

b. Literally "into the ages of the ages"

c. Prov 20:27

d. Lightfoot notes that this refers to the officers of the church.

e. Prov 16:4; Sir 1:27

f. This has shifted from "us" to "them"; here Clement is detailing things the wives should be doing if their husbands are, as the previous verse states, setting their wives on the straight path.

g. 1 Tim 5:21

who walk devoutly with a pure mind. ⁹ For he is a searcher of thoughts and desires; his breath is in us and when he wills, he will take it away.

LEARN THE FEAR OF THE LORD

22.1 And the faith in Christ confirms all these things, for even he himself calls us through the Holy Spirit thus:[a] "Come, children, listen to me, I will teach you the fear of the Lord. ² Who is the one who is wanting life *and* loving to see good days? ³ Make your tongue cease from evil and ₗkeep your lips from speaking deceit,ₗ[b] ⁴ Turn aside from evil and do good. ⁵ Seek peace, and pursue it. ⁶ The eyes of the Lord *are* upon the righteous, and his ears to their prayer, but the face of the Lord *is* against those who do evil, to utterly destroy their memory from the earth. ⁷ The righteous one cried out, and the Lord heard him and delivered him from all of his afflictions."[c] ⁸ "Many *are* the torments of the sinner, but those who hope upon the Lord will be surrounded by mercy."[d]

BE SINGLE-MINDED, NOT DOUBLE-MINDED

23.1 The Father, beneficent and merciful in every way, has compassion upon those who fear him, both kindly and lovingly bestows his gifts on those who draw near to him with a sincere mind. ² Therefore let us not be double-minded and let not our soul entertain strange notions[e] about his excellent and glorious gifts. ³ Let this scripture be far away from us,[f] where it says, "Wretched are the double-minded,[g] those who doubt in their soul, who say, 'We have heard these things even ₗin the days of our fathers,ₗ[h]

----

a. Ps 34:11–17

b. Literally "your lips not to speak deceit"

c. θλίψεων Lake, Ehrman] + πολλαὶ αἱ θλίψεις τοῦ δικαίου καὶ ἐκ πασῶν αὐτῶν ῥύσεται αὐτὸν ὁ κύριος Lightfoot, Holmes. The additional words ("Many are the troubles of the righteous, but the Lord shall deliver him from them all") are missing in the best Greek exemplar, Alexandrinus. Lightfoot (followed by Holmes) posits omission by *homoiteleuton* due to the repeated Πολλαὶ αἱ that begins in verse 8.

d. Ps 34:19

e. Lightfoot glosses as "indulge in caprices and humors."

f. It is a mystery which "scripture" Clement refers to here (the same is referred to in 2 Cl 11:2–3). Lightfoot suggests it is from the lost apocryphal book of Eldad and Modad; others have suggested that Clement here fused together several NT scriptures.

g. Jas 1:8

h. Literally "in our fathers"

and behold we have grown old and none of these things has happened to us.' 4 Oh foolish people! Compare yourselves to a tree. Take a vine: first it indeed sheds its leaves, then a bud comes, then a leaf, then a flower, and after these things an unripe grape, then presents a bunch of grapes." See that in a little time the fruit of the tree [becomes ripe].ab 5 [Truly]c it will be quickly and suddenly accomplished, his desire as the scripture also testifies, that "He will come quickly and [will not stay long];d and the Lord will suddenly come to his temple, even the Holy One whom you expect."e

EXAMPLES OF RESURRECTION

24.1 Let us consider, beloved, how the Master continually points out to us the resurrection that is coming, of which he made the first fruitsf by raising up the Lord Jesus Christ from the dead. 2 Let us pay attention, beloved, to the resurrection, which happens according to season. 3 Day and night reveal a resurrection to us. The night falls asleep; the day wakes up. The day goes; night returns. 4 Let us take the harvest: how and in what manner does the sowing occur? 5 The one who sowsg went out and threw each of the seeds into the soil. Which, falling on the dry and bareh soil, suffer decay.i Then, from the decay, the impressiveness of the provision of the Master raises them up, and from the one seed many more growj and produce fruit.

THE SIGN OF THE PHOENIX

25.1 Let us consider the strange sign which takes place in the eastern regions, that is those regions around Arabia. 2 For there is a bird which is called the Phoenix. This bird, being the one and only of its kind, lives five hundred years. And now having come to its dissolution to death, it makes itself a

---

a. Literally "attains to ripeness"

b. Gen 40:10

c. Literally "In truth"

d. Literally "not will stay awhile"

e. Isa 13:22 (LXX); Mal 3:1

f. 1 Cor 15:20, 23

g. Matt 13:3; Mark 4:3; Luke 8:5

h. 1 Cor 15:36

i. This word occurs once in the NT with the sense of "to disperse" (Acts 5:36) but is commonly used outside the NT with the meaning of "to decay" or even "to destroy."

j. Eph 2:21; Col 2:19

tomb[a] out of frankincense and myrrh and other fragrant spices, into which, after fulfilling the time, it enters and dies. 3 And from the rotting of the flesh, a certain worm is born, which, being nourished by the juices of the dead bird, grows wings. Then, having become strong, it takes away that tomb where the bones of its progenitor are and, carrying them, it continues from the Arabian region as far as Egypt, to the *place* called Heliopolis. 4 And in the daylight, being seen by all, lighting upon the altar of the sun it places them[b] and ₗstarts back again.ₗ[c] 5 Therefore the priests[d] examine the public records of the dates and they find it has come at the fulfillment of the five-hundredth year.[e]

THE WONDER OF THE RESURRECTION

26.1 Therefore do we consider *it* to be great and wonderful if the creator of everything will bring about the resurrection of those who devoutly served him in the confidence of a good faith, ₗwhenₗ[f] he showed us the greatness of his promise through a bird? 2 For it says somewhere, "And you will raise up me and I will praise you"[g] and "I lay down and fell asleep, I awoke because you were with me."[h] 3 And again Job says, "And you will raise up this my flesh which has patiently borne all these things."[i]

THE HOPE OF THE RESURRECTION

27.1 Therefore with this hope let our souls be bound to the one faithful in his promises and righteous in his judgments. 2 The one who commanded *us* not to lie, how much more will he himself not lie? For nothing *is* impossible

---

a. The word σηκός has the sense of both "nest" and "burial place." Here both are used, as BDAG comments: "In the σηκός which the bird Phoenix prepared for itself 1 Cl 25.2, the meanings nest and tomb merge in striking imagery." Holmes translates "coffin-like nest" capturing both senses of the word.

b. The "tomb of bones" carried to the altar of the sun by the phoenix.

c. Literally "thus starts for behind"

d. These are the priests of the temple of the sun.

e. Lake notes: "The same story, with variations, is found in Herodotus (ii. 73), Pliny (*Nat Hist* x. 2), etc. It was supposed by Christians to be sanctioned by the LXX version of Ps 92:12, where there is a confusion between Θοῖνιξ = phoenix, and Θοῖνιξ = palm tree."

f. Literally "since also"

g. Ps 28:7

h. Ps 3:5; 23:4

i. Job 19:26

with God[a] except to lie.[b] 3 Therefore let faith in him be rekindled in us and let us consider that all things are near him. 4 By the word of his majesty he established all things, and by a word he is able to destroy them. 5 "Who will say to him, 'What have you done?' or who will resist the power of his strength?"[c] When he wishes and as he wishes, he will do all things, and nothing decreed by him ₗwill ever pass awayₗ.[de] 6 All things are before him, and nothing escapes the notice of his will, 7 since "The heavens declare the glory of God and the firmament announces the work of his hands. Day utters a word to day, and night announces knowledge to night. And there are no words or speeches whose voices are not heard."[f]

TURN TO GOD

28.1 Therefore, having seen and having heard all things, let us fear him and let us leave behind abominable lusts of evil deeds, that we may be protected by his mercy from the coming judgments. 2 For where are any of us able to flee from his powerful hand? And what world will receive any of those who desert from him? 3 For somewhere the writing[g] says, "Where shall I go, and where shall I be hidden from your face? If I go up to heaven, you are there. If I go away to the ends of the earth, your right hand is there. If I make my bed in the abyss, your Spirit is there."[h] 4 Therefore, where can a person go or where can one run away from the one who embraces all things?

APPROACH GOD WITH WORSHIP AND LOVE

29.1 Therefore let us approach him in holiness of soul, raising pure[i] and undefiled hands to him, loving our gentle and compassionate Father, who

---

a. Matt 19:26; Mark 10:27

b. Heb 6:18; Titus 1:2

c. Wis 12:12

d. Literally "will not pass away"

e. Matt 5:18

f. Ps 19:1–3

g. This use of γραφεῖον may signify that Clement held to a three-fold division of the Hebrew Scriptures, the law, the prophets, and the writings. BDAG notes: "In ecclesiatical usage the plural sometimes designated the third part of the Hebrew canon, also called ἁγιόγραφα. 1 Cl 28.2 may be an early example of this usage." Lightfoot also discusses this.

h. Ps 139:7–10

i. 1 Tim 2:8

made us his own chosen portion. ² For thus it is written, "When the Most High divided the nations, when he scattered the sons of Adam, he established the boundaries of the nations according to the number of the angels of God. His people, Jacob, became the portion of the Lord; Israel the allotment of his inheritance."ᵃ ³ And in another place it says, "Behold, the Lord takes for himself a nation from among the nations, just as a person takes the first fruits from his threshing floor, and the Holy of Holies will come forth from that nation."ᵇ

LIVE IN HARMONY

³⁰·¹ Therefore, being a holy portion,ᶜ let us do ₍everything that pertains to holiness₎,ᵈ fleeing from evil speech,ᵉ both abominable and impure embraces, both drunkenness and rebellions and detestable lusts, loathsome adulteries, detestable haughtiness. ² "For God," it says, "opposes the proud but gives grace to the humble."ᶠ ³ Therefore let us join with those to whom is given the grace from God. Let us put on harmony, being humble-minded, exercising self-control, keeping ourselves far away from all gossip and evil speech,ᵍ being justified by works not by words. ⁴ For it says, "The one who says much will also hear in turn, or does the talkative one suppose that he is righteous? ⁵ Blessed is one born of a woman and who is short-lived. Do not be profuse with words."ʰ ⁶ Let our praise be in God and not of ourselves, for God hates those who praise themselves. ⁷ Let the testimony of our good deeds be given by others,ⁱ just as it was given to our fathers, the righteous ones. ⁸ Arrogance and stubbornness and audacity to those who are cursed by God; gentleness and humility and meekness with those who are blessed by God.

---

a. Deut 32:8–9
b. Deut 4:34; 14:2; Num 18:27; 2 Chr 341:14; Ezek 48:12
c. 1 Pet 1:15
d. Literally "all things of holiness"
e. 1 Pet 2:1
f. Prov 3:34; Jas 4:6; 1 Pet 5:5
g. 2 Cor 12:20; Rom 1:30
h. Job 11:2–3
i. Prov 27:2

CLING TO HIS BLESSING

31.1 Therefore let us cling to his blessing and let us consider what *are* the paths of blessing. Let us untwist in our minds[a] what has happened from the beginning. 2 Why was our father Abraham blessed? Was it not because he brought about righteousness and truth through faith?[b] 3 Isaac, knowing what was about to happen with confidence, gladly was brought as a sacrifice.[c] 4 Jacob with humility departed from his country because of *his* brother and went away to Laban and served *him*,[d] and the scepter of the twelve tribes of Israel was given to him.

RECOGNIZE HIS GREATNESS

32.1 If anyone may sincerely consider each *of these* ₁one by one,₁[e] he will recognize the greatness of the gifts given by him. 2 For from him *come* the priests and all the Levites who minister at the altar of God; from him *comes* the Lord Jesus according to the flesh; from him *come* kings and rulers and governors according to the line of Judah; and his other scepters will be held in no small honor, because God promised that "your seed will be as the stars of the heaven."[f] 3 Therefore all of them were glorified and magnified, not through themselves or their deeds or righteous actions which they accomplished, but through his will. 4 And we, therefore, having been called through his will in Christ Jesus, we are not justified through ourselves, or through our wisdom or understanding[g] or piety or deeds which we accomplished in holiness of heart,[h] but through the faith by which all those ₁since the beginning₁[i] the Almighty God has justified. To him be the glory ₁forever,₁[j] amen.

---

a. The verb τυλίσσω literally means "to roll" or "to twist"; this translation makes the metaphor explicit.

b. Gen 15:6; Rom 4

c. Gen 22:7–8

d. Gen 28

e. Literally "according to one"

f. Gen 15:5; 22:17; 26:4

g. 1 Cor 1:19; Col 1:9; Isa 29:14

h. Titus 3:5

i. Literally "since the age"

j. Literally "into the ages of the ages"

BE DEVOTED TO HIS WILL

[33.1] Therefore what shall we do,[a] brothers? Shall we be idle in good deeds and abandon love? May the master never allow this to happen at least to us but let us be zealous to fulfill every good deed with earnestness and eagerness. [2] For the Creator and Master of everything himself rejoices greatly in his works. [3] For by his most immense power he established the heavens, and by his incomprehensible understanding he set them in order. And he separated the land from the water containing it, and he established it upon the safe foundation of his own will; and the animals moving about within it he commanded to exist by his own decree. Having prepared beforehand the sea and the animals within it, he enclosed *them* by his own power. [4] Above all, the most excellent and by far the greatest *creature* according to his purpose,[b] the human, he formed with holy and blameless hands the stamp of his own image. [5] For God spoke thus: "Let us make humankind according to our image and likeness. And God made humankind, male and female he made them."[c] [6] Therefore, having completed all these things, he praised and blessed them, and he said, "Increase and multiply."[d] [7] Let us consider that all the righteous have been adorned with good works; and even the Lord himself, having adorned himself with good works, rejoiced. [8] Therefore, having this example, let us unhesitatingly devote ourselves to his will; let us work the work of righteousness with all of our strength.

BE IN HARMONY

[34.1] The good worker receives the bread[e] of his work with confidence; the lazy and careless one cannot look his employer[f] in the face.[g] [2] Therefore it is necessary that we be eager for good deeds, for all things are from him.

---

a. Rom 6:1

b. The Greek can be understood two different ways. Lightfoot notes this will mean either "(1) 'in intellectual capacity,' referring to man; or (2) 'as an exercise of his creative intelligence,' referring to God. The former appears to be generally adopted; but the latter seems to me preferable."

c. Gen 1:26–27

d. Gen 1:28

e. The metaphorical use of "bread" to indicate the reward/result/proceeds of one's labor is not directly attested in the NT. A similar use occurs in *Did* 11.6.

f. This is a compound word; according to BDAG the component parts literally translate as "one who gives work."

g. Acts 27:15; Wis 12:14

³ For he warns us, "Behold the Lord! And his reward is before his face, to pay each one according to his work."ᵃ ⁴ Therefore he urges us who believe in him with the whole heart not to be idle or careless in every good work. ⁵ Let our boast and confidence be in him. Let us be subject to his will. Let us consider the whole multitude of his angels, how standing by they serve his will. ⁶ For the scripture says, "Ten thousand ten thousands stood by him, and thousands upon thousands served him, and they cried out, 'Holy, holy, holy is the Lord of Hosts;ᵇ the whole creation is full of his glory.'"ᶜ ⁷ Therefore we too, in harmony ₍together₎,ᵈ being gathered in conscience, as with one mouth we cry out fervently to him, so that we may be sharers of his great and glorious promises. ⁸ For he says, "Eye has not seen and ear has not heard and into the human heart it has not entered what the Lord has prepared for those who wait for him."ᵉ

THE GIFTS OF GOD

35.1 How blessed and wonderful are the gifts of God, beloved! ² Life in immortality, splendor in righteousness, truth with boldness, faith with confidence, self-control in holiness; and all these things fall within our ₍comprehension₎.ᶠ ³ Therefore what, then, are the things being prepared for those who wait? The Creator and Father of the ages, the All-holy oneᵍ himself, knows their magnitude and beauty. ⁴ Therefore let us strive to be found among the number of those who wait, so that we may have a share in the gifts which were promised. ⁵ But how shall this be, beloved? If our understanding is faithfully fixed on God; if we seek out what is pleasing and acceptable to him; if we accomplish what is fitting to his unblemished will and we follow the way of truth, driving away from ourselves all injustice and wickedness, greediness, strife, both malice and deceit, both gossip and slander, hatred toward God, both pride and arrogance, both empty conceit and

---

a. Rev 22:12; Isa 40:10; 62:11; Prov 24:12; Rom 2:6

b. The Greek σαβαώθ (Sabaoth) is a transliteration of an Aramaic term meaning "armies." The sense is that the Lord is Lord over the armies of his angels, also called his "host."

c. Dan 7:10; Isa 6:3

d. Literally "with the same"

e. 1 Cor 2:9; Isa 64:4

f. Literally "understanding"

g. 4 Macc 7:4; 14:7

inhospitality. [6] For those who do these things are hateful to God, and not only those who do them, but also those who approve of them.[a] [7] For the scripture says, "But to the sinner God said, 'Why do you recount my regulations and take up my covenant in your mouth? [8] But you hate instruction and cast out my words ˌbehind youˌ.[b] If you saw a thief, you joined with him, and with adulterers you made your portion. Your mouth multiplied evil and your tongue wove deceit. Sitting down, against your brother you spoke evil and against the son of your mother you put a cause for stumbling. [9] You have done these things and I kept silent; you supposed, O lawless one, that I would be like you. [10] I will convict you and I will set you against your *own*[c] face. [11] Understand these things, then, ones who forget God, lest he seize *you* like a lion, and there be nobody to deliver you. [12] The sacrifice of praise will glorify me, and there is a way which I will show him the salvation of God.'"[d]

THE SALVATION OF CHRIST

[36.1] This is the way, beloved, in which we found our salvation, Jesus Christ, the high priest[e] of our offerings, the defender[f] and helper of our weaknesses.[g] [2] Through this one we look intently to the heights of the heavens; through this one we see as in a mirror his unblemished and lofty face; through this one the eyes of our heart have been opened; through this one our foolish and darkened understanding springs up[h] into the light; through this one the Master has willed the immortal knowledge that we should taste "Who, being the radiance of his majesty, is so much greater

---

a. Rom 1:32

b. Literally "to the back"

c. Lightfoot expands as "I will bring you face to face with yourself, show thee to thyself in your true light."

d. Ps 50:16–23

e. Heb 2:17; 3:1; 4:14, 15

f. Lightfoot notes this is a "guardian, patron, who protects our interests and pleads our cause. To a Roman it would convey all the ideas of the Latin 'patronus,' of which it was the recognized rendering." See also Rom 16:2.

g. Heb 4:15

h. Lightfoot comments: "Our mind, like a plant shut up in a dark closet, had withered in its growth. Removed thence by His loving care, it revives and shoots up toward the light of heaven."

than angels, as he has inherited a more excellent name."[a] [3] For so it is written, "The one who makes his angels spirits and his ministers a flame of fire."[b] [4] But of his Son, thus spoke the Master: "You are my son, I today have begotten you. Ask from me and I will give to you the Gentiles for your inheritance, and for your possession the ends of the earth."[c] [5] And again he says to him, "You sit at my right hand until I make your enemies a footstool for your feet."[d] [6] Who, therefore, *are* the enemies? The evil ones and those who oppose his will.

SOLDIERS OF CHRIST

[37.1] Therefore let us wage war, men *and* brothers, with all earnestness under his faultless commands. [2] Let us consider those who serve as soldiers under those who rule us, how precisely, how readily, how subserviently they fulfill their orders. [3] Not all[e] are prefects or military tribunes or centurions or commanders of fifty or the like, but each[f] in his own rank carries out what is commanded by the king and the rulers. [4] The great ₍cannot exist₎[g] without the small, nor the small without the great. There is a certain combination among all, and usefulness *lies* in this. [5] Let us take our body: the head is nothing without the feet; likewise, ₍the feet are nothing₎[h] without the head. Even the smallest parts of our body are necessary and useful to the whole body, but all work together and experience a mutual subjection, to save the whole body.[i]

DUTIES OF THE SOLDIERS

[38.1] Therefore let our whole body be saved in Christ Jesus, and let each of us be subject to his neighbor, ₍according to the gift given to him₎,[jk] [2] Let the

---

a. Heb 1:3-4
b. Heb 1:7; Ps 104:4
c. Heb 1:5; Ps 2:7-8
d. Heb 1:13; Ps 110:1
e. 1 Cor 12:29-30
f. 1 Cor 15:23
g. Literally "not are able to exist"
h. Literally "neither the feet"
i. 1 Cor 12:12-24
j. Literally "just as he was appointed with his gift"
k. 1 Pet 4:10; 1 Cor 7:7; Rom 12:6

strong care for the weak and let the weak respect the strong. Let the rich provide for the poor and let the poor give thanks to God, that he gave to him *one* through whom he might supply[a] his need. Let the wise one demonstrate his wisdom not with words but with good works. Do not let the humble person testify about himself, but allow him to be testified about by another. Do not let the pure in the flesh boast, knowing that another is the one who provides for his self-control. 3 Therefore, let us consider, brothers, from what kind of matter we were made, who and what we came into the world as, from what kind of grave and darkness the one who made and one who created us brought *us* into his world, having prepared his benefits before we were born. 4 Therefore having all these things from him, we ought to give thanks to him for everything, to whom *be* the glory ⌊forever,⌋[b] amen.

THE FOOLISHNESS OF BOASTING

39.1 Ignorant and senseless and stupid and uninformed people mock[c] and treat us with contempt, desiring to exalt themselves in their thoughts. 2 For what can a mortal do? Or what strength *can* one born of the earth *have*?[d] 3 For it is written, "There was no form[e] before my eyes, but I heard a breath and a voice. 4 What then? Shall a mortal be pure before the Lord? Or by his deeds a blameless man seeing that in his servants he does not trust and he has brought to mind something crooked against his messengers.[f] 5 And heaven *is* not pure before him. Ah, and those who dwell in houses made of clay,[g] of which even we ourselves were made from the same clay. He smashed them like a moth, and from morning until evening[h] ⌊they do not endure.⌋[i] Because they could not help themselves, they perished. 6 He breathed on them and they died because they had no wisdom. 7 But call

---

a. 1 Cor 16:17; Phil 2:30; Col 1:24

b. Literally "into the ages of the ages"

c. Ps 44:14

d. Lightfoot comments: "Altogether we may say that the word (1) signifies originally 'humility and meanness of origin,' and (2) connotes 'separation from and hostility to God.'"

e. Job 4:16–18; 5:15; 4:19–5:5

f. Lightfoot, Lake, and Holmes opt for "angels" as the translation here, but Ehrman's "messengers" seems more contextually appropriate.

g. 2 Cor 5:1

h. Isa 38:12–13

i. Literally "still they are not"

out, if someone will answer you or if you will see any of the holy angels. For wrath destroys even the foolish and jealousy destroys those who go astray. [8] But I have seen the foolish putting down roots, but their house[a] was immediately consumed. [9] May their sons be far away from deliverance, may they be ridiculed at the door of lesser men, and a deliverer will not be *there*. For what has been prepared for these the righteous shall eat, and they themselves shall not be delivered from evil.[b]

DO WHAT HAS BEEN COMMANDED

[40.1] Therefore since these things are evident to us, and we have looked into the depths of the divine knowledge, we ought to do in sequence everything whatever the Master commanded *us* to accomplish, at the times appointed. [2] Both the offerings and services should be accomplished, and he commanded *them* not to be done thoughtlessly or disorderly, but at appointed times and hours. [3] Both where and by whom he wants *them* to be accomplished, he himself has appointed by his most supreme will, that all things being done devoutly in good pleasure may be acceptable to his will. [4] Therefore those who make their offerings at the appointed times *are* both acceptable and blessed, for following the lawful ways of the Master they do not sin.[c] [5] For the proper services are given to the high priest, and the proper position has been appointed to the priests, and the proper ministries have been imposed upon the Levites. The lay[d] person is bound by the laity's commands.

---

a. Job 8:6, 22; 11:14; 39:6

b. Job 4:16–18; 15:15; 4:19–5:5

c. BDAG notes that this action is "of failure to meet divine expectations," hence the translation "sin." The thought is general and not specific, more like a maxim or proverb: "If you follow the Master's lawful ways, you won't sin."

d. The original sense of the word is that of someone acting in an unofficial context. BDAG offers "lay" as a possible gloss, but with clarification: "lay as opposed to appointed officiants, ... Here λ is contrasted with the OT priesthood, but clearly with reference to the situation within the Christian community."

BE PLEASING TO GOD

41.1 Each of us, brothers, in his own group, must be pleasing to God, being in good conscience,[a] not going beyond the appointed rule[b] of his ministry, with dignity. **2** Not everywhere, brothers, are the sacrifices continually offered,[c] or vows or ₍sin-offerings and trespass-offerings₎,[de] but only in Jerusalem, and even there, offerings are made not in every place, but before the temple, at the altar, the offering being examined for blemishes by the high priest and those doing the previously mentioned service. **3** Therefore those who do anything contrary to ₍the duty imposed₎[f] by his will, they experience the death penalty. **4** You see, brothers, as we have been considered worthy of greater knowledge, so we will be exposed to more danger.

ORDER AND AUTHORITY

42.1 The apostles received the gospel for us from the Lord Jesus Christ; Jesus the Christ was sent out from God. **2** Therefore the Christ is from God and the apostles from Christ. Therefore both came forth in good order from the will of God. **3** Therefore, having received commands and being fully convinced by the resurrection of our Lord Jesus Christ, and full of faith in the word of God, they went forth with the full assurance of the Holy Spirit, proclaiming the gospel, that the kingdom of God was about to come. **4** Therefore, preaching among regions and cities, they appointed their first fruits, testing *them* by the Spirit to *be* bishops and deacons ₍of the future believers₎,[g] **5** And this *is* nothing new, for much time since then has been written about bishops and deacons. For somewhere the scripture says as follows: "I will appoint their bishops in righteousness and their deacons in faith."[h]

---

a. Acts 23:1; 1 Tim 1:5, 19; 1 Pet 3:16, 21
b. 2 Cor 10:13–14
c. Exod 29:38; Num 28:3ff
d. Literally "[those] concerning sin and trespasses"
e. Lev 7:37
f. Literally "what is proper"
g. Literally "of those who are going to believe"
h. Isa 60:17

THE FAITHFUL EXAMPLE OF MOSES

[43.1] And what amazement is there if those in Christ, entrusted with work of such a kind from God, appointed those previously mentioned? Since even the blessed Moses, "faithful servant in all his house,"[a] took note of all the orders given to him in the sacred books, which the other prophets also followed, testifying together to the laws given by him. [2] For when that jealousy fell concerning the priesthood and the tribes were rebelling about which of them may be adorned with the glorious title, he commanded the twelve tribal heads to bring rods to him, inscribing each tribe by name. And taking them he bound and sealed them with the rings of the tribal heads. And he put them away inside the tent of the testimony, upon the table of God. [3] And having shut the tent, he sealed the keys just like the rods. [4] And he said to them, "Men, brothers, whichever tribe's rod sprouts leaves, this one God has chosen to the priesthood and to minister to him." [5] And when it was early morning, he called together all Israel, six hundred thousand men, and he showed the seals to the tribal heads, and he opened the tent of the testimony, and he took out[b] the rods and he found the rod of Aaron not only to have sprouted leaves, but also to be bearing fruit.[c] [6] What do you think, beloved? Did Moses not know beforehand that this was about to happen? Most assuredly[d] he knew, but that there might not be insurrection in Israel, he acted this way to glorify the name of the true[e] and only God, to whom be the glory ₍forever₎,[f] amen.

STRIFE IN CORINTH

[44.1] And our apostles knew through our Lord Jesus Christ that there would be strife concerning the title of bishop. [2] Because of this reason, therefore, having received complete foreknowledge, they appointed those previously mentioned and afterward they gave a rule that if they should die, other approved men should succeed their ministry. [3] Therefore, those

---

a. Num 12:7; Heb 3:5

b. This sense of προαιρέω does not occur in the NT. See Jdt 13:15 for a similar example.

c. Num 17

d. While μάλιστα is usually translated "especially," in this context it denotes even more certainty, hence the translation "most assuredly" (cf. BDAG).

e. John 17:3

f. Literally "into the ages of the ages"

who were appointed by them or afterward by other reputable men, those approved of by the whole church and those who ministered blamelessly to the flock of Christ with humility, quietly, and unselfishly; and those who are well spoken of on many occasions by all, these we consider to be unjustly removed from the ministry. 4 For it will be no small sin for us if those who have blamelessly and devoutly offered we remove from the episcopate the gifts. 5 Blessed are those presbyters who died beforehand, who have obtained a fruitful and perfect departure,[a] for they have no fear,[b] lest anyone remove them from their established place. 6 For we see that you have steered some who led their own lives well away from the ministry blamelessly held in honor by them.

MORE EXAMPLES

45.1 Be contentious and zealous,[c] brothers, about the things relating to salvation. 2 You have looked into the holy scriptures, which *are* true, which *were given* by the Holy Spirit. 3 You know that nothing unrighteous or falsified is written in them. You will not find that the righteous have been cast out by holy men. 4 The righteous were persecuted, but by the lawless. They were imprisoned, but by the unholy. They were stoned by the lawless; they were killed by those who have taken to themselves abominable and unrighteous zeal. 5 Suffering these things, they endured gloriously. 6 For what shall we say, brothers? *That* Daniel was thrown into a den of lions[d] by those who feared God? 7 Ananias [sic] and Azariah and Mishael were shut up inside the furnace of fire[e] by those who ministered to the magnificent and glorious worship of the Most High? By no means may this be granted! Who, therefore, *were* those who accomplished these things? The despicable ones, and full of all evil, were roused to such anger that those who served God with holy and unblemished purpose they tortured cruelly,[f]

---

a. Phil 1:23; 2 Tim 4:6
b. 1 Macc 3:30
c. 1 Pet 3:13
d. Dan 6:16
e. Dan 3:19–21
f. Literally "they adorned with torture"

not knowing that the Most High is defender[a] and protector[b] of those who serve his most excellent name with a pure conscience,[c] to whom be the glory ₍forever₎,[d] amen. [8] But they who endured with confidence inherited glory and honor. They were both exalted and they were enrolled by God in his memorial ₍forever₎,[e] amen.

SCHISM IN CORINTH

[46.1] Therefore it is also necessary for us to cling to such examples, brothers. [2] For it is written, "Cling to the holy ones, because those who cling to them will be made holy."[f] [3] And again, in another place it says, "With the innocent one you will be innocent and with the elect you will be elect and with the perverse you will deal perversely."[g] [4] Therefore let us cling to the innocent and the righteous, as these are the elect of God. [5] Why is there strife and anger and dissension and division[h] and war among you? [6] Or do we not have one God and one Christ, and one Spirit of grace which is poured out upon us, and one calling in Christ? [7] Why do we tear and rip apart the members of Christ, and rebel against our own body and get worked up to such a frenzy that we forget that we are members of one another? Remember the words of the Lord Jesus, [8] for it says, "Woe to that person, it would be better for him if ₍he had not been born₎[i] than to cause one of my elect to sin. It would have been better for him to be tied to a millstone and to sink into the sea than to turn away one of my elect."[j] [9] Your schism has turned many away, has plunged many into discouragement, many into doubt; all of us into grief, yet your rebellion is continuous!

---

a. 2 Macc 14:34; Wis 10:20

b. Ps 28:2, 7, 8; 33:10

c. 1 Tim 3:9; 2 Tim 1:3

d. Literally "to the ages of the ages"

e. Literally "for the ages of the ages"

f. The source of this quotation is unknown.

g. Ps 18:25–26

h. Lightfoot notes: "The words are arranged in an ascending scale."

i. Literally "he was not born"

j. Matt 26:24; Luke 17:1, 2

FOLLOW PAUL'S PREVIOUS EXHORTATION

[47.1] Take up the letter of the blessed Paul the apostle. [2] What first did he write to you at the beginning of his gospel? [3] [Truthfully][a] he wrote to you in the Spirit about himself and Cephas and Apollos,[b] because even then you had engaged in partisan strife.[c] [4] But that partisanship brought less sin to you, for you joined with reputable apostles and with a man approved by them. [5] But now consider who has perverted you, and has lessened the respect due to your well-known love for fellow believers. [6] *It is* shameful, beloved, [extremely][d] shameful and unworthy of your conduct in Christ, that it should be reported that the well-established and ancient church of the Corinthians, because of one or two people, is rebelling against the presbyters. [7] And this report has reached not only to us, but even to those who have different allegiances from us, so that even blasphemies are brought upon the name of the Lord because of your foolishness, and you cause danger for yourselves.

REMOVE THE SCHISM

[48.1] Therefore let us remove this [quickly][e] and let us fall down before the Master and let us weep, imploring him that he may be merciful *and* may be reconciled to us and restore us to the honorable, pure way of life,[f] our love for fellow believers. [2] For this gate of righteousness opens to life, just as it is written, "Open to me the gates of righteousness, that entering into them, I may praise the Lord. [3] This is the gate of the Lord; the righteous will enter into it."[g] [4] Therefore, though many gates are open,[h] the one *opened* in righteousness, this one is the one *opened* in Christ, in which are blessed all who enter and direct their course in holiness and righteousness, accomplishing everything without confusion. [5] Let one be faithful, let him be able to express knowledge, let him be wise in the discernment of words,

---

a. Literally "By truth"
b. 1 Cor 3:4–6, 21–22
c. 1 Cor 1:12
d. Literally "even very"
e. Literally "with haste"
f. 2 Tim 3:10
g. Ps 118:19–20
h. Matt 7:13–14

let him be pure in deeds;[a] [6] for to the degree he seems to be even greater he ought to be more humble-minded and to seek the common good of all, and not his own.

LOVE CHRIST AND FOLLOW
HIS COMMANDMENTS

[49.1] The one who has love in Christ, he should do the commandments of Christ. [2] Who is able to explain the bond of the love of God? [3] Who can sufficiently express the greatness of its beauty? [4] The height to which love leads is indescribable. [5] Love unites us with God. Love covers up a multitude of sins.[b] Love bears[c] all things, is patient in all things. *There is* nothing vulgar, nothing arrogant in love; love does not have schism, love does not rebel; love does all things in harmony.[d] All of the elect of God were made perfect in love. Apart from love, nothing is pleasing to God. [6] The Master received us in love. Because of the love that he had for us, he gave his blood for us, Jesus Christ our Lord, by the will of God, and his flesh for our flesh, and his life for our lives.

THE WONDER OF LOVE

[50.1] You see, beloved, how great and wonderful love is? And there is no description of its perfection. [2] Who is sufficient to be found in it, except whomever God considers worthy? Therefore let us beg and plead for his mercy, that we may be found blameless in love, apart from human partisanship. [3] All the generations from Adam until this day have passed away, but those who were perfected in love according to the grace of God have a place among the godly who shall be revealed ˌwhen the kingdom of Christ

---

a. ἤτω ἀγνὸς ἐν ἔργοις Lake, Ehrman] ἤτω γοργὸς ἐν ἔργοις ἤτω ἀγνὸς Lightfoot, Holmes. The difference is between "let him be pure in deeds" and "let him be energetic in deeds, let him be pure." The reading of Lightfoot/Holmes is based on quotations of Clement, and is not found in extant editions of Clement's letter.

b. 1 Pet 4:8; Prov 10:12

c. Of the general nature of verses 5-6, though particularly in this portion of verse 5, Lightfoot comments: "An imitation of 1 Cor 13:4, 7; and indeed the whole passage is evidently inspired by St. Paul's praise of love. The juxtaposition of the language of St. Paul and the language of St. Peter is a token of the large and comprehensive apathies of one who paid equal honor to both these great Apostles, though their rival sectarians claimed them for their respective schools."

d. 1 Cor 13:4–7

comes⌐.[ab] 4 For it is written, "Enter into the inner rooms for a very short while, until my anger and wrath pass away. And I will remember a good day and will raise you up out of your grave."[c] 5 Beloved, we are blessed if we carry out the commandments of God in the harmony of love, so that our sins may be forgiven through love. 6 For it is written, "Blessed *are* those whose trespasses are forgiven and whose sins are covered up; blessed *is* the one the sin of whom the Lord does not take into account, and in his mouth there is no deceit."[d] 7 This blessing was given to those who have been chosen by God through Jesus Christ our Lord, to whom *be* the glory forever⌐,[e] amen.

SCHISM LEADS TO DEATH

51.1 However, then, we have fallen away and *whatever* we have done through any insidious plots ⌐of the opponent⌐,[f] let us ask that we be forgiven. And those also who became leaders of the rebellion and dissension ought to pay careful attention to the common hope. 2 For those who lead their lives with fear and love, they themselves prefer to experience mistreatments rather than their neighbors, and to endure condemnation themselves rather than the harmony being handed down to us rightly and justly. 3 For *it is* better for a person to confess concerning his sin than to harden his heart, just as the heart of those who rebelled was hardened against the servant of God, Moses, the condemnation of whom became evident. 4 For they descended into Hades alive,[g] and death will shepherd them.[h] 5 Pharaoh and his army and all the rulers of Egypt, both the chariots and their riders,[i] were plunged into the Red Sea and perished not because of any other reason, but because their foolish hearts were hardened after the signs and wonders were worked in the land of Egypt by the servant of God, Moses.

a. Literally "with the visitation of the kingdom of Christ"
b. Luke 19:44; 1 Pet 2:12; Wis 3:7
c. Isa 26:20; Ezek 37:12
d. Ps 32:1–2; Rom 4:7–9
e. Literally "into the ages of the ages"
f. Literally "of the one who opposes"
g. Num 16:33
h. Ps 49:14
i. Exod 14:23; Ps 136:15

CONFESS TO THE LORD

52.1 Brothers, the Master has no need ₍of anything at all₎.[a] He requires nothing except confession to him. **2** For the elect one David says, "I will confess to the Lord, and it will please him more than a young calf growing horns and hooves. Let the poor see *this* and rejoice."[b] **3** And again he says, "Sacrifice to God a sacrifice of praise, and pay your vows to the Most High. And call upon me in the day of your affliction, and I will deliver you and you will glorify me.[c] **4** For the sacrifice to God is a broken spirit."[d]

REPENT AND TURN

53.1 For you know and you know well the holy scriptures,[e] beloved, and you have looked into the sayings of God. Therefore we write these things as a reminder. **2** For Moses, having gone up to the mountain and having spent forty days and forty nights in fasting and humiliation, God said to him, "Go down quickly from here, because your people whom you led out of the land of Egypt broke the law. They have deviated quickly from the way which you commanded them; they cast for themselves molten images."[f] **3** And the Lord said to him, "I have spoken to you ₍time and again₎,[g] saying, 'I have seen this people and behold, it is a stiff-necked people!' Let me utterly destroy them and I will blot out their name from under heaven and make you into a nation great and wonderful, and much more than this."[h] **4** And Moses said, "By no means, Lord. Forgive the sin of this people, or also blot me out from the book of the living."[i] **5** O great love! O unsurpassable perfection! The servant speaks boldly to the Lord; he asks forgiveness for the crowd or he demands himself also to be blotted out with them.

---

a. Literally "not of anything"
b. Ps 69:30-32
c. Ps 50:14-15
d. Ps 51:17
e. 2 Tim 3:15; 2 Macc 8:23
f. Deut 9:12; Exod 32:7-8
g. Literally "once and twice"
h. Deut 9:13-14; Exod 32:9-10
i. Exod 32:32

DO WHAT IS RIGHT

54.1 Therefore who among you is noble? Who is compassionate? Who is filled with love? **2** Let him say, "If *there is* rebellion and strife and division because of me, I will depart, I will go away wherever you desire, and will do whatever is commanded by the people; only let the flock of Christ be at peace with its appointed presbyters." **3** The one who does this will win for himself great fame in Christ, and every place will welcome him, for "the earth is the Lord's, and its fullness."[a] **4** These *are the things that* those who lead their lives without regret in the commonwealth of God have done and will continue to do.

EXAMPLES OF NOBILITY

55.1 But moreover let us also bring forward examples of the heathen. Many kings and rulers who, being in times of pestilence, following some oracle, have given over themselves to death so that they might rescue their citizens by their own blood. Many have departed their own cities so that they might not rebel ₍any more₎.[b] **2** We know many among us have given themselves over to imprisonment so that they might ransom others. Many have given themselves over to slavery and having received their price ₍used the proceeds to feed₎[cd] others. **3** Many women, being strengthened by the grace of God, have accomplished many manly deeds. **4** The blessed Judith, when her city was under siege, asked of the elders to permit her to go out into the fortified camp of the foreigners.[e] **5** Therefore, giving herself over to danger, she went out because of love for her country and for the people who were under siege, and the Lord delivered Holophernes into the hand of a woman. **6** Not less also did Esther, perfect in faith, put herself in danger so that she might rescue the nation of Israel, which was about to be destroyed. For through fasting and her humiliation she beseeched the all-seeing Master of the ages, who upon seeing the humility of her soul rescued the people for whose sake she put herself in danger.[f]

---

a. Ps 24:1
b. Literally "against more"
c. Literally "have fed"
d. 1 Cor 13:3
e. Jdt 8
f. Esth 2–6

GOD'S DISCIPLINE AND MERCY

56.1 Therefore, let us also intercede for those who have fallen into any sin[a] so that gentleness and humility may be given to them, so that they may submit, not to us but to the will of God, for so they will have fruitful and perfect remembrance[b] before God[c] and the holy ones with mercy. 2 Let us receive discipline, by which no one should become angry, beloved. The admonition which we make to one another is advantageous and helpful beyond measure, for it unites us with the will of God. 3 For thus says the holy word: "Disciplining, the Lord has disciplined me, yet he has not handed me over to death. 4 For whom the Lord loves he disciplines, and he punishes every [child][d] whom he receives."[e] 5 "For the righteous will discipline me," it says, "with mercy and will correct me, but do not let the oil of sinners anoint my head."[f] 6 And again it says: "Blessed[g] is the one whom the Lord has corrected, and do not reject the admonition of the Almighty, for he himself causes *one* to feel pain, and he restores again. 7 He was wounded, and his hands were healed. 8 Six times he will deliver you from calamity, and the seventh time evil will not touch you. 9 In famine he will rescue you from death, and in war he will set you free from the hand of the sword.[h] 10 And he will keep you safe from the scourge of the tongue, and you will never fear when evils approach. 11 You will laugh at[i] the unrighteous and lawless, and you will not be afraid of the wild beasts, 12 for wild animals will be at peace with you. 13 Then you will know that your house will be at peace, [and the tent of your dwelling][j] [will never fail].[k] 14 And you will know that

---

a. Gal 6:1

b. Exod 28:23; 30:16; 23:18; Sir 50:16; Acts 10:4

c. Lightfoot comments: "The record of them before God and the Church will redound to their benefit, and they will receive pity."

d. Literally "son"

e. Prov 3:12; Heb 12:6

f. Ps 141:5

g. Job 5:17–260

h. While σίδηρος literally means "iron," here it is used metonymically for "sword." A similar English construction might use "blade of steel" but imply "sword," but to translate "hand of the sword" idiomatically as "blade of steel" seems a bit of a stretch.

i. Some editions (Lightfoot, Holmes) insert the break between verses 11 and 12 after this word.

j. Literally "and the habitation of your tent"

k. Literally "not do wrong"

your seed *will be* many, and your children *will be* like ₁all the plants₁[ab] of the field. [15] And you will come to the grave like ripe wheat harvested ₁at the proper time₁,[c] or like a heap on the threshing floor gathered together[d] ₁at the proper hour₁."[ef] [16] You see, beloved, how great the protection[g] is for those disciplined by the Master, for being a kind Father, he disciplines so that we may receive mercy through his holy discipline.

REBELLIOUS LEADERS MUST REPENT

[57.1] Therefore you who laid the foundation of the rebellion, you be subject to the presbyters[h] and be disciplined to repentance, bending the knees of your hearts. [2] Learn to be submissive, putting away the boastful and arrogant stubbornness of your tongue, for it is better for you to be found small and reputable among the flock of Christ than seeming prominent ₁and being deprived of his hope₁.[i] [3] For thus says the all-virtuous Wisdom, "Behold,[j] I will express to you the saying of my breath, and I will teach you my word. [4] Since I called and you did not obey, and I extended words and you did not pay attention but ₁disregarded₁[k] my counsel and disobeyed my correction, therefore I also will laugh at your destruction and will rejoice whenever destruction comes to you and whenever turmoil suddenly reaches you and destruction arrives like a sudden blast of wind or when tribulation and siege come upon you. [5] For it will be when you call upon me, and I will not hear you. Evil ones will seek me and they will not find *me*. For they hated wisdom and they did not choose the fear of the Lord, nor did they desire to pay attention to my counsel but treated my correction with contempt.

---

a. Literally "the herbage"

b. On this usage BDAG comments: "The imagery is that of a field covered in every direction with herbage too thick to count piece by piece. So great in number will be Job's offspring."

c. Literally "according to the time"

d. While συγκομίζω does occur in the NT (Acts 8:2), the usage is metaphoric and means "to bury"; the literal sense of "to bring in for harvest" or "to gather together" does not occur in the NT and hence has no LN assignment.

e. Literally "according to the hour"

f. Job 5:17–26

g. 2 Sam 22:36; Ps 38:35; Lam 3:64

h. 1 Pet 5:5

i. Literally "[and] being driven out from his hope"

j. Prov 1:23–33

k. Literally "made void"

[6] Therefore they will eat the fruit of their own way, and they will be completely filled with their own impiety. [7] For whoever wronged the innocents, they will be killed, and an inquiry will destroy the ungodly. But those who hear me will dwell having confidence in hope, and will rest without fear of any evil."[a]

LISTEN TO THE ADVICE OF THE ROMAN CHURCH

[58.1] Therefore, let us obey his all-holy and glorious name, escaping the threats foretold by Wisdom to those who disobeyed, that being confident, we may dwell upon the most holy name of his majesty. [2] Accept our advice, and there will be nothing for you to regret. For *as* God lives and *as* the Lord Jesus Christ lives and the Holy Spirit (both the faith and the hope of the elect) that he who has done without regret in humility with eager gentleness the regulations and commandments given by God, this one enrolled and included will be within the number of those who are saved by Jesus Christ, through whom is to him the glory ₍forever₎,[b] amen.

GUARD THE ELECT

[59.1] But if some should disobey what has been said by him through us, they must know that they will entangle themselves in no small sin and danger. [2] But we will be innocent of this sin and will ask, making earnest prayer and supplication, that the number of those who are counted among his elect throughout the whole world, the Creator of everything may guard unharmed through his beloved child Jesus Christ, through whom he called us from darkness into light, from ignorance into the knowledge of the glory of his name. [3] *Grant us, Lord*, to hope[c] upon the source of all creation, your name, *and* open the eyes of our hearts to know you, who alone remain highest among the most high[d] *and* holiest among the holy. You who humble the

---

a. Prov 1:23–33

b. Literally "into the ages of the ages"

c. The text is damaged here. Lightfoot provides the following conjecture, which most editions accept: [Δὸς ἡμῖν, Κύριε], ἐλπίζειν; translated "[Grant us, Lord], to hope ...".

d. Isa 57:15

pride of the proud,[a] who destroy[b] the speculation of the nations, who lift[c] the humble to the heights and who humble the proud, who make people rich and make people poor,[d] who kill and who make alive,[e] who alone is the discoverer[f] of spirits and God of all flesh,[g] who look into the depths,[h] the eyewitness of human deeds,[i] the helper of those who are in danger,[j] the Savior of those who are in despair, the creator[k] and guardian of every spirit, who multiply the nations upon earth and chose from all of them those who love you through Jesus Christ your beloved child, through whom you have taught, sanctified, and honored us. 4 We ask you, Master, to be our helper and protector. Save ₗthose of us who are in tribulation₎;[l] on the lowly, have mercy; those who fall, raise; to those who pray, reveal yourself; the sick, heal; those of your people who wander about, turn back; feed those who hunger; ransom our prisoners; raise up[m] those who are weak; encourage those who are discouraged. Let all the nations know you,[n] that you are the only God, and Jesus Christ is your child, and we are your people and the sheep of your pasture.[o]

PRAYER FOR HARMONY

60.1 For you, through ₗyour works₎,[p] have made known the ever-flowing structure of the world. You, Lord, created the world. You are faithful in all generations, righteous in judgments, wonderful in strength and majesty. You are wise in creating and intelligent in establishing what exists. You

---

a. Isa 13:11
b. Ps 33:10
c. Job 5:11; Isa 10:33; Ezek 21:26; 17:24; Matt 23:13; Luke 14:11; 18:14
d. 1 Sam 2:7; Luke 1:53
e. Deut 32:39; 1 Sam 2:6
f. Ps 115:7
g. Num 16:22; 27:16
h. Sir 16:18, 19
i. Ps 33:13
j. Jdt 9:11
k. Zech 12:1
l. Literally "those who [are] in tribulation among us"
m. 1 Thess 5:14
n. 1 Kgs 8:60; 2 Kgs 19:19; Ezek 24:23; John 17:3
o. Ps 100:3
p. Literally "the workings"

are good in the things which are seen and kind in the things which trust in you. Merciful and compassionate one, forgive us our transgressions and unrighteousnesses and our sins and offenses. [2] Do not take into account[a] every sin of your male slaves and female slaves, but cleanse us with the cleansing of your truth, and direct our steps to walk in holiness[b] of heart,[c] and to do what is good and pleasing before you and before our rulers.[d] [3] Yes, Master, let your face shine upon us[e] for *our own* good,[f] in peace, so that we may be protected by your mighty hand, and rescued from all sin by your uplifted[g] arm, and you rescue us from those who hate us unjustly. [4] Give harmony and peace, both to us and to all those who dwell on the earth, just as you have given to our forefathers, when they called upon you reverently, in faith and truth;[h] being obedient to your all-powerful and glorious name, both to our rulers and governors upon the earth.

PRAYER FOR PEACE

[61.1] You, Master, have given the power of the kingdom to them through your magnificent and indescribable power, so that we may know the glory and honor given to them by you, *and* be subject[i] to them, in no way opposing your will. To whom, Lord, give[j] health, peace, harmony, *and* good disposition[k] so that they may administer the government given by you to them without stumbling.[l] [2] For you, heavenly Master, King of the ages,[m] have

---

a. Literally "Do not reckon"

b. ὁσιότητι Lake, Lightfoot, Ehrman] + καὶ δικαιοσύνῃ καὶ ἁπλότητι Holmes. The difference in translation is from "to walk in holiness of heart" to "to walk in holiness and righteousness and purity of heart."

c. 1 Kgs 9:4

d. Deut 13:18

e. Ps 67:1

f. Jer 21:10; Gen 50:20; Deut 30:9

g. Exod 6:1; Deut 4:34; 5:15; 7:19; 9:26; 11:2; 26:8; Jer 32:21; Ezek 20:33–34

h. ἀληθείᾳ Lake, Ehrman] + ὥστε σώζεσθαι ἡμᾶς Lightfoot, Holmes. The reading in Lightfoot and Holmes is an emendation by Lightfoot that can be translated "that we may be saved." There is no direct textual evidence for the emendation.

i. 1 Pet 2:13, 15; Rom 13:2

j. Rom 13:1; Titus 3:1; 1 Pet 2:13; Wis 6:1

k. Lightfoot comments: "The word may mean either 'firmness, steadiness' as a moral quality, or 'stability' as a material result."

l. Lightfoot provides the glosses "without stumbling" and "without any jar or collision."

m. 1 Tim 1:17; Tob 8:6, 10

given to the sons of men glory and honor and power over the things which belong upon the earth. You, Lord, direct their plan according to what is good and pleasing in your presence, so that, piously administering with peace and gentleness the authority given by you to them, they may experience your mercy. [3] The only one able to do these things and even better things for us, to you we give praise through the high priest and defender of our souls, Jesus Christ, through whom *be* glory and majesty to you, both now and ₗfor all generationsₗ[abc] and ₗforever,ₗ[d] amen.

LETTER SUMMARY

[62.1] And we have written enough to you, men *and* brothers, about what is fitting in our worship and what is most beneficial for a virtuous life to those who desire to conduct *their lives* in godliness and righteousness. [2] For concerning faith and repentance and genuine love and self-control and moderation and endurance, we have touched on every aspect, reminding you that it is necessary to reverently please the all-powerful God in righteousness and truth and patience, ₗliving in harmonyₗ[e] without bearing malice, in love and peace with eager gentleness, just as even our fathers who were previously mentioned, being humble-minded, were pleasing to the Father and Creator God, and *to* all people. [3] And we reminded *you* of these things even more gladly since we clearly knew to write to people *who were* faithful and highly regarded and ₗwho had studied,ₗ[f] the sayings of the teaching of God.

HEAR THE WISDOM OF REPENTANCE

[63.1] Therefore it is right, agreeing with examples of such a kind and so many, to risk our necks and to take up the position of obedience, so that ceasing from the futile rebellion, we may attain the goal ₗtruly set before

---

a. Literally "into the generation of generations"

b. Lightfoot clarifies this as "the generation which comprises all generations," further noting that "this is a rare mode of expression."

c. Ps 102:24

d. Literally "into the ages of the ages"

e. Literally "being in agreement"

f. Literally "who had looked into"

us,[a] without any blemish. ² For you will give joy and exultation to us if, being obedient to what was written by us through the Holy Spirit, you do away with the disgusting anger of your jealousy according to the petition which we have made with peace and harmony in this very letter. ³ And we have sent people faithful and prudent from youth until old age who have conducted themselves blamelessly among us, who also shall be witnesses between you and us. ⁴ And we have done this so that you may know that all of our concern also has been and is for you to attain peace ₁very quickly,₁.[b]

CLOSING PRAYER

64.1 Finally, the all-seeing God and Master of spirits, and Lord of all flesh, who chose out[c] the Lord Jesus Christ, and us through him for a specially acquired people, may he give to all souls who call upon his magnificent and holy name faith, reverence, peace, endurance and patience, self-control, purity and moderation,[d] so that being found pleasing to his name through our high priest and defender Jesus Christ, through whom to him *be* the glory and majesty, power and honor, both now and for all ₁eternity,₁[e] amen.

FINAL REQUESTS AND BENEDICTION

65.1 Now those who were sent from us, Claudius Ephebus and Valerius Bito also along with Fortunatus, send *them* back to us ₁very soon,₁[f] in peace[g] with joy, so that they may report quickly the peace and harmony prayed for and greatly desired by us, so that we also may soon rejoice about your stability. ² The grace of our Lord Jesus Christ *be* with you and with everyone everywhere who has been called by God through him, through whom to him *be* the glory, honor, power and majesty, *and* an eternal throne from ₁eternity,₁[h] into ₁eternity,₁[i] amen.

---

a. Literally "which has been set before us in truth"
b. Literally "with quickness"
c. Luke 9:35
d. Titus 2:5
e. Literally "the ages of the ages"
f. Literally "with quickness"
g. 1 Cor 16:11
h. Literally "the ages"
i. Literally "the ages of the ages"

– The Letter of the Romans to the Corinthians

An Early Christian Homily
(The Second Letter of Clement to the Corinthians)

INTRODUCTION

[1.1] Brothers, it is necessary for us to think in this way concerning Jesus Christ: *to think* as concerning God, as concerning the judge of the living and the dead. [a] And it is not proper for us to think little concerning our salvation. [2] For when we think little concerning him, we also hope to receive little. And the ones listening [as if these were][b] little things, they sin and we sin, not knowing from where and by whom and to which place we have been called, nor how great the suffering Jesus Christ endured for us. [3] Therefore what can we give to him as return?[c] Or what fruit[d] worthy of that which he himself has given to us? And how much do we owe[e] holiness to him? [4] For he gave us the light; as a father,[f] he called us sons; when we were being destroyed, he saved us. [5] Therefore what praise shall we give to him? Or *what* wages as return for what we received? [6] Being maimed in our understanding, worshiping stone and wood and gold and silver and brass, human works, and our entire life was nothing if not death. Therefore [being blanketed][g] by darkness and [our vision impaired by such a foggy mist,][h]

---

a. Acts 10:42; 1 Pet 4:5
b. Literally "as concerning"
c. Rom 1:27; 2 Cor 6:13; Ps 116:12
d. The previous verb is assumed here: "Or what fruit [can we give him]."
e. Isa 55:3; Acts 13:34
f. Hos 2:1; Rom 9:26; 2 Cor 6:18; 1 John 3:1
g. Literally "being surrounded"
h. Literally "of such foggy mist, being full in the vision"

we regained our sight, by his will casting off[a] that cloud which ˌenveloped usˌ.[b] 7 For he had mercy on us and having compassion he saved *us*, seeing in us great error and destruction. And we have ˌnot an ounce of hopeˌ[c] of salvation, except through him. 8 For he called[d] us when we did not exist and he willed us out of ˌnon-beingˌ[e] ˌto beˌ.[f]

TEXT AND EXPOSITION

2.1 "Rejoice, O barren woman who has not given birth, break forth and shout, you who have no birth pains, for many *are* the children of the deserted *woman*, more than she who has a husband."[g] The one who says, "Rejoice, O barren woman who has not given birth," speaks to us, for our church was barren before children were given to her. 2 And the one who says, "Shout, you who have no birth pains," means this: offer up our prayers sincerely to God; ˌwe should not grow weary like women in laborˌ.[h] 3 And the one who says, "For many *are* the children of the deserted *woman*, more than she who has a husband," since our people seem to be deserted by God, but now we who have believed have become many more than those who seemed to have God. 4 And another scripture also says that "I have not come to call the righteous, but the sinners."[i] 5 He means this: that we must save those who are perishing. 6 For it is great and marvelous to strengthen not what is established but what has fallen. 7 So also Christ willed to save[j] what was perishing, and he saved many, having come and having called us who were already perishing.

CONFESSING CHRIST

3.1 Therefore, since he has shown so much mercy to us, and that first of all we who are living do not offer sacrifice to dead gods and do not worship

---

a. Heb 12:1; Acts 28:20; Heb 5:2
b. Literally "surrounded us"
c. Literally "no hope"
d. Rom 4:17
e. Literally "not existing"
f. Literally "to exist"
g. Isa 54:1
h. Literally "not as those who have birth pains we should grow weary"
i. This is likely the earliest citation of a passage found in the New Testament as scripture.
j. Luke 19:10; 1 Tim 1:15

them, but through him we know the Father of truth. What is the knowledge (the knowledge about him) [except not denying the one] [a] through whom we know him? [2] And he himself also says, "The one who confesses me before people, I will confess him before my Father." [b] [3] Therefore this is our reward, if only we confess *him* through whom we are saved. [4] But [how] [c] do we confess him? By doing what he says and not disobeying his commandments, and *by* not only honoring him with *our* lips but with *our* whole heart and with *our* whole mind. [d] [5] And he also says in Isaiah, "This people honors me with their lips, but their heart is far away from me." [e]

KEEPING HIS COMMANDMENTS

[4.1] Therefore, let us not merely call him Lord, for this will not save us. [2] For he says, "Not everyone who says to me, 'Lord, Lord!' will be saved, but the one who practices righteousness." [f] [3] So then, brothers, let us confess him with our deeds by loving one another, by not committing adultery or slandering [g] one another or being jealous, but by being self-controlled, merciful, good. [h] And we ought to suffer with one another and not to love money. By these works let us confess him, and not by their opposites. [4] And it is not necessary for us to fear men but God. [i] [5] Because of this, you who do these things, the Lord said, "If you have gathered with me in my bosom and you do not do my commandments, I will throw you out and I will say to you, [Leave me!] [j] I do not know where you are from, you doers of iniquity!'" [k]

---

a. Literally "if not to deny the one"

b. While this quotation occurs in the NT, it here is directly attributed to Jesus. The source could be oral, it could be a collection of sayings, or it could be from one of the two instances in the gospels (Matt 10:32; Luke 12:8).

c. Literally "by what"

d. Mark 12:30

e. Isa 29:13; Matt 15:8; Mark 7:6; see also 1 Cl 15.2

f. Matt 7:21

g. Jas 4:11

h. Titus 2:5; 1 Pet 2:18; 1 Thess 3:6

i. Acts 4:19; 5:29

j. Literally "Go away from me!"

k. Lightfoot (and others) posit the larger quotation may be from the apocryphal Gospel of the Egyptians. The inner quotation could be from either Luke 8:27 or Matt 7:23; though both have ties to Ps 6:9.

CONDUCT YOURSELVES
REVERENTLY AND RIGHTLY

5.1 Therefore, brothers, leaving behind the temporary residence of this world, let us do the will of him who called us and let us not be afraid to go out from this world. 2 For the Lord said, "You will be a like sheep ₍among₎ b wolves." c 3 And answering, Peter said to him, "But if the wolves tear apart the sheep?" 4 Jesus said to Peter, "The sheep have no fear of the wolves after they are dead, and you have no fear of those who kill you and who are able to do nothing more to you, but you fear him who after you are dead has power to throw soul and body into the hell of fire." 5 And you know, brothers, that the sojourn, the one in this world, of this flesh, is small and of short duration, but the promise of Christ is great and wonderful: the rest of the coming kingdom and life eternal. 6 Therefore, what are we to do to obtain them, except to conduct ourselves reverently and rightly, and to consider these worldly things as foreign and not to desire them? 7 For when we desire to acquire these things, we fall away from the way of the righteous.

ONE MASTER, NOT TWO

6.1 And the Lord said, "No slave is able to serve two masters." d If we desire to serve both God and money, it is harmful to us. 2 "For what is the advantage if someone gains the whole world but forfeits his soul?" e 3 And this age and the one about to come are two enemies. 4 This *age* speaks of adultery and corruption f and love of money and deceit, but that one renounces these things. 5 Therefore, we are not able to be friends ₍with both₎, g but it is necessary for us to renounce this one to experience that one. 6 We suppose that it is better to hate the things here because *they are* insignificant, of short duration and corruptible, but to love those good and incorruptible

---

a. While portions of this whole exchange can be found in the canonical Gospels, the entire account as a whole is not present, nor some crucial pieces of it. Some hold it to be from the apocryphal Gospel of the Egyptians (cf. 2 Cl 12.2), though that is supposition. Portions of the larger exchange are found in Matt 10:16, 28; Luke 10:3; 12:4-5.

b. Literally "in the midst of"

c. Matt 10:16; Luke 10:3

d. Luke 16:13; Matt 6:24

e. Matt 16:26; Mark 8:36; Luke 9:25

f. 2 Pet 1:4; 2:12, 19

g. Literally "of the two"

things. [7] For if we do the will of Christ, we will find rest; but if *we do* otherwise, if we disobey his commandments, nothing will rescue us from eternal punishment. [8] And the scripture also says in Ezekiel that "if Noah and Job and Daniel should rise up, they will not rescue their children"[a] in the captivity.[b] [9] But if even righteous men such as these are not able to rescue their children by their own righteousness, if we do not keep our baptism pure and undefiled, with what kind of confidence will we enter into the kingdom[c] of God? Or who will be our advocate if we may not be found to have holy and righteous works?

COMPETING IN THE CONTEST

[7.1] So then, my brothers, let us compete[d] knowing that the contest ⌊is at hand⌋[e] and that many set sail for ⌊contests with a perishable prize⌋,[f] but not all are crowned, except the many who trained hard[g] and competed well. [2] Therefore let us compete so that we all may be crowned. [3] So then, let us run the straight course, ⌊the heavenly competition⌋,[h] and let many of us set sail toward it and let us compete that we may also be crowned. And if we are not all able to be crowned,[i] at least let us come near the crown. [4] We must know that he who competes in the ⌊contest with a perishable prize⌋,[j] if he is found cheating,[k] he is taken away, flogged, and he is thrown

---

a. Ezek 14:14-20

b. Lightfoot notes that "in the captivity" is an addition and it should not be included in the quotation/abridgement from Ezek 14:14-20.

c. Lake translates literally as "palace"; Lightfoot strongly recommends "kingdom" and is followed by Holmes and Ehrman.

d. 1 Cor 9:24-27; Phil 3:12-14; 2 Tim 4:7-8

e. Literally "[is] in the hands"

f. Literally "perishable contests"

g. Lightfoot notes that this is "a word used especially of training for the contest."

h. Literally "the immortal competition"

i. Lightfoot comments: "This seems to point to some public recognition of those who came next after the victor. In the Olympian chariot races there were second, third, and fourth prizes; but in the foot races the notices of any inferior prize or honorable mention are vague and uncertain."

j. Literally "perishable contest"

k. Though φθείρω is found in the NT, this sense ("to violate rules, to cheat") is not attested in the NT and is clearly intended here. Lightfoot notes "the word is used of violating the conditions of the contest, e.g., by making a false start or cutting off a corner or tripping up an adversary or taking any underhanded advantage."

outside the stadium. 5 What do you think? He who cheats in the ₁contest with an imperishable prize₁,ᵃ what will he suffer? 6 For those who have not kept the sealᵇ he says, "Their worm will not die and their fire will not be extinguished and they will be a vision to all flesh."ᶜ

THE TIME TO REPENT

8.1 Therefore, while we are on the earth, let us repent. 2 For we are clayᵈ in the hand of the craftsman. For ₁it is like₁,ᵉ the potter, if he should make a vessel, and it becomes misshapen in his hands or it is broken,ᶠ ₁he reshapes it₁. ⁸ But if he has already put it into the ₁kiln₁,ʰ ₁he will not be able to fix it anymore₁.ⁱ So also with us, while we are in this world, evil which we have done in the flesh, let us repent from *our* whole heart, that we might be saved by the Lord, while we have time for repentance. 3 For after we depart from the world, we are no longer able to confess or even repent in that place. 4 So then, brothers, having done the will of the Father and having kept the flesh pure and having obeyed the commandments of the Lord, we will receive eternal life. 5 For the Lord says in the gospel, "If you did not guard the small things, who will give you the big things? For I say to you that whoever *is* faithful with the least important is also faithful with the very *important*."ʲ 6 Therefore he means this: keep the flesh pure and the seal unstained,ᵏ in order that we may receive eternal life.

LOVE AND REPENTANCE

9.1 And none of you should say that this flesh is neither judged nor raised again. 2 Understand *this*! In what state were you saved? In what state did you regain your sight, except being in this flesh? 3 Therefore it is necessary

---

a. Literally "imperishable contest"
b. The seal of baptism, see 2 Cl 6.9; 8.6
c. Isa 66:24; Mark 9:48
d. Jer 18:4–6; Rom 9:21
e. Literally "in which manner"
f. Rev 2:27
g. Literally "again he forms it"
h. Literally "furnace of fire"
i. Literally "he will help it no longer"
j. Luke 16:10–12; Matt 25:21, 23
k. 1 Tim 6:14; Jas 1:27

for us to guard the flesh as a temple of God. [a] 4 For [just as] [b] in the flesh you were called, [you will also come in the flesh]. [c] 5 If Christ, the Lord who saved us, indeed being [originally] [d] spirit, became flesh and [in this state] [e] called us, thus also we will receive the reward in this flesh. 6 Therefore, let us love one another so that we may all enter into the kingdom of God. 7 While we have opportunity [f] to be healed, let us give ourselves to the one who heals, God, giving recompense to him. 8 Which *recompense*? Repentance from a sincere heart. 9 For he is the one who knows everything beforehand, and knows what is in our heart. [g] 10 Therefore, let us give him praise, [h] not only from the mouth but also from the heart, so that he might welcome us as sons. 11 For the Lord also says, "These are my brothers *and sisters*, the ones who do the will of my Father." [i]

DO THE WILL OF THE FATHER

10.1 So then, my brothers, let us do the will of the Father who called us, so that we may live, and let us instead pursue virtue. But let us give up evil as the forerunner of our sins and let us flee impiety, lest evil overcome us. 2 For if we are eager to do good, peace will pursue us. 3 For because of this, the reason nobody is able to find *peace*, [j] they bring in [k] human fears, preferring instead the present pleasure to the coming promise. 4 For they do not know what great torment the present pleasure brings, and what kind of joy the future promise holds. 5 And if they alone were doing these things,

---

a. 1 Cor 3:16, 17; 6:19; 2 Cor 6:16

b. Literally "in which manner"

c. Literally "and in the flesh you will come"

d. Literally "at first"

e. Literally "thus"

f. Gal 6:10

g. 2 Chr 32:31; Deut 8:2; 1 Sam 9:19

h. αἶνον Lake, Ehrman] + αἰώνιον Lightfoot, Holmes. The translational difference is "praise" vs. "eternal praise." Lightfoot's reading, however, is an emendation. Alexandrinus reads αἶνον; Hierosolymitanus and the Syriac edition have only αἰώνιον; Lightfoot's emendation considers the likeliest solution to be both terms (the omission likely occuring via *homoiteleuton*).

i. Matt 12:50; Mark 3:35; Luke 8:21

j. Holmes' note here is instructive: "The ancient authorities read only 'to find'. The Greek word for 'peace' may have been omitted accidentally owing to its similarity in appearance to the preceding word for 'find.'"

k. This sense of παράγω does not occur in the NT; see LXX 1 Sam 16:9.

it would be bearable, but now they persist in teaching evil to innocent souls, not knowing that they will receive[a] a double punishment, both themselves and those who listen to them.

SERVE GOD WITH A PURE HEART

11.1 Therefore, let us serve God with a pure heart[b] and we will be righteous. But if we do not serve *him* because we do not believe the promise of God, we are wretched. 2 For the prophetic[c] word[d] also says: "Wretched are the double-minded,[e] those who doubt in their heart, who say, 'We have heard these things long ago and ₗin the days of our fathers₎,[f] and we, waiting ₗday in and day out₎,[gh] have seen none of these things.' 3 Foolish people! Compare[i] yourselves to a tree. Take a vine: first it indeed sheds its leaves, then a bud comes, after these things an unripe grape, then presents a bunch of grapes. 4 So also my people experienced insurrection and tribulation; later they will receive good things."5 So then, my brothers, let us not be double-minded, but let us remain in hope in order that we may also receive the reward. 6 For he who promised[j] is faithful to pay to each[k] the recompense of his works. 7 Therefore, if we do what is righteous before God, we will enter into his kingdom and receive the promises which "ear has not heard and eye has not seen and have not entered into the human heart."[l]

---

a. The notion of the teacher also being responsible for those he teaches is common. See 1 Tim 4:16; also see 2 Cl 15.1; 19.1 and Ign Eph 16.1–2

b. 1 Tim 1:5; 2 Tim 2:22; Matt 5:8

c. 2 Pet 1:19

d. The same "scripture" is quoted in 1 Cl 23.3: Lightfoot suggests it is from the lost apocryphal book of Eldad and Modad.

e. Jas 1:8

f. Literally "in our fathers"

g. Literally "day by day"

h. Num 30:15; 2 Pet 2:8

i. While συμβάλλω is used in the NT, the sense of "to compare" is not found in the NT.

j. Heb 10:23

k. Matt 16:27; Rom 2:6; Rev 22:12

l. 1 Cor 2:9; Isa 64:4

THE COMING OF GOD'S KINGDOM

^{12.1} Therefore let us wait for the kingdom of God ˻hour by hour˼ [a] with love and righteousness, since we do not know the day of God's appearance. [2] For when the Lord himself was asked by someone when his kingdom will come, he said, "When the two shall be one, and the outside as the inside, and the male with the female neither male nor female." [b] [3] And "the two are one" when we speak the truth with ourselves, and there is one soul in two bodies with no hypocrisy. [4] And "the outside as the inside" means this: "the inside" means the soul and "the outside" means the body. Therefore in this manner your body is made visible, so also let your soul be evident in good works. [5] And "the male with the female neither male nor female" means this: that a brother, upon seeing a sister, thinks nothing about her *being a* female, nor does she think anything about him *being a* male. [6] When you do these things, he says, the kingdom of my Father will come.

NOW IS THE TIME TO REPENT

^{13.1} Therefore, brothers, now at last let us repent. Let us be self-controlled [c] for the good, for we are full of much folly and wickedness. Let us wipe away [d] from ourselves our former sins and, repenting from the soul, let us be saved. And do not let us become people pleasers, [e] nor let us wish to please ourselves alone, but also those people outside *of us* by righteousness, that the name may not be blasphemed [f] because of us. [2] For the Lord says, "My name is blasphemed ˻continually˼ [g] among all the nations," [h] and again, "Woe *to him* on account of whom my name is blasphemed." [i] ˻How˼ [j] is it blasphemed? By you who do not do what I desire. [3] For when the nations

---

a. Literally "each hour"

b. This saying of Jesus is not found in the NT. It is found in the Gospel of Thomas (§22) and also in Clement of Alexandria's *Stromata* 3.13.92, where the saying is attributed to the Gospel of the Egyptians.

c. 2 Tim 2:26; 1 Pet 4:7

d. Acts 3:19

e. Eph 6:6; Col 3:22

f. 1 Tim 6:1

g. Literally "through it all"

h. Isa 52:5

i. The source of this quotation is unknown, though Lightfoot posits it is an alternate form of the previous quotation from Isa 52:5.

j. Literally "By what"

hear from our mouth the sayings of God, they marvel at *their* beauty and greatness. Later, upon learning our works are not worthy of the words which we speak, they turn from *wonder* to blasphemy, saying it is some myth and deception. ⁴ For when they hear from us that God says, "*It is* no credit to you if you love those who love you, but *it is* a credit to you if you love your enemies and those who hate you." ᵃ When they hear these things, they are astonished at the extraordinary degree of goodness, ᵇ but when they see that not only do we not love those who hate *us*, but that not even those who love *us*, they laugh at us and the name is blasphemed.

CHOOSE THE CHURCH OF THE LIVING

¹⁴·¹ So then, brothers, if we do the will of our Father, God, we will belong to the first church, the spiritual one, which was created before the sun and moon. ᶜ But if we do not do the will of the Lord, we will belong to the scripture which says, "My house became a den of robbers." ᵈ So then, therefore, let us choose ᵉ to belong to the church of life that we may be saved. ² And I do not suppose you to be ignorant that the living church is the body of Christ. For the scripture says, "God made humankind male and female." ᶠ The male is Christ, the female *is* the church. And in addition, the books and the apostles ᵍ say the church does not belong to the present, but *has been* from the beginning. For she was spiritual as *was* also our Jesus, but she was made known ʰ at the last days so that she might save us. ³ And the church, being spiritual, was made known in the flesh of Christ, revealing to us that if any of us guard her in the flesh and do not corrupt *her*, he will receive her back again in the Holy Spirit. For this flesh is a copy of the Spirit. Therefore no one who corrupts the copy will have a share in the

---

a. Luke 6:32, 35

b. Wis 7:26; 12:22; Sir 14:23

c. Ps 72:5

d. Jer 7:11; Matt 21:12; Mark 11:17; Luke 19:46

e. Matt 12:18

f. Gen 1:27

g. "The books and the apostles" is likely a reference to the whole of scripture.

h. The feminine pronoun "she" is used here to make explicit the reference back to "the church." Ehrman translates using a masculine pronoun; but the above translation agrees with Holmes who, while noting the masculine, translates with the feminine pronoun with the further comment that it is "grammatically more probable."

original. As a result, then, he means this, brothers: Guard the flesh so that you may have a share in the Spirit. 4 And if we say the flesh is the church and the Spirit is Christ, ⌐of course⌐[a] the one who abuses the flesh will abuse the church. Therefore, one such as this will not have a share in the Spirit, which is Christ. 5 This flesh is able to have a share in such great life and immortality when the Holy Spirit clings to it; no one is able to express or to speak what the Lord has prepared for his elect.

HEED THE SPEAKER'S ADVICE

15.1 And I do not think that I have given unimportant advice about self-control. ⌐Whoever does it⌐[b] will not regret it,[c] but also will save himself[d] and I who advise him. For it is no small reward to return a wandering and perishing soul to salvation.[e] 2 For this is the recompense we are able to pay to God who created us: if the one who speaks and hears both speaks and hears with faith and love. 3 Therefore, let us remain righteous and holy in what we have believed, so that with confidence we may request of God, who says, "While you are still speaking, I will say, 'Behold, I am here.'"[f] 4 For this saying is a sign of great promise: For the Lord says he is more ready to give than the one who asks. 5 Therefore having a share in such great goodness, let us not begrudge each other the experience of such great benefits. For as much pleasure as these words have for those who do them, they have great condemnation for those who disobey.

RENOUNCE THE WORLD

16.1 So then, brothers, having received no small opportunity to repent, having the chance, let us turn back to the God who called us while we still have one who accepts us. 2 For if we renounce these enjoyments and conquer our soul by not doing its evil lusts, we will have a share in the mercy

---

a. Literally "then"

b. Literally "Which if anyone does"

c. The sense of μετανοέω used here is more along the lines of "to regret" and not that of "to repent" in the typical Christian sense. LN has no entry for this sense, and BDAG classifies it together with "to repent."

d. 1 Tim 4:16

e. Jas 5:20

f. Isa 58:9

of Jesus. [3] But you know that the day of judgment is already coming, like a burning oven, [a] and will melt some of the heavens, and the whole earth will be like lead melting in a fire [b] and then he will make known *both* the secret and public works of people. [c] [4] Therefore charitable giving *is* good; so too *is* repentance from sin. Fasting *is* better than prayer, but charitable giving *is better than* both. And love covers up a multitude of sins, [d] but prayer from a good conscience rescues from death. Blessed *is* everyone who is found complete in these things, for charitable giving ₁lightens the load of sin₁. [e]

REPENT WITH YOUR WHOLE HEART

[17.1] Therefore let us repent with *our* whole heart, so that ₁none₁ [f] of us should perish. For if we have commandments, then let us also do this: draw *them* away from idols and teach *them*. How much more should the soul that already knows God not be able to perish? [2] Therefore let us help ourselves and bring back those who are weak ₁in goodness₁, [g] so that we may all be saved. And let us turn back and admonish one another. [3] And let us think about believing and paying attention not only now when we are being instructed by the presbyters, but also when we have departed to home, let us remember the commandments of the Lord and let us not be dragged away by worldly passions but let us try to come as often as possible, to make progress in the commandments of the Lord, so that all ₁with the same mind₁ [h i] may be gathered together for life. [4] For the Lord said, "I come to gather together all the nations, tribes, and tongues." [j] And he means this: the day of his appearance, upon *his* coming, he will redeem each of us according to his works. [5] And the unbelievers "will see his glory" [k] and power, and they will be astonished, seeing the kingdom of the world ₁given

---

a. Mal 4:1; 1 Pet 3:7, 10
b. Isa 34:4
c. 1 Tim 5:24–25
d. 1 Pet 4:8; Prov 10:12
e. Literally "leads to alleviation of sin"
f. Literally "not any"
g. Literally "concerning the good"
h. Literally "who think the same"
i. Rom 12:16; Phil 2:2
j. Isa 66:18
k. Isa 66:18

to Jesus₁,ᵃ saying, "Woe to us, that it was you and we did not know *it* and did not believe and did not obey the presbyters who informed us about our salvation." "And his worm will not die and his fire will not be extinguished, and they shall be a vision to all flesh."ᵇ ⁶ He means that day of judgment, when they will see those who act impiously among us and who distort the commandments of Jesus Christ. ⁷ But the righteous who have done what is right and who have endured torments and who have hated the pleasures of the soul, when they observe those who have deviatedᶜ and who have denied Jesus by words or by works, how they are punished with severe torments in unquenchable fire, ᵈ they shall give glory to their God, saying that "There will be hope for the one who serves God with *his* whole heart."

PURSUE RIGHTEOUSNESS

¹⁸·¹ Therefore let us also be among those who give thanks, who have served God, and *who are* not among the ungodly who are judged. ² For even I am utterly sinful and have not yet escaped temptation, but am still in the midst of the tools of the devil. I am eager to pursueᵉ righteousness so that I may even be able to be near it, being in fear of the coming judgment.

REPENT AND RECEIVE SALVATION

¹⁹·¹ So then, brothers and sisters, with the God of truth, I am reading to you a request to pay attention to what is written, that you may save both yourselves and ₁your reader₁.ᶠ For the reward I ask you to repent with *your* whole heart, giving yourselves salvation and life. For having done this, we will set a goal for all the younger ones who desire to devote themselves to the piety and the goodness of God. ² And let us, the unwise, not be displeased or indignant when someone admonishes and turns us from unrighteousness to righteousness. For sometimes when we do evil, ₁we are unaware₁ᵍ

---

a. Literally "in Jesus"
b. Isa 66:24; Mark 9:48
c. 1 Tim 1:6; 6:21; 2 Tim 2:18
d. Matt 3:12; Mark 9:43; Luke 3:17
e. 1 Tim 4:11; 2 Tim 2:22; Rom 9:30
f. Literally "he who reads among you"
g. Literally "we do not know"

because of the double-mindedness[a] and unbelief which are in our chests
and we are darkened in our understanding[b] by futile desires. [3] Therefore let
us do righteousness, so that at the end we may be saved. Blessed *are* those
who obey these commandments; though they bear hardship patiently[c] for
a short time[d] in this world, they will harvest[e] the immortal fruit of the resurrection. [4] Therefore, let not the godly one grieve if, at the present time,
he feels miserable — a blessed time awaits him! That one, coming to life
again[f] with the fathers above, he will rejoice at an eternity without sorrow.

COMPETE FOR THE REWARD, DOXOLOGY

[20.1] But do not let it disturb your mind that we see the unrighteous becoming rich and the slaves of God undergoing hardship. [2] Therefore let us
have faith, brothers and sisters! We are competing in the contest of the
living God, and we are being trained in the present life so that we may
be crowned[g] in the *life* to come. [3] None of the righteous receive a reward
quickly, but wait for it. [4] For if God promptly paid the wages of the righteous, we would immediately engage in commerce and not godliness,[h]
for we would seem to be righteous, pursuing not piety but profit. And
because of this, divine judgment injures a spirit that is not righteous and
weighs it down with chains. [5] To the only invisible[i] God, Father of truth,
who sent to us the Savior[j] and Originator of immortality, through whom
also he made known to us the truth and the heavenly life, to him *be* the
glory ₍forever₎,[k] amen.

---

a. Jas 4:8
b. Eph 4:18
c. 2 Tim 1:8; 2:3, 9; 4:5; Jas 5:13
d. 1 Pet 1:6
e. Hos 10:12
f. 2 Macc 7:9
g. 2 Tim 2:5
h. 1 Tim 2:10
i. 1 Tim 1:17
j. Acts 5:31; 3:15; Heb 2:10
k. Literally "into the ages of the ages"

— *Ignatius to the Ephesians*

SALUTATION

Ignatius, ₁who is also called "God-bearer,"[a]₁ to her blessed[b] with greatness by the fullness[c] of God the Father; to her predestined before the ages to be ₁always₁[d] for constant, unchangeable glory, united and chosen through genuine suffering[e] by the will of the Father and Jesus Christ our God; to the church worthily blessed which is at Ephesus in Asia, abundant greetings in Jesus Christ and in blameless joy.

GREETINGS AND BACKGROUND

1.1 Welcoming in God your much-loved name, which you possess by your righteous nature according to faith and love in Christ Jesus our Savior; you are imitators[f] of God, having rekindled by the blood of God your related[g]

---

a. Literally "who [is] also God-bearer"

b. Eph 1:3

c. Lightfoot notes this phrase could be translated "through the plenitude of God the Father," further noting that πλήρωμα "is used, as by St. Paul and St. John, in its theological sense, to denote the totality of the Divine attributes and powers."

d. Literally "through all"

e. On πάθος, Lightfoot notes: "This word has a special prominence in the Epistles of Ignatius. In Christ's passion is involved the peace of one church (*Trall* inscr) and the joy of another (*Philad* inscr). Unto His passion the penitent sinner must return (*Smyrn* 5); from his passion the false heretic dissents (*Philad* 3); into His passion all men must die (*Magn* 5); His passion the saint himself strives to imitate (*Rom* 6); the blood of His passion purifies the water of baptism (*Eph* 18); the tree of the passion is the stock from which the Church has sprung (*Smyrn* 1); the passion is a special feature which distinguishes the gospel (*Philad* 9, *Smyrn* 7). In several passages indeed it is coordinated with the birth or the resurrection (*Eph* 20, *Magn* 11, *Smyrn* 12, etc.); but frequently, as here, it stands in isolated grandeur, as the one central doctrine of the faith."

f. Eph 5:1

g. The translation of the phrase τὸ συγγενικὸν ἔργον is difficult. Lake translates "your brotherly task", Ehrman opts for the verbose "the work we share as members of the same family", Holmes has "the task so natural to you" and Schoedel has "the task suited to you".

task, you completed it perfectly. ² For hearing of ₁my being sent from Syria as a prisoner₁ᵃ for the sake of our common name and hope, hoping by your prayers to attain to fight the wild animals in Rome, so that by the experience I might be able to be a disciple, you were eager to see me. ³ Therefore, since I received your whole congregation in the name of God ₁in the person of Onesimus₁,ᵇ (a man of inexpressible love, and who is your bishop),ᶜ I ask in the name of Jesus Christ that you love him and that all of you ₁resemble him₁.ᵈ For blessed is the one who has graciously granted you, who are worthy, to obtain such a bishop.

REFRESHMENT OF FELLOWSHIP

2.1 But concerning my fellow slave Burrhus, ₁by the will of God₁ᵉ your deacon, who is blessed in all things, I desire him to stay for your honor and the bishop's. And also Crocus, who is worthy of God and of you, who is the embodimentᶠ of love I received from you. He has relievedᵍ me in every way; may the Father of Jesus Christ refresh him ₁in the same way₁,ʰ together with Onesimus and Burrhus and Euplus and Fronto, in whom I have seen you all in love. ² May I have joyʲ in you ₁always₁,ᵏ if indeed I am worthy. Therefore it is fitting in every way to glorify Jesus Christ, who has glorified you, so that having been put into proper conditionˡ in one act of obedience, and

---

a. Literally "being imprisoned from Syria"

b. Literally "in Onesimus"

c. ἐπισκόπῳ Lake] + ἐν σαρκὶ Lightfoot Holmes Ehrman. Lightfoot actually brackets it, noting its unsure nature. The phrase would then be translated "earthly bishop" or "bishop in the flesh."

d. Literally "to be in his likeness"

e. Literally "according to God"

f. Lightfoot notes: "The Latin 'exemplar,' 'exemplarium,' is properly a copy, not in the sense of a thing copied from another, but a thing copied by others. ... As a law term, it denoted one of the authoritative originals where a document was written in duplicate. ... It was natural that a provincial, like Ignatius, should adopt from Latin a word which was a law term, just as he elsewhere adopts others which are military terms."

g. 1 Cor 16:18; Phlm 7, 20

h. Literally "as also"

i. 2 Tim 1:16

j. Phlm 20

k. Literally "in all"

l. Of this usage, BDAG refers to Epictetus, where the word is used "of a trainer who adjusts parts of the body." Lightfoot further mentions that the word is a surgical term for "setting bones," used by Galen and others.

being subject to the bishop and to the council of elders,[a] you may be sanctified in every way.

ENCOURAGING, NOT ORDERING

3.1 I do not give orders to you ₁as if I am someone important₁, for if I am also a prisoner because of the name, I am not yet complete in Jesus Christ. For now I am beginning to be a disciple, and I speak to you as my fellow disciples. For I need to be anointed by you with faith, admonition, enduranc,e and patience. 2 But since love does not permit me to be silent concerning you, because of this I have taken it upon myself to encourage you, so that you may run together in harmony with the mind of God. For even Jesus Christ, our inseparable life, the mind of the Father, as also the bishops who have been appointed ₁throughout the world₁ are in the mind of Jesus Christ.

RUN TOGETHER IN HARMONY

4.1 Therefore it is fitting for you to run together in harmony with the mind of the bishop, which indeed you also do. For your council of elders, which is worthy of the name and worthy of God, thus is attuned with the bishop as strings to the lyre. Because of this, in your unanimity and harmonious love Jesus Christ is sung. 2 Now you must join the chorus, each of you₁,[bc] so that being in harmonious unanimity, taking your pitch[d] from God you may sing in unity, in one voice through Jesus Christ to the Father, so that he may also hear and may recognize you through ₁your good actions₁,[e] being members of his Son. Therefore it is useful for you to be in blameless unity, so that you may also always share with God.

---

a. 1 Tim 4:14

b. Literally "by the man"

c. On the phrase οἱ κατ' ἄνδρα, Lightfoot comments: "'the individual members' of the Church, who are to 'form themselves' (γίνεσθε) into a band or chorus."

d. Lightfoot comments: "The term χρώματα 'hues' applied to sounds is only one illustration of the very common transference, by analogy, of ideas derived from one sense to another. ... The word χρῶμα, then, as a musical term, designated an interval between two full tones. ... Hence it gave its name to the chromatic scale ... as distinguished from the two other scales used by the Greeks, the diatonic and enharmonic."

e. Literally "what you do well"

DO NOT OPPOSE THE BISHOP

5.1 For if I in a short time experienced such fellowship with your bishop which was not human but spiritual, how much more do I count you blessed who are so united with him as the church with Jesus Christ, and as Jesus Christ with the Father, so that all things may be harmonious in unity. **2** Let no one be deceived: unless someone is within the sanctuary,[a] he lacks the bread of God.[b] For if the prayer of one or two[c] has such great power, how much more that of both the bishop and the whole church? **3** Therefore he who does not join with the congregation,[d] this one is already arrogant and has distinguished himself. For it is written, "God opposes the proud."[e] Let us be careful, therefore, not to oppose the bishop, so that we may be subject to God.

REGARD THE BISHOP AS THE LORD

6.1 And the more one sees the bishop being silent, the more one should fear him. For everyone whom the master of the house[f] sends ₍to manage his own house₎[g] it is necessary[h] for us to welcome him like this: as the one who sent him. Therefore it is clear that we must regard the bishop as the Lord himself. **2** Therefore indeed Onesimus himself highly praises your good discipline in God, because you all live according to the truth and that no heresy dwells among you, but you do not even so much as hear anyone unless he speaks ₍truthfully₎[i] about Jesus Christ.[j]

---

a. Lightfoot comments: "The θυσιαστήριον here is not the altar, but the enclosure in which the altar stands, as the preposition ἐντός requires. This meaning is consistent with the sense of the word, which (unlike βῶμος) signifies 'the place of sacrifice'; and it is supported by examples of use as applied to Christian churches. ... The reference here is to the plan of the tabernacle or temple. The θυσιαστήριον is the court of the congregation, the precinct of the altar, as distinguished from the outer court."

b. John 6:33

c. Matt 18:19–20

d. Literally "with it," the pronoun refers back to the "entire church" in the previous verse.

e. Prov 3:34; Jas 4:6; 1 Pet 5:5

f. Matt 21:33.

g. Literally "to his own management"

h. John 13:20; Matt 10:40

i. Literally "in truth"

j. On this clause, Holmes notes: "An editor's emendation. One ancient authority reads 'except Jesus Christ speaking in truth'; another has a grammatically impossible reading." Lightfoot is the source of the emendation; as Lightfoot comments: "I have ventured so to

BEWARE THOSE UNWORTHY OF GOD

[7.1] For some are accustomed to bear the name with wicked deceit, doing some other things unworthy of God; whom it is necessary for you to shun as wild beasts. For they are rabidly mad dogs that bite stealthily; it is necessary for you to be on guard against them, ₁as their bite is hard to cure₁.[ab] [2] There is one[c] physician, both fleshly[d] and spiritual, born and unborn,[e] God in man,[f] true life in death,[g] both of Mary and of God, first subject to suffering and then free of suffering, Jesus Christ our Lord.

DO NOT BE DECEIVED

[8.1] Therefore do not let anyone deceive you, indeed, as not even you have been deceived, belonging completely to God. For when no strife is firmly rooted among you, which is able to torture you, then indeed you do live according to God. I, your humble[h] sacrifice, also dedicate myself to you Ephesians, a church of eternal renown. [2] The fleshly ones[i] are not able to do spiritual things, nor the spiritual ones fleshly things;[j] so too neither faith the things of unbelief, nor unbelief the things of faith. But even

---

emend the text, as the Armenian Version suggests, and as the sense seems to require, substituting ΗΠΕΡΙΗΣΟΥ for ΗΠΕΡΙΗΣΟΥ."

a. Literally "being hard to cure"

b. Lightfoot comments: "their madness is a virulent disease which is hard to cure and which they communicate to others by their bite."

c. 1 Tim 2:5–6

d. Lightfoot comments: "The antithesis of σαρκικὸς and πνευματικὸς is intended to express the human and the Divine nature of Christ respectively." See also Ign. *Smyrn* 3.

e. On the phrase γεννητὸς καὶ ἀγέννητος, Lightfoot adds: "'generate and ingenerate,' i.e. 'generate as regards His human nature and ingenerate as regards His deity.'"

f. ἐν ἀνθρώπῳ θεός Lightfoot, Lake, Holmes] ἐν σαρκὶ γενόμενος θεός Ehrman. The difference in translation is "God in man" versus "God come in the flesh." On this text-critical issue, Lightfoot notes: "This reading [ἐν ἀνθρώπῳ θεός] is demanded alike by the great preponderance of authorities and by the antithetical character of the sentence. The substitution ἐν σαρκὶ γενόμενος θεός may have been due to the fear of countenancing the Apollinarian doctrine that the Logos took the place of the human νοῦς in Christ."

g. Lightfoot comments: "For his death is our life, his passion is our resurrection. ... Here again there is reference to his two natures. He died as man: He lives and gives life as the Eternal Word."

h. From Lightfoot: "literally, 'filth, scum, offscouring,' was used, like κάθαρμα, περικάθαρμα, especially of those criminals, generally the vilest of their class, whose blood was shed to expiate the sins of the nation and to avert the wrath of the gods."

i. 1 Cor 2:14

j. Rom 8:5, 8

what you do according to the flesh, this is spiritual,[a] for you do all things in Jesus Christ.

FELLOW TRAVELERS

9.1 But I have learned that some[b] from elsewhere have passed by,[c] having evil doctrine. Your ear did not permit them to sow among you, your ears[d] being plugged, so that you might not receive what was sown by them, as being stones of the temple[e] of the Father, having been prepared for the building of God the Father, hoisted up to the heights by the crane[f] of Jesus Christ, which is the cross, using as a rope the Holy Spirit, and your faith lifts you up, and love is the way that leads to God. 2 Therefore you all are also fellow travelers, God-bearers and temple-bearers,[g] Christ-bearers,[h] bearers of holy things,[i] having been adorned[j] in every way with the commandments of Jesus Christ, in whom also I rejoice greatly, I have been considered worthy through what I write to converse and to rejoice with you, that you love nothing in human life except only God.

---

a. This whole notion is interpreted by Lightfoot as "even your secular business is exalted into a higher sphere, is spiritualized, by your piety."

b. Lightfoot notes: "These are the itinerant false teachers who are described in Ign *Eph* 7"

c. Ezek 36:34; Wis 1:8; 2:7; 5:15; 16:24; 10:8

d. Acts 7:57

e. Eph 2:20-22; 1 Pet 2:5

f. BDAG describes the metaphor: "The figure is carried out thus: the parts of the 'crane of Christ' are the cross ... and the Holy Spirit, the latter being the rope. The crane brings the stones, symbolizing Christians, to the proper height for the divine structure." Lightfoot describes the metaphor similarly: "The framework, or crane, is the Cross of Christ; the connecting instrument, the rope, is the Holy Spirit; the motive power, which sets and keeps the machinery in motion, is faith; the path, (conceived here apparently as an inclined plane) up which the spiritual stones are raised that they may be fitted into the building, is love."

g. Lightfoot explains: "The metaphor is taken from the portable shrines (containing the image of the patron deity), which were made either to be carried about in processions, or to be purchased by pilgrims to any famous sanctuary as reminisces of their visit and worn about the person as amulets. ... Of the latter the miniature representations of the shrine of Ephesian Artemis furnish the best illustration, and we may suppose that Ignatius had these more or less in mind; see Acts 19:24."

h. 2 Cor 4:10

i. Lightfoot comments these are "'bearers of holy things,' such as sacred treasures, votive offerings, and the like, which it was customary to carry in procession."

j. 1 Pet 3:3; 1 Tim 2:9

PRAY UNCEASINGLY

10.1 But you also pray unceasingly on behalf of others,[a] for there is in them a hope of repentance that they may find God. Therefore allow them at least by your deeds, to be disciples. **2** In response to[b] their anger, your gentleness; in response to their arrogant rhetoric, your humility; in response to their abusive speech, your prayer; in response to their deception, your steadfast faithfulness; in response to their violence, your gentleness; not being eager to imitate them. **3** Let us be found to be by gentleness[c] their brothers and sisters, and let us be eager to be imitators[d] of the Lord. Who was treated more unjustly? Who was more cheated?[e] Who was more rejected? So that some weed[f] of the devil may not be found in you, but with all purity and self-control you may remain outwardly[g] and inwardly in Jesus Christ.

THE LAST TIMES

11.1 These are the last times.[h] Therefore let us be ashamed, let us fear the patience of God, that it not turn into our judgment. For either let us fear the coming wrath or let us love the present grace, one of the two; only to be found in Christ Jesus, to the true life.[i] **2** Apart from this one, let nothing be pleasing[j] to you, in whom I carry about these chains, my spiritual pearls, in which may it be granted to me to rise up[k] in your prayer, of which may

---

a. 1 Thess 5:17

b. Matt 5:44; Luke 6:27, 28; Rom 12:14ff; 1 Pet 2:21, 22

c. Lightfoot comments: "The word ἐπιείκεια, as denoting the spirit of concession and forbearance, which contrasts with strict justice, strict retaliation, is highly appropriate here. ... It was moreover especially characteristic of Christ (2 Cor 10:1), whose example is enforced here."

d. Lightfoot expands and paraphrases: "The right way of showing our brotherhood with them is not by imitating their conduct, but by evincing our regard. Our imitation must be of Christ, not of them."

e. 1 Cor 6:7

f. While βοτάνη is a generic word for "plant," the context here is negative and so the translation of "weed" is appropriate. See also Lightfoot, Holmes, and Ehrman.

g. 2 Cor 7:1

h. 1 John 2:18; 1 Cor 7:29

i. Lightfoot notes of this particular infinitive: "... the infinitive being treated as a substantive," further noting the exact phrase τὸ ἀληθινὸν ζῆν occurs in Ign *Trall* 9 and Ign *Smryn* 4.

j. Lightfoot comments: "'glitter in your eyes,' i.e. 'have any attraction for you'; ... The word is thus a preparation for the imagery of 'the spiritual pearls' which follows. Ignatius would say, 'Do not value any decoration apart from Christ.'"

k. Lightfoot discusses this: "He can hardly mean that he desired literally to rise in his chains; but that he hoped through the prayers of the Ephesians to remain steadfast to the

it be granted to me always to be a sharer, that I may be found in the lot of the Christians of the Ephesians, who also have always agreed with the apostles in the power of Jesus Christ.

THE FOOTSTEPS OF PAUL

12.1 I know who I am and to whom I write. I am condemned; you have received mercy. I am in danger; you are secure. 2 You are the highway[a] of those who are being killed for the sake of God, fellow-initiates[b] of Paul, who was sanctified, who was well spoken of, who is worthy of blessing, (may it be granted to me to be found in his footsteps[c] when I reach God); who in every letter mentions you in Christ Jesus.

MEET AND GIVE THANKS

13.1 Therefore make every effort to come together[d] as often as possible to give thanks[e] and glory to God. For when you gather ₁together₁[f] frequently, the powers of Satan are destroyed and his destruction is brought to an end by the unanimity of your faith. 2 There is nothing better than peace by which all war[g] in heaven and on earth is abolished.

---

end, and to so appear at the resurrection invested with the glory of discipline and suffering, of which his chains were the instrument and the symbol."

a. On the phrase πάροδός ἐστε, Lightfoot writes: "[The Ephesians] had escorted St. Paul first, and now they were escorting Ignatius on his way to martyrdom. Their spiritual position, he seems to say, corresponds to their geographical position. As they conducted the martyrs on their way in the body, so they animated their souls with fresh strength and courage. The reference to St. Paul will hardly be satisfied by the interview with the Ephesian elders in Acts 20:17, for he was not then on his way to death, if (as is most probable) he was liberated from his first captivity: but the notices in the Pastoral Epistles show that he was again at Ephesus shortly before his final trial and martyrdom (1 Tim 1:3; 2 Tim 1:18). Probably Ignatius was thinking of other martyrs also of whom we know nothing."

b. Lightfoot comments: "i.e. 'fellow recipients, fellow-students, of the mysteries, with Paul.' ... This was signally true of the Ephesians, among whom St. Paul resided for an exceptionally long time (Acts 19:10; 20:31), with whom he was on terms of the most affectionate intimacy (Acts 20:18, 37), and who were the chief, though probably not the sole, recipients of the most profound of all his epistles."

c. 1 Pet 2:21

d. Heb 10:25

e. Ehrman provides an alternate translation of this phrase: "to celebrate the Eucharist and give glory to God." Lightfoot also mentions the possibility that an allusion to the Eucharist was intended.

f. Literally "with the same"

g. Lightfoot explains: "It is not the war between the powers of heaven and the powers of earth, but the war of his spiritual (ἐπουράνιοι) and his carnal (ἐπίγειοι) enemies alike against

DO WHAT YOU PROFESS

14.1 Nothing of which escapes your notice if you have perfect faith and love toward Jesus Christ, which are the beginning and end of life; the beginning is faith and the end is love.[a] And the two having come together in unity are God; ₁and everything else₁[b] leading to nobility of character ₁follows after₁.[c][a] No one professing faith sins, nor possessing love hates. "The tree is known by its fruit,"[d] so those who profess to be Christ's will be seen through what they do. For the deed[e] is not ₁a matter of what one now professes₁[f] but if one be found in the power of faith to the end.[g]

NOTHING ESCAPES HIS NOTICE

15.1 It is better to be silent and to exist than to be speaking and to not exist. It is good to teach if the one speaking does what he says. Therefore there is one teacher who spoke and it happened.[h] And even what he has done while remaining silent is worthy of the Father. 2 He who truly possesses the word[i] of Jesus is also able to hear his silence, so that he may be perfect, so that he may act through what he says, and he may be known through what he does not say. 3 Nothing escapes the notice of the Lord, but even our secrets are near him. Therefore we should do everything because he is dwelling in us, that we may be his temples[j] and he may be our[k] God in

---

the Christian, of which Ignatius speaks."

a. 1 Tim 1:5

b. Literally "and all the other things"

c. Literally "it is a follower"

d. Matt 12:33; Luke 6:34

e. Lightfoot comments: "'For now (i.e., in these evil times, in this season of persecution) the work is not a mere matter of profession.' For this absolute use of τὸ ἔργον, meaning 'the preaching and practice of the Gospel,' ... see also Acts 15:38; Phil 2:30."

f. Literally "the present promise"

g. Lightfoot expands: "but [is realized only] if a man be found in the power of faith (with an effective faith) to the end."

h. Lightfoot explains: "Thus Ignatius says in effect, 'It is true of Christ's work on earth, as the Psalmist says of God's work in the universe, that he word was equivalent to the deed.' This reference (Ps 33:9) explains the following clause: 'The effects of His silence also, not less than of His speech, are worthy of the Father.'"

i. Of this phrase, Lightfoot paraphrases: "He who has truly mastered the spoken precepts of Christ is best able to appreciate and copy His silence."

j. 1 Cor 3:16, 17; 2 Cor 6:16

k. ἡμῶν Lake, Holmes, Ehrman] — Lightfoot. The omission would make the translation "God in us" instead of "our God in us." Lightfoot notes that "ἡμῶν, which is added in some

us,[a] which indeed he is and he will be made known ₁before our very eyes₁[b] by which we may rightly love[c] him.

THE UNQUENCHABLE FIRE

[16.1] Do not be deceived, my brothers; destroyers of families[d] will not inherit the kingdom of God.[e] [2] Therefore if those who do this according to the flesh die, how much more if someone corrupt[f] the faith of God with evil teaching, for which Jesus Christ was crucified! Such a person, having made himself foul, will go to the unquenchable fire;[g] so too the one who listens to him.

REJECT THE RULER OF THIS AGE

[17.1] Because of this, the Lord received ointment on his head[h] so that he might breathe incorruptibility[i] on the church. Do not be anointed with the stench of the teaching of the ruler of this age, lest he take you captive from the life set before you. [2] But ₁why₁[j] do we not all become wise, receiving the knowledge of God which is Jesus Christ? Why do we foolishly perish, ignoring the gift that the Lord has truly sent?

---

texts, interferes slightly with the sense," but the textual evidence seems to be on the side of inclusion.

a. 1 Cor 3:16

b. Literally "in our presence"

c. 1 Cor 15:34

d. Of the word in this instance, Lightfoot notes: "It denotes those who violate the temple of their hearts and bodies, which is God's house, by evil thoughts or evil habits." See also BDAG, which discusses this instance in depth.

e. 1 Cor 6:9–10; Gal 5:21

f. On supplying "someone" (which all translations do in some form) Lightfoot notes: "This omission of τις in classical writers is not unfrequent."

g. Matt 3:12; Luke 3:17; Mark 9:43

h. Matt 26:6–13

i. This could also be "immortality," but "incorruptibility" seems more appropriate based on the preceding chapter's mention of corruption.

j. Literally "because of what"

THE NATURE OF CHRIST

[18.1] My spirit is a humble sacrifice[a] for the cross, which is a cause for stumbling[b] to unbelievers, but salvation and eternal life to us. Where is the wise?[c] Where is the debater? Where is the boasting of the so-called intelligent ones?[d] [2] For our God, Jesus the Christ, was conceived[e] by Mary according to the plan[f] of God, both from the seed of David and the Holy Spirit, who was born[g] and was baptized so that by his suffering[h] he might purify the water.

GOD IN HUMAN FORM

[19.1] And the virginity of Mary and her giving birth escaped notice of the ruler of this age; likewise also the death of the Lord. Three mysteries to be loudly acclaimed[i] which were accomplished in the silence of God. [2] Therefore how was he made known to the ages? A star[j] in heaven shone

---

a. See also Ign *Eph* 8:1: Lightfoot explains: "Here also the idea is twofold, abasement and self-sacrifice: 'My spirit devotes itself for the sake of the cross,' and 'My spirit devotes itself for the sake of the Cross.' 'I am content,' Ignatius would say, 'to give up everything, and to become myself as nothing for that Cross in which others find only a stumbling block.'"

b. Lightfoot comments: "The Cross was still a stumbling block, as it had been in the apostolic age; but the persons who stumbled at it were different. The stumblers to whom Ignatius seems especially to allude to in σκάνδαλον here are the docetists."

c. 1 Cor 1:20; see also Isa 33:18

d. Literally "of those called intelligent"

e. Eccl 11:5

f. Lightfoot comments: "The word οἰκονομία came to be applied more especially to the Incarnation because this was par excellence the system or plan which God had ordained for the government of his household and the dispensation of his stores. Hence in the province of theology, οἰκονομία was distinguished by the fathers from θεολογία proper, the former being the teaching which was concerned with the Incarnation and its consequences, and the latter the teaching which related to the eternal and divine nature of Christ."

g. Luke 1:13, 57; 23:29

h. The sense of "suffering" is not found in the NT, thus it is not catalogued by LN. The sense is, however, prevalent in Ignatius' letters and also found in *Ep Barn* 6:7.

i. BDAG comments: "The three 'mysteries' are the virginity of Mary, her childbearing, and the death of Jesus. In contrast to God's quiet performance, Ignatius appears to have in mind their public proclamation in a religious setting as part of the divine design, with a responsory cry of acclamation." Lightfoot further notes that "κραυγή is the correlative to ἡσυχία, as revelation is to mystery."

j. Matt 2:2

brighter than,ᵃ ˻the rest of the stars,˼ᵇ and its light was inexpressible,ᶜ and its newness caused astonishment. And all the remaining stars, together with the sun and moon, formed a chorus with that star, and it was easily outshining over them all with its light, and there was perplexity: where had this new thing so unlike them come from? ³ By this all magic was destroyed, and every bond of wickednessᵈ disappeared. Ignorance was torn down. The old kingdom was annihilated. God, being made known in human form to the newness of eternal life, and that which had been prepared by God received its beginning. From then on, all things were stirred up because the abolitionᵉ of death was taking place.

FUTURE CORRESPONDENCE

20.1 If I am considered worthy of Jesus Christ by your prayer, and it be his will,ᶠ in the second small book,ᵍ which I am about to write to you, I will further explain to you what I have begun to explain, the divine plan with reference to the new man Jesus Christ, in his faith and in his love, in his suffering and resurrection, ² especially if the Lord should reveal to me that you all meet together commonly, ˻each of you,˼ʰ in grace, by name, in one faith and in Jesus Christ, who according to the fleshⁱ was from the family of David, the Son of Man and Son of God, so that you obey the bishop and the council of elders with an undisturbed mind,ʲ breakingᵏ one bread, which

---

a. Literally "shone beyond"

b. Literally "all the stars"

c. 1 Pet 1:8

d. There are two possible translations as the "wickedness" (κακία) could modify either δεσμός (chain/bond/fetter) or ἄγνοια (ignorance). Here I side with Lake and Ehrman with "every bond of wickedness disappeared." Lightfoot and Holmes translate something like "... every kind of spell was dissolved, the ignorance so characteristic of wickedness vanished."

e. Lightfoot comments: "The actual destruction of death is the last scene of all; but the appearance of the star was the signal for the commencement of the war destined so to end."

f. Ignatius commonly uses the word θέλημα, "will," to refer to God's will.

g. There is no known "second small book" of Ignatius to the Ephesians, so this intention was likely never fulfilled.

h. Literally "according to man"

i. Lightfoot comments: "This is inserted as a protest against docetic error, by which their unity was threatened. But this emphatic mention of the human nature requires a counter-balance. Hence he adds that Christ is not only 'Son of man' but also 'Son of God.'"

j. Wis 16:11; Sir 41:1; cf. 1 Cor 7:35

k. Acts 2:46; 20:7, 11; 1 Cor 10:16

is the medicine[a] of immortality, the antidote that we should not die but live in Jesus Christ ˌforeverˌ.[b]

FAREWELL

21.1 I am your ransom[c] and of those you have sent for the honor of God to Smyrna, from where I also write to you, giving thanks to the Lord and loving Polycarp, ˌas I have also loved youˌ.[d] Remember me as Jesus Christ also remembers you. **2** Pray for the church in Syria, from where, being imprisoned, I am led away to Rome, being the least of the faithful there, even as I have been considered worthy to be found ˌhonorable to Godˌ.[e] Farewell in God the Father and in Jesus Christ, our common hope.

---

a. While in the NT φάρμακον has a negative connotation (spells, sorcery, potions), it does has a positive connotation (medicine, remedy). This positive aspect of φάρμακον is what Ignatius intends here.

b. Literally "throughout all"

c. Lightfoot notes: "Ἀντίψυχον is properly 'a life offered for a life,' 'a vicarious sacrifice.'"

d. Literally "as also you"

e. Literally "in the honor of God"

— *Ignatius to the Magnesians*

SALUTATION

Ignatius, ₗwho is also called "God-bearer,"ₗ[a] to her blessed with the grace of God the Father in Christ Jesus our Savior, in whom I greet the church which is at Magnesia on the Maeander, and I wish *her* abundant greetings in God the Father and in Jesus Christ.

DESIRE TO CORRESPOND

1.1 Having learned of the great orderliness of your ₗgodly love,ₗ[b] rejoicing greatly I determined[c] to speak with you in the faith[d] of Jesus Christ. 2 For being considered worthy of a most godly name, in the chains which I carry about, I sing the churches,[e] in which I desire a union of flesh and spirit of Jesus Christ, our ₗeverlastingₗ[f] life, ₗand a union of faith and love,ₗ[g] to which nothing is preferable, and what is more essential,[h] ₗa union of Jesus,ₗ[i] and

---

a. Literally "who [is] also God-bearer"

b. Literally "of love toward God"

c. Prov 21:25; 2 Cor 9:7

d. Lightfoot paraphrases this last clause: "as a Christian speaking to Christians, to converse with you (by letter)."

e. On the phrase "I sing the churches," Schoedel comments: "'I sing (ᾄδω) the churches' has a poetic ring. When Ignatius uses the verb elsewhere, the image of choral singing is in the background (Ign *Eph* 4.1, 2; Ign *Rom* 2.2) and in one of these passages he leads over to the usage before us when he says that 'Jesus Christ is sung' (Ign *Eph* 4.1). It is especially the extension of such praise to the churches that brings to mind the role of ancient poets in 'singing' (the praises of) places, persons, and gods."

f. Literally "throughout all"

g. Literally "and of faith and love"

h. This is κύριος as a comparative adjective, not as a noun or proper noun, which leads to the translation "what is more essential/important."

i. Literally "of Jesus"

the Father. In[a] whom, enduring all the abuse of the ruler of this age and escaping, we will attain God.

SUBJECT TO THE BISHOP AND THE COUNCIL

2.1 Therefore, since I have been considered worthy to see you through Damas, your godly bishop, and through your worthy presbyters, Bassus and Apollonius, and my fellow slave, the deacon Zotion, whom I would enjoy because he is subject to the bishop as to the grace of God, and to the council of elders as to the law of Jesus Christ.

HONOR THE BISHOP

3.1 But it is fitting for even you to not presume upon[b] the ₁youth₁[cd] of the bishop, but, according to the power of God the Father, show him all respect, just as I have also learned that the holy presbyters have not taken advantage of his outwardly[e] youthful appearance[f] but as a result deferring to him in godly wisdom[g] and not to him, but to the Father of Jesus Christ, to the bishop of all. 2 Therefore, concerning the honor of that one who desired us, it is fitting to be obedient ₁without any₁[hi] hypocrisy, since it is not that someone deceives this bishop who is seen, but deludes the unseen one. And in such a case his account is not with the flesh but with God, who knows the secret things.[j]

---

a. Schoedel adds a break for verse 3 here; however, Lightfoot, Lake, Holmes, and Ehrman do not (their verse 2 is equivalent with Schoedel's verse 2–3).

b. Lightfoot comments: "The word signifies either (1) 'to use together with another' ... or (2) to use constantly or fully or familiarly."

c. Literally "maturity"

d. 1 Tim 4:12

e. Lighfoot comments: "Ignatius therefore says that, though apparently from his years Damas belongs to the category of youth, yet his godly wisdom takes him out of this category."

f. 1 Tim 4:12

g. φρονίμους Lake] φρονίμῳ Lightfoot, Holmes, Ehrman. The difference is in the referent; with Lake it is the presbyters who are wise in their deferring to Damas; with the reading taken by others (which I prefer) it is Damas who is wise.

h. Literally "with no"

i. Eph 6:6; Col 3:22

j. Ps 43:22

BE CHRISTIANS

4.1 Therefore it is fitting not only to be called Christians but also to be Christians, just as also some indeed recognize the bishop, but they do everything without him. But ones such as these appear to me to be without a conscience, because they gather together invalidly[a] according to the commandment.[b]

DIE IN HIS SUFFERING

5.1 Therefore since these matters have an end, and two things lie together before us, both death and life, and each is about to go to one's own place,[c] **2** for just as there are two coinages,[d] one which is of God, another which is of the world, and each has its own stamp impressed upon it: the unbelievers bear ₍the stamp of this world,₎[e] but the believers in love bear the stamp[f] of God the Father through Jesus Christ, through whom, unless we voluntarily choose to die in his suffering,[g] his life is not in us.

LOVE ONE ANOTHER

6.1 Therefore, since I have by faith seen and loved,[h] in the people mentioned above, the whole congregation, I urge you: be eager to do everything in the harmony of God, the bishop presiding in the place of God, and the presbyters in the place of the council of the apostles, and the deacons, who to me are especially dear, entrusted with the ministry of Jesus Christ, who before the ages was with the Father and has been revealed at the end. **2** Therefore you all, having received a divine agreement in your convictions,[i] have respect for one another, and let no one consider his neighbor

---

a. Lightfoot comments: "The presence of the bishop was necessary for the validity of these gatherings. The persons here enounced held unauthorized meetings for sectarian purposes."

b. Heb 10:24–25

c. Acts 1:25

d. Matt 22:19

e. Literally "of this world"

f. Heb 1:3

g. Rom 6:5; 8:17, 29; 2 Cor 4:10; Phil 3:10; 2 Tim 2:2

h. Lightfoot comments: "The word here refers to external tokens of affection, according to its original meaning."

i. Lightfoot translates the phrase as "moral conformity with God."

according to the flesh, but ₎always₎[a] love one another in Jesus Christ. Let there be nothing in you which ₎is capable of dividing you₎,[b] but be united with the bishop and those who preside over you, as an example[c] and lesson of incorruptibility.[d]

RUN TOGETHER

7.1 Therefore, just as the Lord did nothing without the Father,[e] being united with him, either through himself or through the apostles, in this way ₎you are not to do anything without the bishop and the presbyters₎.[f] Do not even attempt anything that appears reasonable ₎to yourselves₎,[g] but, ₎for the common purpose₎,[h] one prayer, one petition, one mind, one hope in love in the blameless joy, which is Jesus Christ, ₎nothing is better than him₎.[i] 2 You run together all as to one temple of God, as to one altar, to one Jesus Christ, who from one Father came forth, and was with[j] the one, and returned to the one.[k]

DO NOT BE DECEIVED

8.1 Do not be deceived by strange doctrines or ancient myths[l] which are useless. For if until now we live according to Judaism, we admit[m] ₎that we have not received₎[n] grace. 2 For the divine prophets lived according to Christ Jesus. Because of this they were also persecuted, being inspired[o] by his grace, to

---

a. Literally "through everything"

b. Literally "will be able to divide you"

c. Rom 4:17

d. Lightfoot notes that "The idea of ἀφθαρσία in Ignatius … is not merely immortality, but moral incorruption as carrying with it immortal life."

e. John 8:28; 10:37

f. Literally "not even you, you are to do nothing without the bishop and the presbyters"

g. Literally "on our own"

h. Literally "for the same"

i. Literally "whom nothing is better than"

j. John 1:18

k. John 16:28

l. 1 Tim 4:7; Titus 1:14; 3:9

m. Gal 5:4; Col 1:6

n. Literally "not to have received"

o. Literally, ἐπνέω is "to breathe out" but this instance in Ignatius is using it figuratively to show the source of the strength (their inspiration) of the divine prophets of old (cf. BDAG).

fully convince the disobedient that there is one God who revealed himself through Jesus Christ his Son, who is his Word[a] that came forth from silence, who in everything pleased the one who sent him.

BE FOUND TO BE DISCIPLES

9.1 Therefore, if those who lived in ancient customs came to newness of hope, no longer keeping the Sabbath but living according to the Lord's day,[b] on which our life also arose through him and his death, (which some deny) through which mystery we came to believe, and because of this we endure so that we may be found to be disciples of Jesus Christ, our only teacher. 2 How will we be able to live without him, who even the prophets, being disciples in the Spirit, expected him as their teacher? And because of this, the one whom they rightly awaited, ₍when he came₎[cd] he raised them up from the dead.

LEARN TO LIVE ACCORDING TO CHRISTIANITY

10.1 Therefore, we should not fail to see his goodness, for if he should imitate us, do just as we do, ₍we are lost₎.[ef] Because of this, having become his disciples let us learn to live according to Christianity. ₍For whoever₎[g] is called a name other than[h] this is not of God. 2 Therefore do away with the bad yeast,[i] which has become old and sour, and turn to the new yeast,[j] which is Jesus Christ. Be salted[k] in him, so that no one among you is corrupted,

---

a. John 1:1

b. Rev 1:10

c. Literally "arriving"

d. Lightfoot comments on this last clause: "This refers to the 'descensus ad inferos,' which occupied a prominent place in the belief of the early Church. Here our Lord is assumed to have visited (παρὼν) the souls of the patriarchs and prophets in Hades, and to have taught them the truths of the Gospel and to have raised them either to paradise or heaven."

e. Literally "we are no longer"

f. 2 Sam 22:26, 27; Ps 18:25, 26

g. Literally "For who else"

h. Lightfoot translates "beyond." Here πλέον functions as a basic comparative, giving the meaning that whatever name is called other than that of "Christian" is not of God. More literal translations (i.e., "greater than, more than") do not really provide the exclusivity in this use, hence "other than" (which is also used by Lake, Ehrman, and Holmes).

i. 1 Cor 5:7

j. Matt 13:33; Luke 13:21

k. Matt 5:13; Mark 9:50; Luke 14:34

since you will be corrected by your odor. ³ It is absurd to speak of Jesus
Christ and to live like Jews, for Christianity did not believe in Judaism, but
Judaism in Christianity, in which every tongue that believes in[a] God was
brought together.[b]

THESE THINGS REALLY HAPPENED

[11.1] And I say these things, my beloved, not because I have learned that any
from you are acting in this way, but as less than you, I desire to protect[c]
you, ₁that you not be snagged₁[d] by the fishhooks of worthless delusion,[e] but
to be fully convinced of the birth and the suffering and the resurrection,
which took place in the time of the rule of Pontius Pilate. ₁These things
were really and truly done₁[f] by Jesus Christ, our hope, from which ₁may
none of you ever turn away₁.[g]

PRISONER AND FREE

[12.1] May I enjoy you in every way, if indeed I am worthy. For even though I
am a prisoner I am not comparable to one of you who has been set free. I
know that you are not puffed up,[h] for you have Jesus[i] Christ in yourselves,
and even more when I praise you, I know that ₁you blush₁,[jk] as it is written
that "the righteous is his own accuser."[l]

---

a. There is a question as to where the prepositional phrase attaches. Some (e.g., Ehrman,
also Lake) translate "every tongue that believes in God has been gathered together." Others
(e.g., Holmes, also Lightfoot) translate "every tongue believed and was brought together to
God."

b. Isa 66:18

c. Lightfoot glosses this as "should be on your guard beforehand."

d. Literally "not to be snagged"

e. Lightfoot translates "foolish opinion," drawing a distinction from the sense of κενοδοξία
encountered in Phil 2:3.

f. Literally "These things were done truly and certainly"

g. Literally "may it be granted that none of you turn away"

h. 1 Cor 4:6, 18, 19; 5:2; 8:1; 13:4; Col 2:18; cf. 2 Cor 12:20

i. 2 Cor 8:5

j. Literally "you are ashamed"

k. The middle and passive voices of ἐντρέπω are typically translated as "to be ashamed";
the active voice is "to respect." The line here is blurred. Schoedel's translation of "you blush"
is best.

l. Prov 18:17 (LXX)

MAKE EVERY EFFORT

13.1 Therefore make every effort to be confirmed in the ordinances[a] of the Lord and the apostles,[b] in order that whatsoever you do you may prosper[c] in all things: flesh and spirit, faith and love, in the Son and the Father and in the Spirit,[d] in the beginning and in the end, with your most esteemed bishop and that worthily woven spiritual crown, your council of elders and your ⌊godly⌋[e] deacons. 2 Be subject to the bishop and to one another[f] as Jesus Christ was to the Father,[g] and the apostles were to Christ and to the Father, in order that there may be unity, both of flesh and of spirit.[h]

A BRIEF EXHORTATION

14.1 Knowing that you are full of God, I have exhorted you briefly. Remember me in your prayers, that I may reach God, and remember the church in Syria, from which I am not worthy to be called. For I need your united prayer and love so that in God the church in Syria may be considered worthy of being refreshed with dew[i] by your church.[j]

GREETINGS AND FAREWELL

15.1 The Ephesians greet you from Smyrna, from where I also write you. They are here for the glory of God, ⌊just like you are⌋[k] They in all things have refreshed me, together with Polycarp, bishop of the Smyrnaeans. And the

---

a. Also perhaps "precepts"; Lightfoot also refers to them as "authoritative sayings.".

b. Acts 14:4

c. Ps 1:3

d. 2 Cor 13:14

e. Literally "according to God"

f. 1 Pet 5:5; Eph 5:21

g. πατρὶ Lake, Holmes, Ehrman] πατρὶ [κατὰ σάρκα] Lightfoot. Lightfoot brackets κατὰ σάρκα, noting that he thinks it dubious but worthy of inclusion. No other editions include the text. The difference is that Lightfoot's text has Jesus submitting "to the Father [according to the flesh]."

h. Eph 4:4

i. Deut 32:2; Prov 19:12

j. ἐκκλησίας Lake, Ehrman] ἐκτενείας Lightfoot, Holmes. The difference is between "by your church" or "by your fervent prayers." Lightfoot's reading is a conjecture which he introduced loosely based on the Armenian edition of Ignatius' letters; it has no direct basis in the Greek editions.

k. Literally "just as also you"

other churches also greet you in honor[a] of Jesus Christ. Farewell in godly harmony to you who possess an undivided spirit, which is Jesus Christ.

---

a. Lightfoot comments: "not the honor which is implied in the ordinary greetings of men, but the honor which belongs to the sphere of which springs from Jesus Christ."

– *Ignatius to the Trallians*

SALUTATION

Ignatius, ₗwho is also called "God-bearer,"ₗᵃ beloved by God the Father of Jesus Christ, to the holy church which is at Tralles in Asia, elect and worthy of God, being at peace in flesh and spirit through the suffering of Jesus Christ our hope through resurrection to him, which I also greet in the fullness in the apostolic manner and I offer abundant greetings.

ABOUT THE TRALLIANS

1.1 I have learned that you possess a blameless understanding and are unwavering in endurance, not from habit but by nature, just as Polybius your bishop revealed to me, who visited in Smyrna, by the will of God and of Jesus Christ, and so rejoiced with me, being a prisoner in Christ Jesus, that I saw your whole congregation in him. 2 Therefore, having received your ₗgodlyₗᵇ kindnessᶜ through him, I gave glory to God,ᵈ having found you were, as I had learned, imitators of God.

SUBJECT TO THE BISHOP

2.1 For when you are subject to the bishop as to Jesus Christ, you appear to me not to be living ₗin a human wayₗᵉ but according to Jesus Christ, who died for us so that believing in his death you may escape death. 2 Therefore it is necessary (just as you already do) for you to do nothing without the bishop, but be subject also to the council of elders as to the apostles of

---

a. Literally "who [is] also God-bearer"

b. Literally "according to God"

c. Lightfoot comments: "The Trallians appear to have sent some substantial proofs of their goodwill by the hands of Polybius."

d. Lightfoot notes this usage is absolute and recommends "I gave glory to God."

e. Literally "according to human standards"

Jesus Christ our hope. ₗIf we live in him, we will be found in himₗ.[a] 3 And it is also necessary that those who are deacons of the mysteries[b] of Jesus Christ please[c] everyone in every[d] way. For they are not deacons of food[e] and drink but servants of the church of God. Therefore they must guard against accusation as against fire.

RESPECT THE DEACONS

3.1 Likewise, let everyone respect the deacons as Jesus Christ, as also the bishop is an example of the Father, and the presbyters as the council of God and as the band[fg] of apostles. Without these things ₗa group is not recognized as a churchₗ.[hi] 2 About these things, I am persuaded that ₗyou have the same viewₗ.[j] For I have received the embodiment of your love and have it with me in your bishop, whose very behavior is a great lesson[k] and his gentleness a miracle. I think even the godless respect him. 3 In love I spare you, being able to write more sharply[l] about this matter. Concerning this, I did not think that being condemned, I should give you orders as an apostle.

SEEK GENTLENESS

4.1 I have many thoughts[m] in God, but ₗI keep myself within boundsₗ[n] that I might not destroy myself with boasting. For now it is necessary for me to fear even more and not to pay attention to those who puff me up. For those speaking to me are whipping me. 2 For I desire to suffer, but I do not know

---

a. Literally "in whom living we will be found"

b. 1 Cor 4:1

c. 1 Tim 3:8, 10

d. 1 Cor 10:33

e. Act 6:2; Rom 14:17; Col 2:16; Heb 9:10

f. The sense "band, college" (a figurative extension of BDAG sense 4) is that of a group or entity united by a common bond.

g. Acts 8:23

h. Literally "a church is not called"

i. For this phrase, Lightfoot offers the expanded translation: "Without these three orders no church has a title to the name, deserves to be called a church."

j. Literally "you so consider"

k. 1 Pet 3:1

l. Lightfoot glosses as "more urgently."

m. Phil 2:5

n. Literally "I take measure of myself"

if I am worthy. For the zeal is not apparent to many, but it fights against me all the more. Therefore I need the gentleness by which the ruler of this age will be destroyed.

HEAVENLY THINGS

5.1 Am I not able to write to you heavenly things? But I am afraid to, lest (you being infants)[a] I should cause you harm. And make allowances for me, lest not being able ₁to swallow₁,[b] you are choked.[c] 2 For even me, though I am a prisoner and I am able to comprehend the heavenly things and the ranks[d] of the angelic beings[e] and the hierarchies of the celestial commanders,[f] both visible and invisible,[g] because of this I am not even now a disciple, for much lacks in us so that we may not lack God.

STAY AWAY FROM HERESY

6.1 Therefore I urge you (not[h] I, but the love of Jesus Christ) only make use of Christian food, and abstain from the foreign plant,[i] which is heresy. 2 These people, while seeming trustworthy, mingle Jesus Christ with them-selves like those who produce a deadly drug with honeyed wine,[j] which the ignorant one gladly takes hold of in evil pleasure, to his death.

---

a. 1 Cor 3:1-2

b. Literally "to receive"

c. Tob 2:3

d. Lightfoot notes that this is "their distribution in their several ranks or in the several celestial spheres."

e. On this phrase, BDAG notes: "αἱ τοποθεσίαι αἱ ἀγγελικαί probably refers to the celestial positioning of the angelic hosts."

f. Lightfoot glosses this phrase as "the assemblages, musterings, of the heavenly rulers."

g. Col 1:16

h. 1 Cor 7:10

i. In other places Ignatius refers to heresy as a weed: Ign *Eph* 10; Ign *Phld* 3.

j. The idea here is that of something deadly mixed with something sweet in order to make it more palatable. Those who are teaching heresy are mixing Jesus Christ (the honeyed wine) with themselves (the heresy, the deadly drug). While sweet to drink, the heresy will produce death.

BE ON YOUR GUARD

[7.1] Therefore be on guard against such as these. And so it will be for you, not being puffed up and being inseparable from God,[a] from Jesus Christ and from the bishop and from the injunctions of the apostles. [2] The one who is inside of the sanctuary[b] is pure, but the one who is outside of the sanctuary is not pure. That is, whoever does anything without the bishop and the council of elders and the deacons, this one ₗdoes not have a clear conscience₎.[cd]

ANTICIPATE THE DEVIL'S SNARES

[8.1] Since I do not know of anything of such a kind among you, but I am protecting you, being my beloved, anticipating the snares of the devil.[e] Therefore you, adopting gentleness,[f] regain your strength[g] in faith which is the flesh of the Lord and in love which is the blood of Jesus Christ. [2] Let none of you hold a grudge against his neighbor. Give no excuse to the heathen, lest, because of a few foolish ones, the congregation of God be blasphemed. For "woe to him through whom my name is blasphemed ₗout of folly₎[h] among anyone."[i]

---

a. θεοῦ Lightfoot, Lake, Ehrman] — Holmes. This reading is questionable; Lightfoot brackets it, noting its dubiousness, and comments that the word should probably be omitted due to the witness of the Armenian version. Addtionally, there is question as to how to translate it. Lake takes θεοῦ Ἰησοῦ Χριστοῦ as successive ("from God, from Jesus Christ") but Ehrman takes it as appositive/epexegetical ("from God—that is, Jesus Christ"). Schoedel does not translate θεοῦ, so his source must omit it. Lightfoot further notes: "If θεοῦ be retained, it should perhaps be separated from Χριστοῦ, 'of God, of Jesus Christ, and of the bishop, etc.'; but the absence of the connecting particle is hardly consistent with the genius of the Greek language."

b. On θυσιαστηρίου in this context, Lightfoot notes: "It symbolizes the congregation lawfully gathered together under its duly appointed officers."

c. Literally "is not pure in his conscience"

d. 1 Tim 3:9; 2 Tim 1:3

e. 1 Tim 3:7; 6:9; 2 Tim 2:26

f. 1 Tim 6:11

g. This could also be translated "renew yourselves" (Lake, Schoedel).

h. Literally "by futility"

i. Isa 52:5; see also Rom 2:24; 1 Tim 4:1; Titus 2:5

FOCUS ON JESUS CHRIST

9.1 Therefore be deaf whenever anyone speaks to you apart from Jesus Christ,[a] the one of the family of David, the one of Mary, he who truly was born, both ate and drank, truly was persecuted by Pontius Pilate, truly was crucified and died, being seen by those in heaven and on earth and under the earth, 2 who also truly was raised from the dead, his Father having raised him. In the same way he also, his Father, will likewise raise up us who believe in him in Christ Jesus, without whom we do not have true life.

CHRIST'S SUFFERING WAS REAL

10.1 But if, just as some who are atheists (that is, unbelievers) say, his suffering was in appearance only, (it is they who are in appearance only),[b] why am I in chains? And why also do I wish to fight the wild animals? Therefore I die for no cause. As a result, then, I am telling lies about the Lord.

AVOID THE EVIL FRUIT

11.1 Therefore flee from these evil offshoots,[c] which bear death-dealing fruit, which if someone tastes, ₍he immediately dies₎.[d] For these are not the planting of the Father. 2 For if they were, they would appear as branches of the cross and their fruit would be imperishable, by which in his suffering he calls you who are his members.[e] Therefore the head ₍cannot₎[f] be born without limbs; God promises unity, which he himself is.

CONTINUE IN PRAYER

12.1 I greet you from Smyrna together with the churches of God that are present with me, who in all things have refreshed me both in the flesh and in the spirit. 2 My chains, which I carry about for the sake of Jesus Christ

---

a. The description of Jesus Christ that follows, which centers on physical characteristics and earthly events, argues directly against the heretical docetist teaching that Jesus was a spirit, and not a physical being.

b. This exact comparison about suffering "in appearance only" is also found in Ign Smyrn 2:1

c. Lightfoot notes "The word is used of an adventitious shoot or other growth of a plant. ... This word occurs several times in the LXX, where however it is not used with any precision."

d. Literally "by it he dies"

e. Rom 12:4; 1 Cor 6:15; Eph 5:30; 1 Cor 12:12

f. Literally "is not able to"

while praying to reach God, urge you: continue in your unanimity and in prayer for one another. For it is fitting ₗthat each,ⱼᵃᵇ of you, especially even the presbyter, refresh the bishop to the honor of the Father,ᶜ of Jesus Christ and of the apostles. ³ I desire that you listen to me in love that I may not be a witnessᵈ against you by having written. And pray also for me, having need of your love in the mercy of God so that I may be considered worthy of the lot which I am appointed to obtain, that I not be found disqualified.ᵉ

FAREWELL

¹³·¹ The love of the Smyrnaeans and of the Ephesians greets you. Remember in your prayers the church in Syria, of which also I am not worthy to be considered, being the least of them. ² Farewell in Jesus Christ. Be subject to the bishop as to the commandment, likewise also to the council of elders, and love one another, ₗeach of you,ⱼᶠ with an undivided heart. ³ My spirit is dedicated to you, not only now but also when I reach God. For I am still in dangerᵍ but the Father is faithfulʰ in Jesus Christ to fulfill my request and yours, in whomⁱ may you be found blameless.

---

a. Literally "according to one"

b. Eph 5:33

c. πατρός Lake, Ehrman. + καὶ εἰς τιμὴν Lightfoot, Holmes. The effect of Lightfoot/Holmes is to explicitly delineate "to the honor of the Father, and the honor of Jesus Christ," while Lake and Ehrman have "to the honor of the Father, of Jesus Christ" (or possibly, as Schoedel, without the comma).

d. Matt 8:4; 10:18; 24:14; Mark 1:44; 6:11

e. 1 Cor 9:27

f. Literally "according to each person"

g. Lightfoot comments: "There is still the risk that either by his own weakness or by the interposition of others he may be robbed of the martyr's crown."

h. 1 Cor 1:9; 20:13; 2 Cor 1:18; 1 Thess 5:24; 2 Thess 3:3; 1 Tim 1:15; 1 Tim 3:1; 1 Tim 4:9; 2 Tim 2:11; Titus 3:8

i. Lake translates as "which," but it should be "whom" (as Lightfoot, Holmes, Ehrman) as it refers back to "Jesus Christ."

— *Ignatius to the Romans*

SALUTATION

Ignatius, [who is also called "God-bearer,"][a] to her who has obtained mercy in the grandeur of the Father Most High and Jesus Christ his only son, to the church beloved and enlightened by the will of the one who willed all things which exist, according to the love of Jesus Christ our God, which also is preeminent[b] in the place of the district of the Romans, worthy of God, worthy of honor, worthy of blessing, worthy of praise, worthy of success, worthy of sanctification, and preeminent over love, named after the Christ,[c] named after the Father,[d] which also I greet in the name of Jesus Christ, the Son of the Father, to those united in flesh and spirit, to every commandment of his, being filled with the grace of God without wavering and being filtered from every foreign color abundant greetings without blame, in Jesus Christ our God.

PLEA TO THE ROMANS

1.1 Since by praying to God I have managed to see your godly faces, as even more than I asked to receive, for being imprisoned in Christ Jesus I hope to greet you, if indeed it be *his* will to consider me to be worthy to the end. [e] 2 For the beginning is well ordered, if indeed I may obtain the grace to receive my lot unhindered. For I am afraid of your love, lest it treat me

---

a. Literally "who [is] also God-bearer"

b. Lightfoot glosses: "has the chief-seat, presides, takes the precedence"; he further notes: "The word is used of preeminence or superiority generally in writers of about this time."

c. χριστώνυμος Lake] χριστόνομος Lightfoot, Holmes, Ehrman. The difference is between "named after the Christ" and "observing the law of Christ." Lake's reading is most likely the wrong one as it has the weakest textual evidence, makes the least sense in context, and is easily explained as an assimilation with the following word πατρώνυμος.

d. Eph 3:14-15

e. Luke 11:7

unjustly. For it is easy for you to do what you will, but it is difficult for me to reach God, if indeed you do not spare[a] me.

IGNATIUS' DESIRE

2.1 For I do not want you to be a people-pleaser[b] but to please God, just as indeed you are doing. [c] For neither will I ever have such an opportunity to reach God, nor will you, if you are silent, a better work have ascribed to you. For if you are silent about me, I am a word of God; [d] if but you love my flesh, ₁I will once again be just a sound₁. [e] **2** Grant me nothing more than to be poured out as an offering to God, while an altar is still ready, that becoming a chorus in love, you may sing to the Father in Christ Jesus that God has considered the bishop of Syria worthy to be found ₁at the setting of the sun₁ [f] having summoned him ₁from the rising of the sun₁. [g] It is good to set [h] from the world to God, that I may rise to him.

PRAY FOR STRENGTH

3.1 You have never envied anyone; you have taught others. But I desire that those things which you command when teaching disciples be in force. **2** Only pray for strength for me, both inward and outward, so that ₁I do not

a. Lightfoot comments: "To Ignatius martyrdom is life. ... Whoever stands between him and this his true life, does him a wrong. Such a person grudges him a blessing. Hence in his nomenclature the meaning of words is reversed. To 'spare' means to deliver to death, because death is life."

b. Lightfoot comments: "By 'pleasing men' he means abetting those friends who desired to save him or gratifying the merely human cravings of his own nature."

c. Outside of the NT, the semantic range of ἀρέσκω is wide. BDAG notes it is "a favored term in the reciprocity-conscious Mediterranean world, and frequently used in honorary documents to express interest in accommodating others by meeting their needs or carrying out important obligations. ... The use of the term in a good sense in our literally contributes a tone of special worth and dignity to some of the relationships that are depicted."

d. On the relationship between being "a word of God" and "just a sound," Lightfoot comments: "The saint's career, if it is left to work out its course and ends in martyrdom, will be a word of God; it will be an expressive testimony to the gospel, a manifestation of the divine purpose: but, if interfered with, it will be reduced to a mere inarticulate meaningless cry."

e. Literally "again I will be a voice"

f. Literally "in the west"

g. Literally "from the east"

h. Lightfoot comments: "He was following the course of the sun; his life would set to the world in the far west; but as the sun rises, so it also would rise again to God."

just talk about it, [a] but ,I also want to do it,, [b] that ,I am not just called, [c] a Christian but ,I may also be found to be a Christian,. [d] For if I may be *so* found and I am able to be *so* called, and then to be faithful when I am not visible to the world. ³ Nothing visible is good. For our God Jesus Christ, being in the Father, is made more visible. Christianity is not the work of persuasion [e] but of greatness when it is hated by the world. [f]

BECOMING A DISCIPLE

⁴⁺¹ I am writing to all the churches and giving instructions to everyone that I die willingly for God, if indeed you do not hinder *me*. I urge you do not be an ill-timed kindness to me. [g] Allow me to be food for beasts, through whom it is possible to reach God. I am God's wheat, and I am ground by the teeth of beasts, that I may be found pure bread of Christ. ² Instead, coax the beasts that they may become a tomb for me and leave nothing of my body, that ,I may not be a burden to anyone when I die,. [h] Then I will truly be a disciple of Jesus Christ, when ,the world will not even see my body,. [i] Petition Christ on my behalf that through these tools, I may be found a sacrifice. ³ I give orders to you, not as Peter and Paul; they *were* apostles, I *am* a convict; they *were* free, but I until now *am* a slave. But if I suffer I will be a freedperson [j] of Jesus Christ, and I will rise up free in him. For now, being imprisoned, I am learning to desire nothing.

TO REACH JESUS CHRIST

⁵⁺¹ From Syria to Rome I am fighting with wild beasts, by land and sea, night and day, being imprisoned by ten leopards (that is, a company of soldiers)

---

a. Literally "I not only speak"

b. Literally "I also desire"

c. Literally "not only am I called"

d. Literally "also I may be found"

e. 1 Cor 2:4; 1 Thess 1:5; Gal 5:8

f. John 7:7; 15:18, 19; 17:14; 1 John 3:13

g. Lightfoot, Lake, and Holmes note that this is likely an allusion to an ancient proverb recorded by Zenobius, "An unseasonable kindness is no different than hostility" (Holmes' translation).

h. Literally "I may not be burdensome to anyone when I fall asleep"

i. Literally "not even the world will see my body"

j. 1 Cor 7:22

who also, being treated kindly, [a] become even worse. But in their mistreatments I am becoming more of a disciple, but I have not been justified ₍by these mistreatments₎. [b] [c] [2] May I enjoy the beasts that have been made ready for me, and I pray ₍they might deal with me speedily₎. [d] I will also entice them to devour me quickly, not as with some who were so cowardly they have not touched. But even if they are themselves unwilling I will force *them* myself. [3] Grant me this favor. I know what is best for me. Now I am beginning to be a disciple. May nothing visible or invisible envy me, so that I may reach Jesus Christ. Fire and cross and battles with beasts, mutilation, being torn apart, scattering of bones, mangling of limbs, grinding of the whole body, cruel tortures of the devil; let these come upon me, only that I may reach Jesus Christ.

BETTER TO DIE FOR CHRIST

[6.1] Neither the ends of the earth [e] nor the kingdoms of this age [f] will be of benefit to me. It is better [g] for me to die in Christ Jesus than to reign over the ends of the earth. I seek that one who died on my behalf. I desire that one who rose up on our account. But the pains of childbirth [h] are upon me. [2] ₍Be in agreement with me₎, [i] brothers, do not hinder me from living, do not wish me to die. Do hand over not to the world one who desires to belong to God, and do not deceive him with material things. [j] Allow me to receive the pure light; arriving there I will be a man. [3] Allow me to be an imitator of the suffering of my God. If anyone has him in himself, let him understand what I want and let him sympathize with me, knowing what constrains me.

---

a. Lightfoot paraphrases, "The more they receive in gratuities, the harsher and more extortionate they become."

b. Literally "because of these"

c. 1 Cor 4:4

d. Literally "they be found prompt for me"

e. Lightfoot notes: "In the LXX, τὰ πέρατα τῆς γῆς (τῆς οὐκουμένης) is a common expression, see especially Ps 2:8, which well illustrates the meaning of Ignatius here."

f. Matt 4:8; Luke 4:5

g. 1 Cor 9:15; Matt 18:8, 9; Mark 9:43, 45

h. Gal 4:19

i. Literally "join your minds with mine"

j. In addition to the sense of "wood" or "forest," the word ὕλη can also generally represent "matter" or "stuff." Cf. BDAG ὕλη sense 3.

COME TO THE FATHER

7.1 The ruler of this age wants to abduct [a] me and to corrupt my mind toward God. Therefore let none of you who are present help him. Instead ˌbe on my sideˌ, [b] that is, ˌGod's sideˌ. [c] Do not speak of Jesus Christ but desire the world. 2 Do not let envy dwell in you. If I myself, being present, urge you, do not be persuaded by me, but instead be persuaded by this: what I write to you. For I write to you while living, strongly desiring [d] to die. My passion has been crucified and there is no fire of love for material things in me, but water [e] living and speaking in me, saying within me, "Come to the Father." 3 I take no pleasure in food of corruption or the pleasures of this life. I desire the bread [f] of God, which is the flesh of Jesus Christ, who is from the seed of David; and for drink I desire his blood, which is imperishable love. [g]

FINAL PLEA

8.1 I no longer desire to live according to human standards, and this will happen, if you so desire. Desire it, so that you also may be desired! 2 I ask you by brief letter: believe me! And Jesus Christ, the unerring mouth by whom the Father has truly spoken, will make this known to you, that I speak truly. 3 Plead for me, that I may reach God. [h] I write to you not according to the flesh but according to the mind of God. If I suffer, you desired it; if I am rejected, you hated me. [i]

---

a. When used of persons, διαπράζω has the sense of "to steal away, to snatch, to abduct." Cf. BDAG διαπράζω.

b. Literally "be for me"

c. Literally "for God"

d. Gal 6:14

e. John 4:10-11

f. John 4:33

g. Lightfoot comments: "As the flesh of Christ represents the solid substance of the Christian life, so the blood of Christ represents the element of love which circulates through all its pores and ducts, animating and invigorating the whole."

h. When Ignatius uses ἐπιτυγχάνω, he is almost always talking about "reaching God"; suffering the death of a martyr and by this becoming a true disciple.

i. In this last portion of the verse, Ignatius is telling the Romans that his fate as a martyr is in their hands. If he suffers the martyr's death it will be because the Romans also wanted this and did not prevent him from this path. If he is rejected as a martyr, it will be because the Romans intervened on his behalf. Ignatius views such intervention as hate because it would prevent him from his goal of "reaching God."

REMEMBER THE SYRIAN CHURCH

9.1 Remember in your prayer the church in Syria which has God as shepherd [a] in my place. Jesus Christ alone will oversee [b] it and your love. 2 But
I myself am ashamed to be called one of them, for I am not worthy, being
the least of them and an untimely birth. [c] But I have found mercy [d] to be
someone, if I may reach God. 3 My spirit greets you as *does* the love of the
churches that welcomed me in the name of Jesus Christ, not as one passing by. [e] For even those *churches* not present on my physical route [f] went
before me from city to city. [g][h]

FAREWELL

10.1 And I write you these things from Smyrna by the Ephesians, who are
worthy of blessing. And Crocus, a name very dear to me is also together
with me, along with many others. 2 Concerning those who preceded me
from Syria to Rome to the glory of God, I believe you have information. Tell
them I am also near. For they are all worthy of God and of you. It is fitting
for you to give rest to them in every way. 3 And I write you these things
the twenty-fourth of August. [i] Farewell until the end, in the endurance [j2]
of Jesus Christ.

---

a. 1 Pet 2:25; 5:2; see also Ezek 34:11

b. This could also be translated "will be its bishop."

c. Lightfoot comments: "The idea in the metaphor, as used by St. Paul and Ignatius, is
twofold: (1) irregularity of time, referring to an unexpected, abrupt, conversion; and (2)
imperfection, immaturity, weakness of growth. Ignatius, like St. Paul, we must suppose, had
been suddenly brought to a knowledge of the Gospel. ... It is very possible that his early life
had been stained with the common immoralities of heathen society; but at all events this
expression throws a flood of light on his position and explains the language of self-depreci-
ation which he uses so freely."

d. 1 Tim 1:13

e. Ezek 36:34

f. Literally "route according to the flesh"

g. Literally "according to city"

h. Luke 7:1, 4; Acts 15:21; 20:23

i. Literally "on the ninth day before the calends of September"

j. 2 Thess 3:5; Rev 1:9; 1 Thess 1:3; Rom 8:25

— Ignatius to the Philadelphians

SALUTATION

Ignatius, [who is also called "God-bearer,"[a] to the church of God the Father and of the Lord Jesus Christ which is in Philadelphia in Asia, which has obtained mercy and is established in harmony of God, and which rejoices greatly in the suffering of our Lord without wavering, and is fully convinced by all mercy in his resurrection, whom I greet in the blood of Jesus Christ, which[b] is eternal and abiding joy, especially if they are in unity with the bishop and with the presbyters and deacons with him, who have been appointed in the purpose[c] of Jesus Christ, who, according to his own will, [he securely established][d] by his Holy Spirit.

EXAMPLE OF THE BISHOP

1.1 I know that your bishop, neither from himself[e] nor through people, but by the love of God the Father and the Lord Jesus Christ, acquired a ministry which pertains to the common good and not to delusion. I was amazed at his gentleness, who, by keeping silent, is able to do more than those who speak empty words. 2 For he is attuned to the commandments as a lyre to its strings. Therefore my soul blesses his [godly][f] mind (recognizing it is virtuous and perfect), [his solid and angerless character,][g] living in all [godly][h] gentleness.

---

a. Literally "who [is] also God-bearer"
b. 1 Tim 3:15
c. Lightfoot glosses this as "with the approval"
d. Literally "he established in strength"
e. Gal 1:1
f. Literally "in God"
g. Literally "his steadfast character and his lack of anger"
h. Literally "of God"

FLEE FROM DIVISION

2.1 Therefore, children of the light of truth, flee from division and evil teaching. And where the shepherd is, there follow like sheep. **2** For many seemingly trustworthy wolves[a] take God's runners captive[b] by evil pleasure, but they will not have a place in your unity.

LIVE IN ACCORDANCE WITH JESUS CHRIST

3.1 Refrain from the evil plants which Jesus Christ does not cultivate because they are not a planting[c] of the Father. Not that I have found division among you, but a filtering out.[d] **2** For as many as belong to God and Jesus Christ, these are with the bishop. And as many who repent and come to the unity of the church, these will belong to God, so that they may be living in accordance with Jesus Christ. **3** Do not be deceived, my brothers: if anyone follows a schism-maker he does not inherit the kingdom of God.[e] If anyone walks in a strange mindset, this one has no part[f] in the Passion.[g]

UNITY

4.1 Therefore be eager to use one Eucharist[h] (for there is one flesh[i] of our Lord Jesus Christ and one cup for unity through his blood; there is one altar as there is one bishop together with the council of elders and the deacons, my fellow slaves) in order that whatever you do, do it in accordance with God.

---

a. Acts 20:29; John 10:12

b. 2 Tim 3:6; Gal 5:7

c. Matt 15:13

d. Lightfoot comments: "The false teachers had been at Philadelphia; but the Philadelphian Christians had strained out these dregs of heresy. They had separated themselves from the heretics; but this separation deserved the name of 'filtering' rather than of 'division.'"

e. 1 Cor 6:9–10

f. Literally "does not agree"

g. Here the implicit reference is to the suffering of Christ, so it is translated as "Passion."

h. 1 Cor 11:18, 20

i. 1 Cor 10:16–17

APOSTLES AND PROPHETS

5.1 My brothers, ₗI am overflowingₗ[a] with love to you and rejoice greatly as I ensure your safety;[b] and not me but Jesus Christ, in whom being imprisoned I am all the more fearful as I am still imperfect, but your prayer to God will complete me, so that I may reach the portion in which I have found mercy,[c] having fled for refuge to the gospel as to the flesh of Jesus and to the apostles[d] as the council of elders of the church. 2 And we also love the prophets because ₗtheir proclamation also anticipated the gospel,ₗ[e] and set their hope on him and awaited him, in whom also by believing they were saved being in the unity of Jesus Christ, holy ones worthy of love and worthy of admiration, being well spoken of by Jesus Christ and numbered together in the gospel of the common hope.[f]

ONLY JESUS CHRIST

6.1 But if anyone should interpret Judaism to you, do not hear him. For it is better to hear Christianity from a man who is circumcised than Judaism from ₗsomeone who is uncircumcised,ₗ[g] But if ₗneither of them speakₗ[h] about Jesus Christ, these ones represent to me tombstones[i] and graves of the dead, upon which are written only the names of people. 2 Therefore flee from the evil designs and snares[j] of the ruler of this age, lest being afflicted by his mind-set you grow weak in love. But all of you come ₗtogetherₗ[k] with an undivided heart. 3 But I give thanks to my God that I have a good conscience among you and ₗno one can boast,ₗ[l] either privately or publicly, that

---

a. Literally "I give very abundantly"

b. Neh 3:15; Wis 13:15

c. 2 Cor 4:1; 1 Tim 1:13, 16; Rom 11:30, 31; 1 Pet 2:10

d. Lightfoot notes: "The expression ('the apostles') obviously points to some authoritative writings of the New Testament. The 'Apostles,' like the 'Prophets,' must have been represented in some permanent form to which appeal could be made."

e. Literally "they also made proclamation to the gospel"

f. 1 Tim 1:1

g. Literally "an uncircumcised person"

h. Literally "both do not speak"

i. Matt 28:27

j. 1 Tim 3:7; 6:9; 2 Tim 2:26

k. Literally "to the same"

l. Literally "do not have anyone to boast"

I was a burden[a] to anyone in small things or in great things. But I pray also for everyone among whom I spoke that they may not bring it upon themselves as a witness.

BE IMITATORS OF JESUS CHRIST

7.1 For even if some desired to deceive me according to the flesh, the spirit is not deceived, being from God. For it knows from where it came and where it is going[b] and it exposes the hidden things.[c] I shouted out, being in your midst; I spoke with a loud voice, the voice of God: "Pay attention to the bishop and to the council of elders and deacons." 2 But those who suspected me of saying this because I knew beforehand of the division of some. But my witness, in whom I am a prisoner, that I have not known from ₁any human being₁,[d] but the Spirit was preaching, saying this:[e] "Do nothing without the bishop. Keep your body as the temple of God. Love unity. Flee from divisions. Be imitators of Jesus Christ, as also he is of his Father."

JESUS CHRIST IS THE ARCHIVE

8.1 Therefore I was doing ₁my part₁[f] as someone who was set on unity. But where there is division and anger God does not dwell. Therefore the Lord forgives all who repent if they turn in repentance to the unity of God and the council of the bishop. I believe in the grace of Jesus Christ who will loose[g] every bond from you. 2 But I urge you to do nothing according to selfish ambition but according to the teaching of Christ. For I heard some saying that "Unless I find it in the archives,[h] I do not believe it in the gospel." And when I said to them that "It is written,"[i] they answered me, "That ₁is

---

a. 2 Cor 11:9; 12:16; 1 Thess 2:9; 2 Thess 3:8; 2 Sam 12:3

b. John 3:8

c. 1 Cor 2:10

d. Literally "a human body"

e. On the sayings in this chapter, Lightfoot notes: "Ignatius is plainly speaking throughout this passage of a spiritual revelation to himself."

f. Literally "my own"

g. Isa 58:6

h. Lightfoot comments: "The opponents of Ignatius refuse to defer to any modern writings, whether Gospels or Epistles, as a standard of truth; they will submit only to such documents as have been preserved in the archives of the Jews, or in other words, only to the Old Testament Scriptures."

i. Here meaning the Old Testament Scriptures.

exactly the question¸."[a] But to me the archives are Jesus Christ, the sacred archives his cross and death and his resurrection and the faith which is through him; in these things I desire through your prayer to be justified.

JESUS CHRIST OUR SAVIOR

9.1 And the priests were good, but the high priest[b] is even better: he has been entrusted with the Holy of Holies, who alone has been entrusted with the hidden things of God; he is the door of the Father through which Abraham and Isaac and Jacob and the prophets and apostles and the church enter. All of these are brought into the unity of God. 2 But the gospel has something distinctive: the coming[c] of the Savior, our Lord Jesus Christ, his suffering and resurrection. For the beloved prophets preached with reference to him, but the gospel is the consummation of immortality. All things together are good if you believe in love.

ANTIOCH AT PEACE

10.1 Since, according to your prayers and according to the compassion which you have in Christ Jesus, it has been reported to me the church which is in Antioch of Syria is at peace, it is fitting for you as a church of God to appoint a deacon ¸to go on a mission there as God's ambassador¸[d] to rejoice with those gathered ¸together¸[e] and to glorify the name. 2 Blessed in Jesus Christ is he who will be considered worthy of such a ministry, and you yourselves will be glorified. And ¸if you have the will¸[f] it is not impossible for you to do this on behalf of the name of God as also the churches nearby have sent bishops, and others[g] have sent presbyters and deacons.

---

a. Literally "lies before [us]"

b. Heb 2:17; 3:1; 4:14; 5:5, 10; 6:20; 7:7-26; 8:1; 9:11

c. 2 Pet 1:16

d. Literally "to be an ambassador there, an ambassador of God"

e. Literally "to the same"

f. Literally "desiring"

g. Lightfoot comments: "presumably those which were not so near and whose bishop could not be spared."

GREETINGS AND FAREWELL

11.1 Now concerning Philo, the deacon from Cilicia, a man well spoken of, who also now serves me in the word[a] of God, together with Rheus Agathopous, an elect man who is following me from Syria, having renounced this life; they also speak well[b] of you. And I give thanks to God on your behalf, that you received them as also the Lord received you. But may those who shamed them be redeemed by the grace of Jesus Christ. **2** The love of the brothers who are in Troas greets you; from there also I write to you through Burrhus, who was sent together with me from the Ephesians and Smyrnaeans as ₁a mark of honor₁.[cd] The Lord Jesus Christ will honor them; on him they hope in flesh, in soul, in spirit, in faith, in love, and in harmony. Farewell in Christ Jesus, our common hope.

---

a. Acts 6:2; Col 1:25; Rev 1:9

b. 3 John 5–6

c. Literally "a word of honor"

d. Most translations have "a mark of honor," "a pledge of honor," or "a token of honor." Lightfoot glosses as "to do me honor."

— *Ignatius to the Smyrnaeans*

SALUTATION

Ignatius, ₁who is also called "God-bearer,"₁[a] to the church of God the Father and of the beloved Jesus Christ, which has obtained mercy in every gift, which has been filled with faith and love, which is not lacking in any gift, most worthy of God and bearing holy things, which is in Smyrna of Asia, abundant greetings in a blameless spirit and the word[b] of God.

ESTABLISHED IN FAITH

1.1 I give glory to Jesus Christ, the God who has made you so wise.[c] For I have perceived that you have been established in immovable faith just as if having been nailed[d] on the cross[e] of the Lord Jesus Christ, both in flesh and spirit, and having been established in love by the blood of Christ, having been fully convinced about our Lord that he is truly from the family of David according to the flesh, the Son of God according to the will and power of God, having been born truly of a virgin, having been baptized by John that all righteousness might be fulfilled by him,[f 2] truly nailed to the tree in the flesh for us under Pontius Pilate and Herod the tetrarch[g] (we are from

---

a. Literally "who [is] also God-bearer"

b. 1 John 1:10; 2:14

c. 2 Tim 3:15

d. Col 2:14; Gal 2:20

e. On this comparison, Schoedel notes: "For evidently the point is that the Smyrnaeans are committed to the reality of the passion. The thought is expressed with an odd play on words. The immovability of their orthodox faith is traced to the fact that they have been nailed (so to speak) to the cross. Their being nailed explains their 'immovability,' their being nailed to the cross indicates their acceptance of the passion. Underlying both levels of meaning is the Pauline theme of being crucified with Christ (Gal 2:19)."

f. Matt 3:15

g. Luke 23:7-12

its fruit, from his suffering blessed by God) that he might raise a banner[a] to the ages through the resurrection to his holy and faithful ones, whether among Jews or among Gentiles, in the one body, his church.

AGAINST THE DOCETISTS

2.1 For he suffered all these things because of us, that we might be saved. And he truly suffered as he also truly raised himself up, not as some unbelievers say, his suffering was in appearance only (it is they who are in appearance only).[b] And just as they think, so also will it happen to them, being bodiless and ghost-like.[c]

FLESH AND SPIRIT

3.1 For I know and believe he was in the flesh even after the resurrection. **2** And when he came to those with Peter, he said to them, "Take hold. Touch me and see that I am not a bodiless demon."[d] And immediately they touched him and they believed, being closely united with his flesh and spirit.[e] Because of this they despised even death, and were found to be above death. **3** And after the resurrection he ate with them and drank with them[f] as fleshly, although being united spiritually with the Father.

OUR TRUE LIFE

4.1 And I urge you of these things, beloved, knowing that you are also like-minded. But I am protecting you from the beasts in human form, whom you must not only not receive, but, if possible, not even meet, but only

---

a. Isa 49:22; 62:10

b. This exact comparison about suffering "in appearance only" is also found in Ign *Trall* 10.1.

c. Ignatius here, in his arguing against docetism, puts the outcome of the docetists back on themselves. As the docetists believe in separation of body and spirit, Ignatius assents and agrees with them that in their eternal torment, apart from the glory of Christ, they will be bodiless and ghost-like (also could be translated "demonic").

d. Luke 24:39

e. πνεύματι Lake, Ehrman] αἵματι Lightfoot, Holmes. The choice here is between "his flesh and spirit" (Lake and Ehrman) or "his flesh and blood" (Lightfoot and Holmes). While Lightfoot and Holmes seem more attractive for the anti-docetic context, the notion of "mixing" along with the fact that the only Greek witness is to "his flesh and spirit" seems to favor the reading of Lake and Ehrman.

f. Acts 10:41; Luke 24:30, 35, 42, 43; John 21:12, 13

pray for them, if they might somehow repent, which indeed is difficult. But Jesus Christ, who is our true life, has authority over this. [2] For if these things were accomplished by our Lord in appearance only, I also am a prisoner in appearance only, and why also have I allowed myself to be given over to death, to fire, to the sword, to beasts? Instead nearer to the sword is nearer to God; in the midst of beasts is in the midst of God. I endure[a] all things in the name of Jesus Christ alone so that I may suffer with him; the perfect human himself strengthening me.

DOCETISTS UNABLE TO BE CONVINCED

[5.1] Some unknowingly deny him but instead[b] were denied by him, being advocates of death rather than of the truth. The prophecies[c] have not persuaded them, nor the law of Moses, and[d] not even until now the gospel nor our ₍individual₎[e] suffering. [2] For they even think the same thing about us. For what does anyone benefit me if he praises me but he blasphemes my Lord, not confessing he was clothed in flesh? But he who says this denies him completely, being clothed in a corpse.[f] [3] And their names, being unbelievers, I am not disposed to write down, but may it be granted to me not to remember them until which time they might repent concerning the passion, which is our resurrection.

---

a. 2 Tim 2:10

b. 2 Tim 2:12

c. Of the opponents, Lightfoot notes: "As Judaizers they professed the greatest respect for the Law and the Prophets, and yet they ignored the testimony borne by them to Christ's passion."

d. The use of ἀλλά here shows a comparison between "the prophecies and the law of Moses" and "the gospel and individual suffering." While the prophecies and the law point to Christ, gospel and individual suffering do even more so; Ignatius' point is that not even the gospel or the witness of individual suffering (including the testimony of martyrs) convince these people of Christ.

e. Literally "according to each person"

f. On the interplay between σαρκοφόρον (clothed in flesh) and νεκροφόρος (clothed in a corpse), BDAG notes: "Ign[atius] uses it in a play on words to reject the views of the docetists, who deny that Christ was a σαρκοφόρος. Whoever does this, he says, is himself a νεκροφόρος, evidently meaning that he is clothed in a corpse rather than in flesh."

FAITH AND LOVE ARE EVERYTHING

6.1 Let no one be deceived: even the heavenly things and the glory of the angels and the rulers, both visible and invisible, ₍unless they believe₎[a] on the blood of Christ, judgment is also theirs. He who can accept this, let him accept it.[b] Let an office puff up no one, for faith and love are everything, to which nothing is preferable. **2** But observe those who hold divisive opinions concerning the grace of Jesus Christ that came to us; how opposed they are to the mind of God. For love does not concern them, no concern for the widow,[c] none for the orphan, none for the afflicted, none for the ones imprisoned or the ones set free, none for the hungry or the thirsty.

THE PASSION HAS BEEN REVEALED

7.1 They abstain from the Eucharist and prayer because they do not confess the Eucharist to be the flesh of our Savior Jesus Christ who suffered for our sins, whom the Father raised up by his goodness. Therefore those[d] who oppose the gift[e] of God, being disputers, they die. But it would be better for them to love, that they might also rise up.[f] **2** It is fitting to refrain from such as these and not to speak about them ₍privately₎[g] or publicly. But consider the Prophets and especially the gospel, in which the passion has been revealed to us and the resurrection has been accomplished.[h] But flee from divisions as the beginning of evil.

THE ROLE OF THE BISHOP

8.1 All of you follow the bishop as Jesus Christ follows the Father, and follow the council of elders as the apostles. And have respect for the deacons as the commandment of God. No one does anything that pertains to the church without the bishop. Consider valid that Eucharist which is held under the

---

a. Literally "if they do not believe"
b. Matt 19:12
c. Acts 6:1; 9:38, 41; 1 Tim 5:3–16; Jas 1:27
d. Some translations (Lightfoot, Ehrman) begin section 7 here.
e. Rom 5:15; 2 Cor 9:15
f. Lake translates "they may attain to the Resurrection."
g. Literally "according to one's own"
h. Some editions (Lightfoot, Holmes) begin section 8 here.

bishop or whomever he ₍appoints₎.[a] [2] Wherever the bishop appears, let the congregation be there; just as wherever Jesus Christ is, the catholic church is there. It is not permitted either to baptize or to hold a love feast without the bishop, but whatever that one approves, this also is pleasing to God, that everything which you do may be safe and secure.

BE REFRESHED

[9.1] Finally, it is reasonable for us to return to our senses[b] while we still have opportunity to repent to God. It is good to know[c] God and the bishop. He who honors the bishop will be honored by God. He who does anything without the knowledge of the bishop serves the devil. [2] Therefore let all things abound to you in grace, for you are worthy. You have refreshed me in all things; may Jesus Christ also refresh you. In absence[d] and presence you have loved me. God is your reward; ₍if you endure everything for his sake₎,[e] you will attain him.

ENCOURAGEMENT

[10.1] You did well to receive Philo and Rheus Agathopous, who followed after me in the word of God, as deacons of God; who also give thanks to the Lord on your behalf, that you have refreshed them in every way. Nothing to you ₍will ever be lost₎.[f] [2] May my spirit be a ransom for you, and my chains, which you did not treat with arrogance nor were you ashamed. Neither will the perfect hope, Jesus Christ, be ashamed of you.[g]

AN AMBASSADOR TO SYRIA

[11.1] Your prayer came to the church which is in Antioch in Syria; from there, being imprisoned with most godly chains, I greet everyone, not being worthy to be from there, being the least of them. But according to the divine

---

a. Literally "permits"
b. 2 Tim 2:25
c. 1 Thess 5:12
d. Phil 2:12
e. Literally "enduring all things through him"
f. Literally "will not ever be lost"
g. Mark 8:38

will I am considered worthy not by my own complicity[a] but by the grace of God which I pray be given to me in perfection, that by your prayer I may reach God. [2] Therefore, that your work may be perfect both on earth and in heaven, it is fitting for your church to appoint, to the honor of God, a godly ambassador to go to Syria, to rejoice with them that they are at peace and have recovered their proper greatness, and their proper corporate life has been restored. [3] Therefore it appeared to me a deed worthy of God to send someone from your number with a letter that he might join in praising the tranquility which happened to them according to God, and that they were already experiencing a haven by your prayer. As you are perfect you also think perfect things. For to you who desire to do well, God is ready to help.

GREETINGS

[12.1] The love of the brothers who are in Troas greets you, from where also I write to you through Burrhus, whom you sent with me, together with the Ephesians your brothers, who has relieved me in every way. Would that[b] all were imitators of him, being a living example of the ministry of God. Grace will reward him in every way. [2] I greet the godly bishop and venerable council of elders and my fellow slaves the deacons and all ⌊individually⌋[c] and in common, in the name of Jesus Christ and in his flesh and blood, both his passion and resurrection, both physical[d] and spiritual, in unity with God and with you. Grace to you, mercy, peace, and endurance ⌊forever⌋.[e]

FURTHER GREETINGS AND FAREWELL

[13.1] I greet the households of my fellow believers with wives and children, and the virgins[f] who are called widows. I bid you farewell in the power

---

a. Lightfoot notes: "The expression might have either of two meanings: (1) 'of conscience,' i.e., 'not that my conscience pronounces me worthy,' compare 1 Cor 4:4; or (2) 'of consent, complicity,' i.e., 'it was God's sole doing.' ... The latter is perhaps the more probable sense here."

b. 1 Cor 4:8; 2 Cor 9:1; Gal 5:12; Rev 3:15

c. Literally "by person"

d. Lightfoot notes: "A spiritual resurrection was not denied by the docetists. Hence Ignatius asserts both."

e. Literally "through all"

f. This is a confusing phrase; after all, how can virgins be called widows? The basic thought is that the virgins could be supported by the church through the existing office of widow. Schoedel comments: "The solution once advanced by many (including Lightfoot) that Ignatius means widows who may be regarded as virgins fails because of the order in

of the Father. Philo greets you, being with me. ² I greet the household of Tavia,ᵃ who I pray is established in faith and love, both physical and spiritual. I greet Alce, a name very dear to me, and the incomparable Daphnus, and Eutecnus, and all ₁individual₁,ᵇᶜ Farewell in the grace of God.

---

which the terms occur and because the expression τὰς λεγομένας ('called') indicates that the term 'widow' is used of the virgins in an unusual or improper sense. The correct solution is probably that argued most forcefully by Zahn: the order of 'widows' (cf. 1 Tim 5:3-16) was opened up also to virgins (especially older women) who had no other means of support."

a. Ταουΐας Lake, Ehrman] Γαουΐας Lightfoot, Holmes. This is a simple difference in proper name; "Tavia" or "Gavia." Lightfoot prefers Gavia because it is well attested in inscriptions even though no Greek editions witness it for this variation.

b. Literally "by name"

c. 3 John 15

– *Ignatius to Polycarp*

SALUTATION

Ignatius, ₁who is also called "God-bearer,"₁[a] to Polycarp, bishop of the church of the Smyrnaeans, or rather, who is being bishopped by God the Father and the Lord Jesus Christ; abundant greetings.

GREETING AND EXHORTATION

1.1 Welcoming your ₁godly way of thinking,₁[b] which is firmly established as if upon an immovable rock,[c] I glory exceedingly, having been considered worthy ₁to see your blameless face,₁[d] which I have benefited from[e] in God. **2** I urge you, by the grace with which you are clothed, to proceed on your course[f] and to urge all so that they might be saved. Vindicate your position[g] with all care, both physical and spiritual.[h] Be intent on unity, of which nothing is better. Bear with everyone, like the Lord also bears with you.[i] Endure all in love, just as you also do. **3** Be diligent with unceasing prayer. Ask for ₁greater understanding than₁[j] you have. Be on the alert, possessing an always active spirit. Speak ₁to each individual₁[k] with agreement in God's

---

a. Literally "who [is] also God-bearer"

b. Literally "godly mind"

c. Matt 7:24, 25; Luke 6:48

d. Literally "of your blameless face"

e. Phlm 20

f. Lightfoot notes the sense of προσθεῖναι τῷ δρόμῳ is that of "to run the race with increased vigor." Paul uses a similar metaphor in Acts 13:25; 20:24; 2 Tim 4:7. Ignatius uses it elsewhere as well; see Ign *Rom* 2.

g. The sense here is of position or office.

h. Lightfoot notes this could also be "secular as well as spiritual." Ignatius uses this phrase elsewhere, e.g., Ign *Eph* 10.

i. Isa 53:4; Matt 8:17

j. Literally "understanding greater than which"

k. Literally "those by man"

convictions. Bear the sicknesses of all like the perfect athlete. Where the trouble is greater, the gain is great.

WISE, INNOCENT AND GRACIOUS

2.1 If you love good disciples, it is no credit to you; rather bring the more troublesome ones into submission with gentleness. Not every wound is healed with the same treatment.[a] Relieve attacks of fever with cold compresses. 2 Be wise like the serpent in all things, and always innocent like the dove.[b] For this reason[c] you are physical and spiritual, so that you may deal graciously with[d] whatever is visible before your face; and ask that the invisible be revealed to you, so that you may lack[e] nothing and you may abound in every gift. 3 The time seeks for you, like shipmasters[f] seek for wind and like storm-tossed sailors seek for harbor, to reach to God. Be self-controlled, like God's athlete. The prize[g] is immortality and eternal life, about which you also have been persuaded. I am your ransom in every respect and also my chains, which you loved.

STAND FIRM

3.1 Those who appear to be trustworthy yet teach strange doctrines,[h] do not let them amaze you. Stand firm,[i] like an anvil being struck with a hammer.[j] It is the mark of[k] a great athlete to endure punishment[l] and to achieve

---

a. Lightfoot notes this could be translated as "plaster" or "salve."

b. Matt 10:16

c. Literally "Because of this"

d. Lightfoot notes: "The advice here is not very different from St. Paul's maxim of 'becoming all things to all men.' The things of this world are to be 'coaxed' into conformity with the will of God."

e. Jas 1:4; 1 Cor 1:7

f. Lightfoot notes: "This is the earliest example of a simile which afterward was used largely by Christian writers."

g. Lightfoot adds: "The θέμα was a prize of money, as distinguished from the στέφανος."

h. 1 Tim 1:3; 6:3

i. 1 Cor 7:37

j. Job 41:15

k. Translations (Lake, Ehrman, Holmes) regularly supply "the mark of" or "the task of" to make the contrast of the passive and active infinitive verbs more evident. Also, while "great athletes" may achieve victory, Ignatius here is noting the quality, not the athlete in particular.

l. 1 Cor 9:26

victory. But especially ₍for God's sake₎[a] we must endure all things, so that
he may also endure us. [2] Be more diligent than you are. Mark the seasons.[b]
Wait for the one above the seasons: the timeless one,[c] the invisible one,[d]
who because of us is visible, the intangible one, the unsuffering one, who
because of us suffers, who because of us endured in every way.

WIDOWS AND SLAVES

[4.1] Do not let the widows be neglected.[e] After the Lord, you yourself be
their protector.[f] Let nothing happen without your consent, nor do anything yourself without God, as indeed you do not do. Be firm. [2] Let your
meetings be[g] as often as possible. Seek out everyone by name. [3] Do not treat
male or female slaves arrogantly, but ₍do not puff them up either₎,[h] instead
let them serve even more to the glory of God, that they may experience a
better freedom from God. Let them desire not to be set free ₍at the church's
expense₎,[ij] that they not be disclosed as slaves of lust.

---

a. Literally "because of God"

b. Matt 16:3; Luke 12:56

c. cf. Lightfoot, "beyond the limits of time."

d. 1 Tim 1:17

e. 1 Tim 5:3

f. Lightfoot describes this as "... a semi-technical term ... It corresponds to the Latin
'curator' ... Like 'curator' it may refer to the guardianship of orphans or widows, etc., as here,
or to the direction of public words, or to the management of finance ... where the officer
intended was probably 'curator' (or 'procurator') 'fisci' to this prince."

g. Heb 10:25

h. Literally "neither puff them up"

i. Literally "through the common fund"

j. It was possible for slaves in these times to purchase their freedom. Lighfoot explains:
"As the money available for this purpose was limited, it was necessary to select cases of special
hardship; and a general anxiety of slaves to obtain their emancipation this way was to be
deprecated."

HUSBANDS AND WIVES

5.1 Flee from the evil arts;[a] instead, preach a sermon about them. Tell my sisters to love the Lord and to be content with their husbands[b] in flesh and in spirit. In the same way, also command my brothers in the name of Jesus Christ to love their wives like the Lord loved the church.[c] **2** If anyone is able to remain in purity to honor the flesh of the Lord,[d] let him do so ₁without boasting₁.[e] If he boasts, he has been lost; and if it becomes known to any beyond the bishop, he is ruined. But it is fitting for ₁men and women who marry₁[f] with the consent of the bishop to make their union, that the marriage may be in accordance with the Lord[g] and not in accordance with lust. Let all things be done for the honor of God.

FURTHER EXHORTATIONS

6.1 Pay attention to the bishop, that God also may pay attention to you. I am a ransom for those who are subject to the bishop, presbyters, and deacons; and may it be granted to me to have my part with them[h] in[i] God. Labor

---

a. On κακοτεχνία, BDAG provides the following: "At Ign *Pol* 5.1, where there is no reference to the devil, and where Polycarp is advised to make κακοτεχνίαι the subject of preaching, the word seems to mean 'evil arts', i.e., the arts and trades which are forbidden for a Christian, especially magic. In favor of this interpretation is the fact that the context of this passage deals with conjugal relations in a manner that suggests a warning against recourse to magical formulae that feature erotic themes." Consider also Lightfoot's discussion, "It was used especially of 'magical arts' and of these most commonly as connected with heretical teaching. ..." There is something to be said for giving it this very definite sense "here. ...Witchcraft, sorcery, and the like were highly attractive in these regions; and against them Christians waged internecine war from the first (see Acts 19:19)."

b. Lightfoot notes: "The word σύμβιος is common for a husband or a wife in this age and even earlier.... In the inscriptions during the Roman period it is especially frequent. In those of Smyrna alone, to which place this letter was written, I find it several times. ... To the Christians it would perhaps be an especially welcome term, because it would cover those unions of slaves which are called 'contubernia' and which the Christian Church regarded as not less sacred and inviolable than wedlock among the free-born, though the Roman law did not recognize such a thing as marriage among slaves."

c. Eph 5:25, 29

d. 1 Cor 6:15

e. Literally "with freedom from boasting"

f. Literally "men who marry and women who are married"

g. 1 Cor 7:39

h. Matt 24:51; Luke 12:46; Rev 21:8

i. ἐν Lake, Ehrman] παρά Lightfoot, Holmes. The difference is from "in God" to "in the presence of God," according to Lightfoot.

together[a] with one another, compete together, run together, suffer together, die together, rise up together, as God's managers[b] and assistants and servants. [2] Please the one whom you serve as a soldier,[c] from whom you also receive wages. Let none of you be found a deserter. Keep your baptism as weaponry,[d] your faith as a helmet, your love as a spear, your endurance as a full set of armor.[e] ₍Let your works be your war-time deposits,₎[fg] so that you may receive your deserved savings.[h] Be patient, therefore, with one another, in gentleness, as God is with you. May I enjoy you ₍always₎.[i]

A COURIER TO ANTIOCH

[7.1] Since the church which is in Antioch of Syria is at peace, as has been revealed to me, through your prayer, I too have become more encouraged in ₍a God-given freedom from earthly cares₎[j] if through suffering I may reach God so that I am found to be your disciple in the resurrection.[k] [2] It is fitting,

---

a. Col 1:29; 1 Tim 4:10

b. Titus 1:7; 1 Cor 4:1; 1 Pet 4:10

c. 2 Tim 2:4

d. Lightfoot and Holmes translate ὅπλα as "shield"; Lightfoot with the added note that this is "as the context requires. ... This sense explains μενέτω; 'Hold out your baptismal vows, your baptismal privileges, as a shield before you.'" Yet BDAG does not note "shield" as a sense of ὅπλον, seeing it as more generic weaponry, both defensive and offensive. Regarding this specific instance, BDAG offers: "let baptism remain as your arms ('remain' in contrast to the deserter, who throws his weapons away)." It seems best to follow BDAG and treat this generally.

e. Lightfoot comments: "Here 'the complete body armor,' breast-plate, greaves, etc.: for nothing else remains. Patience protects the whole spiritual man, wherever the blow is aimed."

f. Literally "your war-time deposits as your works"

g. From BDAG: "Latin loanword 'deposita'; military technical term. When gifts of money were given the army on special occasions, the individual soldier received only half of what was due him; the rest was deposited to his credit in the regimental treasury, and he received it (as ἄκκεπτα, q.v.) if and when he was honorably discharged." Lightfoot further comments: "The deposits, however, as entered in the name of any soldier, would include other items besides, e.g., other portions of donatives voluntarily so deposited, prize money, etc."

h. From BDAG: "Technical term of military finance: a sum credited to a Roman soldier and paid upon his discharge." This is the disbursement of the δεπόσιτα (deposit of money) mentioned earlier. Lightfoot further comments that it was also possible that instead of the saved up amount, "an equivalent in land [could also be] given to him. ... Those who deserted or were dismissed for misconduct would forfeit all this accumulated property."

i. Literally "through all"

j. Literally "a freedom by God from cares"

k. ἀναστάσει Lake, Ehrman] αἰτήσει Lightfoot, Holmes. Lightfoot/Holmes would read "a disciple by means of your prayer," whereas Lake/Ehrman reads "your disciple in the resurrection." Lightfoot gives some credence to this option, but ultimately prefers the other because of a similar passage in Ign Smryn 11.

O Polycarp, most blessed by God, to convene a council, most pleasing to God, and to appoint someone whom you consider very beloved and untiring, who will be able to be called God's courier.[a] Consider this one worthy that, going to Syria, he may honor your untiring love to the glory of God. [3] A Christian does not have authority over himself, but he devotes himself to God. This is the work of God, and of yourselves, when you complete it. For by grace I trust that you are ready for a good work that concerns God. Knowing your intense desire for the truth, ₁I have urged you with only a few words₁.[b]

GREETINGS AND FAREWELL

[8.1] Since I could not write to all the churches because of my sudden sailing from Troas to Neapolis, as the divine will commands, you are to write ₁the churches ahead of me₁[cd] as one possessing the mind of God, that they also may do likewise. Some can send messengers, others letters through those being sent by you, so that you may be glorified by an eternal work, as you are worthy. [2] I greet everyone by name, including ₁the wife₁[e] of Epitropus,[f] with her whole house and her children. I greet Attalus, my dear friend. I greet him who is about to be considered worthy to go to Syria. Grace will be with him ₁always₁,[g] and with Polycarp who is sending him. [3] I bid you farewell ₁always₁[h] in our God Jesus Christ; may you remain in him in the unity and care of God. I greet Alce, a name very dear to me. Farewell in the Lord.

---

a. From Lightfoot: "The word is used here in reference to the special mission, which he was promptly to execute."

b. Literally "I have urged you during a few words"

c. Literally "the churches before"

d. Lightfoot notes that these are churches "nearer to Syria than Smyrna itself. The writer naturally imagines himself looking toward Antioch, whither the delegates are to be sent. Ignatius had been unable himself to write any of these, except Philadelphia, since they lay at too great a distance from Troas." Holmes translates "on this side" and further notes, "i.e., Antioch in Syria. Ignatius has in mind the churches between Smyrna and Antioch: Ephesus, Magnesia, and Tralles. He himself had been able to communicate with Philadelphia about sending a delegation to Antioch."

e. Literally "she"

f. Lake translates "the Procurator"; Lightfoot notes that the name Ἐπίτροπος is rare and Lake's alternative is a possibility. Lightfoot also mentions the possibility that "the wife of Epitropus" is a widow, as the following words seem to indicate.

g. Literally "through all"

h. Literally "through all"

— *Polycarp to the Philippians*

SALUTATION[a]

Polycarp and the presbyters with him, to the church of God, the one temporarily residing in[b] Philippi. Mercy to you and peace from God the all-powerful and Jesus Christ our Savior be multiplied.

THANKSGIVING

1.1 I rejoice with[c] you greatly in our Lord Jesus Christ, having welcomed the replicas of true love and having sent on their way,[d] as was incumbent upon you, those confined by chains fitting for saints which are the crowns of those truly chosen by God and our Lord [2] and because of the secure root of your faith, being proclaimed from ancient[e] times, ₁still continues,[f] and bears fruit[g] to our Lord Jesus Christ, who endured because of our sins, to reach even death, whom God raised up having loosed the birth pains of Hades.[h] 3 In whom,[i] not having seen, you believe with joy inexpressible and glorious, which many[j] long to experience, knowing that by grace[k] you have been saved, not by works, but the will of God through Jesus Christ.

---

a. The full title of the letter is "Letter of Saint Polycarp, Bishop of Smyrna and Holy Martyr, to the Philippians."

b. The idea is that "Christians are alien in this world" (Lightfoot).

c. Phil 4:10; 2:17

d. Acts 15:3

e. Acts 15:7; 21:16; Phil 4:15; Rom 1:8

f. Literally "until now continues"

g. Col 1:6

h. Acts 2:24; also 2 Sam 22:6; Ps 18:5; 116:3

i. 1 Pet 1:8

j. 1 Pet 1:12; cf. Matt 13:17; Luke 10:24

k. Eph 2:5, 8, 9

PREPARE YOURSELVES

2.1 Therefore ₁prepare yourselves,₁[ab] Serve God in reverence and truth,[c] leaving behind empty, fruitless talk[d] and the deception of the crowd, believing[e] in the one who raised our Lord Jesus Christ from the dead and gave him glory[f] and a throne at his right hand, to whom all things in heaven and earth are subject,[g] whom every breathing thing[h] worships, who is coming as judge of the living and dead,[i] whose blood God will require[j] from those who disobey him. 2 But the one who raised[k] him from the dead also will raise us if we do his will and follow in his commandments and love the things he loved, refraining from all unrighteousness, greediness, love of money, evil speech, and false witness, not paying back evil for evil or abuse for abuse[l] or blow for blow or curse for curse, 3 but remembering[m] what the Lord said when he taught: Do not judge so that you may not be judged;[n] forgive and then you will be forgiven;[o] show mercy so that you will be shown mercy;[p] with what measure you measure out it will be measured again to you;[q] and blessed are the poor and those being persecuted for the sake of righteousness; for theirs is the kingdom of God.[r]

---

a. Literally "gird up your loins"

b. 1 Pet 1:13; cf. Eph 6:14; Isa 11:5

c. 1 Pet 1:13 (cf. Ps 2:11)

d. 1 Tim 1:6; Titus 1:10; cf. 1 *Cl* 9.1

e. 1 Pet 1:21; Eph 1:20

f. 1 Pet 1:21

g. 1 Cor 15:28; Phil 3:21; 2:10

h. 1 Kgs 15:29; Ps 150:6; Isa 57:16

i. Acts 10:42

j. Gen 42:22; 2 Sam 4:11; Ezek 3:18, 20; 33:6, 9; Luke 11:50, 51

k. 2 Cor 4:14; cf. 1 Cor 6:14; Rom 8:11

l. 1 Pet 3:9

m. Acts 20:35

n. Matt 7:1; Luke 6:37

o. 1 *Cl* 13.2

p. 1 *Cl* 13.2

q. Matt 7:2; Luke 6:38

r. Matt 5:10 (cf. Matt 5:3; Luke 6:20)

REMEMBER PAUL'S WORDS

3.1 Brothers, I write these things to you concerning righteousness ₁not on my own initiative,[a] but because you requested this of me. **2** For neither I nor another like me is able to follow after[b] the wisdom[c] of the blessed and glorious Paul,[d] who, when he was with you in the presence of the people at that time, he taught the word of truth accurately and reliably, who also being absent he wrote letters to you regarding which, if you examine them ,you will be able to build yourselves up in the faith given to you **3** which is the mother of all of us;[e] hope follows after and the love which is for God and Christ and for the neighbor goes before. For if ₁anyone is in their company,₁[f] he has fulfilled[g] the commandment of righteousness, for he who has love is a long way from all sin.

FOLLOW IN THE COMMANDMENT
OF THE LORD

4.1 But the beginning of all difficulty is the love of money.[h] Knowing, therefore, that we have brought nothing into the world, and neither are we able to take out anything,[j] let us arm ourselves[k] with the weapons of righteousness and let us teach ourselves first to follow in the commandment of the Lord. **2** Then also teach your wives to walk in the faith given to them, and in love and in purity, feeling affection for their own husbands in all fidelity and loving all others equally in all chastity,[l] and to instruct their children with the instruction[m] of the fear of God. **3** The widows, being

---

a. Literally "not myself having permitted"

b. Luke 23:55; Acts 16:17

c. 2 Pet 3:15

d. "The blessed and glorious Paul"; similar language is used in Pol 11.3 and in 1 Cl 47.1; see also Ign Eph 12.2.

e. Gal 4:26

f. Literally "anyone may be within these"

g. Rom 8:8, 10; Gal 5:14

h. On this phrase, note the translation within BDAG's entry for χαλεπος: "everything that is acrimonious begins with love of money."

i. 1 Tim 6:10

j. 1 Tim 6:7

k. Eph 6:13; Rom 13:12; see also Rom 6:13

l. See BDAG on εγκρατεια for the sense of "chastity" used here.

m. Sir 1:27

sensible concerning the faith of the Lord, interceding[a] unceasingly for everyone, being far removed from all slander,[b] evil speech, false witness, love of money, and every kind of evil, knowing that they are an altar of God, and that each *sacrifice*[c] is examined for blemishes and nothing escapes his notice, neither reasonings nor thoughts nor any secrets of the heart.[d]

WALK IN A MANNER WORTHY

[5.1] Understanding, therefore, that God is not mocked,[e] we ought to walk in a manner worthy of his commandment and glory. [2] Likewise, deacons[f] must be blameless in the presence of his righteousness, as servants of God and Christ and not of people, not slanderers, not insincere, not lovers of money, *but* self-controlled[g] in all things, compassionate,[h] careful, walking according to the truth of the Lord, who became the servant of all.[i] If we please him in this present age, we will receive also that which is to come, just as he promised us, to raise us from the dead, and that if we conduct our lives in a manner worthy of him, we will also reign with him,[j] if indeed we have faith. [3] Likewise also, the younger men must be blameless in all things; above all being concerned about purity and holding themselves in check[k] from all evil. For it is good to abstain from sinful passions in the world because all sinful passion wages war against the spirit,[l] and neither the sexually immoral, nor the passive homosexual partner, nor the dominant homosexual partner will inherit the kingdom of God;[m] nor

---

a. 1 Tim 5:5

b. 1 Tim 3:11; Titus 2:3

c. Here "sacrifice" is implied based on the sacrifice/offering language of the present context.

d. 1 Cor 14:25

e. Gal 6:7

f. 1 Tim 3:1–13

g. Here "but" is supplied to make explicit the contrast from negative items to positive items.

h. Eph 4:32; 1 Pet 3:8

i. Matt 20:28; Mark 9:35

j. 2 Tim 2:12

k. Jas 1:26; 3:2

l. 1 Pet 2:11; cf. Gal 5:17

m. 1 Cor 6:9, 10

those who engage in perversity.[a] Therefore it is necessary to refrain from all these things, being subject to the presbyters and deacons as to God and Christ. The virgins[b] must conduct themselves with a blameless and pure conscience.

BE COMPASSIONATE AND MERCIFUL

6.1 And the presbyters also must be compassionate, merciful to all, turning back those who have gone astray,[c] caring for[d] all sick, neglecting neither widow nor orphan nor the poor, but always taking thought for the good before God and people,[e] refraining from all anger, partiality, unjust judgment, being far removed from all love of money, not quickly believing against anyone, not relentless[f] in judgment, understanding that we are all debtors in the matter of sin. **2** Therefore if we ask[g] the Lord to forgive us we are obligated to forgive also, for we are before the eyes of the Lord and God, and we must all stand before the judgment seat of Christ, and each must give an account of oneself.[h] **3** So, then, let us serve[i] him with fear and all reverence, just as he himself has commanded, as did the apostles who proclaimed the gospel to us and the prophets who publicly proclaimed[j] the coming of our Lord. Let us be enthusiasts[k] concerning the good, refraining from those who cause others to stumble and the false brothers and those bearing the name of the Lord in hypocrisy,[l] who mislead foolish people.

---

a. Job 27:6; 34:12; Prov 30:20; 2 Macc 14:23; Luke 23:41

b. The widest sense of the word is that of "young women" or "maidens"; however, the context here indicates that "virgins" is more appropriate.

c. Ezek 34:3, 4; 1 Pet 2:25; Sir 18:13

d. Ezek 34:11; also Zech 10:3

e. 2 Cor 8:21; also Rom 13:17; 1 Tim 5:8

f. Wis 6:6

g. Matt 5:12, 14, 15; also Matt 18:35

h. Rom 14:10, 12 and 2 Cor 5:10

i. Ps 2:11

j. Acts 7:52

k. 1 Pet 3:13; Titus 2:14

l. 1 Tim 4:2

CONFESS CHRIST

7.1 For everyone who does not confess that Jesus Christ has come in the flesh is an antichrist,[a] and whoever does not confess the testimony of the cross is from the devil,[b] and whoever twists the sayings of the Lord for one's own sinful passions, and says that there is neither resurrection[c] nor judgment, this one is the firstborn of Satan. 2 Therefore, leaving behind the idle speculation[d] of the crowd and their false teachings, let us turn back to the word which was delivered to us from the beginning,[e] being self-controlled with regard to prayer[f] and being persistent in fasts, making petitions of the all-seeing God to lead us not into temptation,[g] just as the Lord said, "The spirit is indeed willing, but the flesh is weak."[h]

BE IMITATORS OF CHRIST

8.1 Therefore we should persevere unceasingly in our hope and down payment[i] of our righteousness, which is Christ Jesus, who bore our sins in his own body on the tree,[j] who committed no sin, and no deceit was found in his mouth,[k] but because of us, in order that we might live in him, endured all things. 2 Therefore let us be imitators of his endurance, and if we should suffer[l] because of his name, we should glorify him. For this is the example he set for us in himself, and this we have believed.

---

a. 1 John 4:2–3

b. 1 John 3:8; also John 8:44

c. 2 Tim 2:18

d. On "idle speculation," see the BDAG entry for ματιστης.

e. Jude 3

f. 1 Pet 4:7

g. Matt 6:13; Luke 9:4

h. Mark 14:38; Matt 26:41

i. 2 Cor 1:22; 5:5; Eph 1:14

j. While the lexical value "cross" best fits the context due to the NT allusion, the translation "tree" best fits the specific context, again due to the implicit allusion to 1 Pet 2:24.

k. 1 Pet 2:22, 24

l. 1 Pet 4:16

YOU DO NOT RUN IN VAIN

[9.1] Therefore I urge all of you to obey the word of righteousness[a] and ₍to practice endurance to the limit₎[b] which also you saw with your own eyes not only in the blessed Ignatius and Zosimus and Rufus,[c] but also in others ₍from your number₎[d] and in Paul himself, and the other apostles. [2] Having confidence that ₍none of them ran in vain₎,[ef] but in faith and righteousness, and that they are with the Lord in the place which they are due, with whom they also suffered.[g] For they did not love the present age,[h] but the one who died on our behalf and on account of us was raised up by God.

BE SUBJECT TO ONE ANOTHER

[10.1] Stand fast therefore in these things and follow the example of the Lord, firm and unchangeable in faith,[i] loving the brotherhood,[j] cherishing one another, joined together in the truth, giving way to one another in the gentleness of the Lord, despising no one. [2] When you can do good do not defer it, for charity sets free from death. All of you be subject one to the other,[k] having your conversation blameless among the Gentiles, that you may receive praise for your good works[l] and the Lord may not be blasphemed in you. [3] But woe to him through whom the name of the Lord is blasphemed. Therefore teach self-control to all and show it forth in your own lives.

KEEP FROM THE LOVE OF MONEY

[11.1] I am deeply sorry for Valens, who was once a presbyter among you, that he so little understands the place which was given to him. I advise,

---

a. Heb 5:13

b. Literally "to practice all endurance"

c. This Rufus is likely not either Rufus mentioned in the New Testament (Mark 15:21; Rom 16:13).

d. Literally "who from you"

e. Literally "these not all ran in vain"

f. Phil 2:16

g. Rom 8:17

h. 2 Tim 4:10

i. 1 Cor 15:58

j. 1 Pet 2:17

k. Eph 5:21

l. 1 Pet 2:12

therefore, that you keep from love of money[a], and be pure and truthful. Keep yourselves from all evil. [2] For how may he who cannot attain self-control in these matters preach it to another?[b] If any man does not abstain from love of money, he will be polluted by idolatry, and shall be judged as if he were among the Gentiles who know not the judgment of God.[c] Or do we "not know that the saints shall judge the world"[d] as Paul teaches? [3] But I have neither perceived nor heard any such thing among you, among whom the blessed Paul labored, who are praised in the beginning of his epistle. For concerning you he boasts in all the churches[e] who then alone had known the Lord, for we had not yet known him. [4] Therefore, brothers, I am deeply sorry for him[f] and for his wife; may the Lord grant them true repentance. Therefore you yourselves should also be moderate in this matter, and do not regard such people as enemies,[g] but call them back as fallible and straying members, that you may make whole the body of you all. For in doing this you edify yourselves.

LET YOUR ANGER BE REMOVED, AND PRAY

[12.1] For I am confident that you are well versed in the Scriptures, and nothing is hid from you; but to me this is not granted. Only, as it is said in these Scriptures, "be angry but do not sin,"[h] and "do not let the sun go down on your anger."[i] Blessed is the one who remembers this, and I believe that it is so with you. [2] Now may God the Father of our Lord Jesus Christ, and the eternal Priest himself, Jesus Christ, the Son of God, build you up in faith and truth, and in all gentleness, and without wrath, and in patience, and in longsuffering, and endurance, and purity, and may he give you a share and place with his saints, and to us with you, and to all under heaven who shall believe in our Lord and God Jesus Christ and in his Father, who raised

---

a. 1 Tim 6:10
b. 1 Tim 3:5
c. Jer 5:4
d. 1 Cor 6:2
e. 2 Thess 1:4
f. The pronoun "him" refers to Valens, not to Paul.
g. 2 Thess 3:15
h. Eph 4:26, quoting Ps 4:5
i. Eph 4:26

him from the dead. [3] Pray for all the saints.[a] Pray also for the kings, and for magistrates, and princes, and for those who persecute you and hate you,[b] and for the enemies of the cross[c] that your fruit may be evident among all people,[d] that you may be perfected in him.

IGNATIUS' LETTERS

[13.1] Both you and Ignatius have written me that if anyone should depart into Syria, he should take along also the letters from you, which I will do if I have suitable opportunity, either myself or the one whom I send to represent us and also ₗto represent you₎.[e] [2] We have sent to you, just as you requested, the letters of Ignatius which were sent to us by him, and others, as many as we had ₗin our possession₎.[f] They are appended to this letter, from which you will be able to benefit greatly, for they contain faith and endurance and all edification which pertains to our Lord.

CLOSING AND COMMENDATIONS[g]

[14.1] I have written this to you by Crescens, whom I commended to you when I was present, and now commend again. For he has behaved blamelessly among us, and I believe that he will do the same with you. His sister shall be commended to you when she comes to you. Farewell in the Lord Jesus Christ in grace, with all who are yours. Amen.

---

a. 1 Tim 2:1
b. Matt 5:44
c. Phil 3:18
d. 1 Tim 4:15
e. Literally "on behalf of you"
f. Literally "with us"
g. Section 14 is extant only in Latin.

– The Didache
(The Teaching of the Twelve Apostles)

TITLE

The teaching of the Lord through the twelve apostles to the nations.

THE WAY OF LIFE

1.1 There are two ways, one of life and one of death, and there is a great difference between the two ways. 2 Therefore the way of life is this: first, to love the God who made you; second, your neighbor as yourself;[a] [and whatever[b] you would wish not to happen to you, then you do not do this to others.[c] 3 Now, the teaching of these words is this: bless those who curse you and pray for your enemies[d] and fast for those who persecute you. For what is the benefit if we love those who love us? Do not even the Gentiles do this?[e] But you, you love those who hate you and you will not have an enemy. 4 Refrain from fleshly and bodily desires. If someone gives you a blow on the right cheek, turn the other to him also and you will be perfect. If someone compels you to go one mile, go with him for two. If someone takes away your cloak, also give him your shirt. If someone takes away from you what is yours, do not demand for you are not able.[f] 5 To all who ask of you give and do not demand repayment.[g] For the Father desires to give gifts to everyone from his own gracious gifts. Blessed is the one who gives according to the command, for he is without guilt. Woe to the one

---

a. Mark 12:30–31; Lev 19:18
b. Literally "and all that"
c. Matt 7:12; Luke 6:31
d. Matt 5:44
e. Matt 5:46
f. Luke 6:30
g. Matt 5:26; Luke 6:30

who receives, for if anyone having need receives he is innocent. But the one
not having need will give an account: why has he received, and for what
purpose? Having been put into prison he will be interrogated concerning
what he did and he will not be set free from there until he has paid back
the last cent.[a] 6 Surely, concerning this also it has been said your charitable gift must sweat in your hands until you come to know to whom you
should give it.

THE COMMANDMENTS

2.1 And the second commandment of the teaching is this: 2 Do not murder,
do not commit adultery, do not sodomize, do not commit sexual immorality, do not steal, do not practice magic, do not use potions, ₍do not murder
a child by abortion₎,[b] do not kill the just-born one, do not yearn after the
things of your neighbor. 3 Do not commit perjury, do not bear false witness, do not speak evil of anyone, do not bear a grudge. 4 You will be neither double-minded nor double-tongued; for being double-tongued is a
snare of death. 5 Your speech should not be false or empty, but filled with[c]
action. 6 Do be not greedy, or vicious, or a hypocrite, or spiteful, or proud.
Do take up not an evil plan against your neighbor. 7 Do not hate any person,
but some you should correct, others you should pray for, and others you
should love even more than your own life.

FLEE FROM EVIL

3.1 My child, flee from every evil and from everything like it. 2 Do not be
inclined to anger, for anger leads to murder; neither zealous, nor quar-
relsome, nor easily stoked to anger, for from all of these murder is born. 3
My child, do not be lustful, for lust leads to sexual immorality; neither be
filthy-mouthed, nor have eyes prone to desire, for from all of these adultery is born. 4 My child, do not be a soothsayer, because it leads to idolatry;
neither an enchanter, nor an astrologer, nor a magician, nor desire to see
the same, for from all of these idolatry is born. 5 My child, do not be a liar,

---

a. Matt 5:26

b. Literally "do not murder a child by destroying"

c. The sense is almost that of "verified," but the contrast between "empty" (κενός) and
"filled with" brings out the same idea.

because lying leads to theft; neither a lover of money,[a] nor conceited, for from all of these theft is born. **6** My child, do not be a grumbler because it leads to blasphemy; neither be arrogant, nor evil-minded, for from all of these blasphemy is born. **7** But be gentle, because the gentle ones will inherit the earth.[b] **8** Be even-tempered and merciful and innocent and quiet and good, ₍always₎[cd] trembling at the words which you have heard. **9** Do not exalt yourself, neither grant arrogance to your soul. Do not let your soul be joined with the haughty, but be associated with the just and humble ones. **10** ₍Whatever₎[e] happens to you, accept it as good knowing that nothing takes place apart from God.

SEEK PEACE AND SERVE OTHERS

4.1 My child, the one who speaks the word of God to you, remember him night and day, and honor him as the Lord: for where the Lord's nature[f] is discussed, there the Lord is. **2** But seek out ₍each day₎[g] the presence of the saints, so that you may find comfort in their words. **3** Do not strive after division, but bring peace to the ones who fight. Judge justly; ₍do not show favoritism₎[h] when bringing sins to light. **4** Do not be of two minds,[i] whether it will occur[j] or not. **5** Do not first reach out your hands to receive, only to pull back from giving. **6** If you have something because of your hands, offer it as a ransom[k] for your sins. **7** Do not hesitate to give nor grumble while giving, for you will come to know who is the good paymaster of the reward.

---

a. I Tim 6:10

b. Matt 5:5

c. Literally "throughout all things"

d. Some editions (e.g., Ehrman, Bihlmeyer) omit δια παντος.

e. Literally "The activity that"

f. This sense of κυριότης does not occur in the NT. Cf. BDAG κυριότης 1 (page 579) which defines κυριότης as "the essential nature of the κυριος."

g. Literally "according to the day"

h. Literally "do not receive the presence"

i. This word does not occur in the New Testament. BDAG adds the qualifying statement that the word is used "of indecision about becoming a Christian or believing in specific Christian teachings or hopes, etc." (BDAG 253).

j. This whole verse is problematic because the referent is unclear. There are references to prayer in other parallels, though it may also refer to judging mentioned in Did 4.3 above. Indeed, Holmes translates it this way, "You shall not waver with regard to your decisions." Also see Neiderwimmer 106 for more discussion on this issue.

k. Mark 10:45; 1 Tim 2:6

[8] Do not reject the needy ones, but share everything with your brother and do not say it is your own, for if you are a sharer in the immortal, how much more in the mortal? [9] Do not withhold[a] your hand from your son or from your daughter, but from their youth teach them the fear of God. [10] Do not command your male slave[b] or female slave who are hoping in the same God in your bitterness, lest ₗthey cease to fear₎[c] the God over you both, for he does not come to call ₗwith partiality₎[d] but to whom the spirit prepares. [11] And slaves, you shall be subject to your master as to a copy of God, in modesty and fear. [12] Hate all hypocrisy and everything that is not pleasing to the Lord. [13] Do not ever forsake the commandments of the Lord, but guard what you have received, neither adding to nor taking away from. [14] In church you shall confess your sin and you shall not enter into your prayer with an evil conscience. This is the way of life.

THE WAY OF DEATH

[5.1] But the way of death is this: First of all, it is filled with evil and cursing, murders, adulteries, expressions of lust, acts of sexual immorality, thefts, idolatries, acts of magic, use of potions, robberies, false witnessing, acts of hypocrisy, acts of duplicity, deceit, pride, malice, stubbornness, greediness, abusive language, jealousy, arrogance, haughtiness, boastfulness. [2] Persecutors of the good, hating the truth, loving the lie, not knowing the reward of righteousness, not joining the good or the righteous judgment, not caring for the good but for the evil, from whom gentleness and patience are far removed, loving what is worthless, pursuing reward, not having mercy on the poor, not toiling for the downtrodden, not knowing the one who made them, murderers of children, corrupters of the creatures of God, rejectors of the needy ones, oppressors of the afflicted, defenders of the rich, lawless judges of the poor, people steeped in sin. Be delivered, children, from all such as these.

---

a. On the phrase, "Do not withhold your hand from," Holmes notes this could also be interpreted as "Do not neglect your responsibility to."

b. Normally δουλος would not merit the translation "male slave," but as the context includes a comparison to female slave/servant (παιδικη), "male" is included in the translation of δουλος.

c. Literally "not not they will fear"

d. Literally "according to person"

DO WHAT YOU ARE ABLE

6.1 See to it that no one leads you astray from this way of the teaching, since he teaches[a] you apart from God. **2** For if you are able to bear the whole yoke of the Lord, you will be perfect. But if you are not able, whatever you are able, this you must do. **3** And concerning food, you bear what you are able, but regarding food sacrificed to idols be scrupulously on your guard,[b] for it is worship of dead gods.

BAPTISM

7.1 And concerning baptism, baptize in this way: having reviewed all of these things, baptize in the name of the Father, and of the Son, and of the Holy Spirit,[c] in running water. **2** But if you do not have access to running water, baptize in other water. And if you are not able to baptize with cold water, then baptize with warm water. **3** But if you possess neither, pour water on the head three times, in the name of the Father, and of the Son, and of the Holy Spirit. **4** And before the baptism the baptizer should fast beforehand, and the one being baptized and any others who are able. Call upon the one being baptized to fast beforehand for one or two days.

FASTING AND PRAYING

8.1 Do not have your fasts with the hypocrites. For they fast on Mondays and Thursdays;[d] but you should fast on Wednesdays and Fridays.[e] **2** Neither are you to pray as the hypocrites, but as the Lord commanded in his gospel, "Pray in this way: Our Father who is in heaven, may your name be holy, may your kingdom come, may your will be done as in heaven, so also upon earth; give to us today our daily bread, and forgive us our debt as also we forgive our debtors, and do not lead us into temptation but deliver us from the evil one, because yours is the power and the glory forever."[fg] **3** Pray in this way three times each day.

---

a. This could also be translated more interpretatively as "such a one teaches."
b. Literally "you be very much concerned"
c. Matt 28:19
d. Literally "on the second [day] of the week and on the fifth [day]"
e. Literally "on the fourth [day] and on the day of preparation"
f. Literally "into the ages"
g. Matt 6:9–13

THE LORD'S SUPPER

9.1 Now, concerning the Eucharist, practice it as follows. **2** First, concerning the cup: We give thanks to you, our Father, for the holy vine of David your son, which you made known to us through Jesus your son, glory to you ₁forever₁.ᵃ **3** Next, concerning the broken bread: We give thanks to you, our Father, for the life and knowledge which you made known to us through Jesus your son, glory to you ₁forever₁.ᵇ **4** Just as this broken bread was being scattered over the mountains and being brought together it became one; likewise bring together your church from the ends of the earth into your kingdom, so that yours is the glory and the power through Jesus Christ ₁forever₁.ᶜ **5** But none shall eat or shall drink from your Eucharist but those baptized in the name of the Lord; for also concerning this the Lord has said, "Do give not what is holy to the dogs."ᵈ

THANKSGIVING

10.1 And after you have been satisfied with food, give thanks as follows: **2** We give thanks to you, O Holy Father, for your holy name which you caused to dwellᵉ in our hearts and for the knowledge and faith and immortality which you made known to us through Jesus your child; to you be the glory ₁forever₁.ᶠ **3** You, All-Powerfulᵍ Master, you have created all things for the sake of your name. Both food and drink you have given to the people for enjoyment, so that they might give thanks to you. But to us you have graciously given spiritual food and drink and life eternal through your son. **4** Above all, we give thanks to you because you are powerful. To you be the glory ₁forever₁.ʰ **5** Remember, Lord, your church, to deliver her from all evil and to perfect her in your love and gather her from the four windsⁱ (she

---

a. Literally "into the ages"

b. Literally "into the ages"

c. Literally "into the ages"

d. Matt 7:6

e. This same word is translated "make a nest" in Matt 13:32, of birds making nests (or perhaps finding shelter) in the branches of the bush grown from a mustard seed.

f. Literally "into the ages"

g. The vocative is used here as it is used in verse 2 above. The reference is obviously to God, which is why the words are capitalized.

h. Literally "into the ages"

i. Matt 24:31

that has been sanctified) into your kingdom, which you prepared for her, for yours is the power and the glory ⌊forever⌋.[a] **6** Come, grace, and let this world pass away. Hosanna to the God of David! If anyone is holy let him come. If anyone is not he must repent. ⌊Maranatha⌋![bc] Amen. **7** But allow the prophets to give thanks as much as[d] they desire.

TRUE AND FALSE PROPHETS

11.1 Therefore whoever comes and teaches you all these things which were mentioned before, welcome him. **2** But if the one teaching is himself turning away so that he may teach a different doctrine leading to destruction, do not listen to him. But if his teaching is for the increase of righteousness and knowledge of the Lord, welcome him as the Lord. **3** Now, concerning the apostles and prophets, act in this way, according to the ordinance of the gospel: **4** Every apostle coming to you, let him be welcomed as the Lord. **5** He will not stay ⌊more than⌋[e] one day and, if it is necessary, another. But if he stays three days he is a false prophet. **6** When going out, the apostle is to receive nothing ⌊except⌋[f] bread until his lodging is located. And if he asks for money, he is a false prophet. **7** And any prophet speaking in the Spirit, do not test or judge, for every sin shall be forgiven, but this sin shall not be forgiven. **8** But not everyone who speaks in the Spirit is a prophet, only if he has the manner of the Lord. Therefore, from his manner you shall distinguish between the false prophet and the prophet. **9** And any prophet who orders a meal in the Spirit will eat not from it, and if he does otherwise, he is a false prophet. **10** But any prophet teaching the truth, if he does not do what he teaches, he is a false prophet. **11** But any prophet having been proven genuine who is making the church into a worldly mystery, but not teaching them to do whatever he himself does, he shall not be judged by you. For with God he has his judgment, for even the ancient prophets acted in the same way. **12** But whoever should say in a spirit, "Give me money"

---

a. Literally "into the ages"
b. Literally "O Lord, come"
c. 1 Cor 16:22
d. This could also be translated "however" (Holmes) or "as often as" (Ehrman).
e. Literally "if not"
f. Literally "if not"

or something else, do not listen to him. But if, concerning others being in need, he should say to give, no one should judge him.

WELCOME EVERYONE

12.1 But everyone who comes in the name of the Lord,[a] let him be welcomed. And then, having tested him you will know him. ₁Then you will be able to distinguish whether he is true or false₁.[b] 2 If the one coming is a traveler help him as much as you are able. But he shall remain not among you ₁more than₁[c] two or three days, if he has need. 3 And if he desires to stay with you, being an artisan, let him work and let him earn his keep.[d] 4 And if he has no craft, take this into consideration according to your understanding how he shall live among you as a Christian[e] without being idle. 5 And if he does not want to act in this way, he is a Christmonger.[f] Beware of such as these.

HONOR TRUE PROPHETS AS HIGH PRIESTS

13.1 But every true prophet wishing to reside among you is worthy of his food. 2 Similarly a true teacher is himself also worthy, just as the worker, of his food.[g] 3 Therefore, collecting all the first fruits of the produce of the winepress and threshing floor, both of cattle and of sheep, you shall give the first fruits to the prophets, for they are your high priests. 4 And if you do not have a prophet, give your first fruits to the poor. 5 If you make bread,[h] collecting up your first fruits give them according to the commandment. 6 Likewise, upon opening a jar of wine or olive oil, collecting up your first fruits give them to the prophets. 7 And of money and of clothing and of

---

a. Ps 118:26; Matt 21:9

b. Literally "Then you will be able to have understanding of right and left"

c. Literally "if not"

d. The sense is less like the literal "to eat" and more along the lines of "to earn a living" or "to earn his keep." Louw and Nida class a similar idiom in 57.190, but the vocabulary is not the same here.

e. An alternate and less likely rendering of this last portion of the verse could be "how no idle Christian shall live among you" (cf. also Ehrman).

f. That is, one who trades on Christ. He uses the name of Christ primarily for his own personal temporal benefit.

g. Matt 10:10

h. This infrequent word is apparently only found in Christian writings (cf. BDAG). While the word is literally "dough" when it is the object of a verb like "make," it is better to translate as "bread."

every possession, collecting up your first fruits ⌊as seems proper to you⌋,[a] give them according to the commandment.

CONFESS AND FORGIVE

14.1 And coming together on the Lord's day, break bread and give thanks,[b] confessing beforehand your sins so that your sacrifice may be pure. 2 And everyone having a quarrel with his fellow member, do not let them gather with you until they have reconciled so that your sacrifice may not be defiled. 3 For this is what was said by the Lord: "In every place and time, offer me a pure sacrifice because I am a great king, says the Lord, and my name is great among the nations."[c]

APPOINT OVERSEERS AND DEACONS

15.1 Therefore, appoint for yourselves overseers and deacons worthy of the Lord, men who are gentle and not lovers of money and truthful and well-proven, for to you they themselves also minister the ministry of the prophets and teachers. 2 Therefore you must not disregard them, for they are your honorable ones, along with the prophets and teachers. 3 And correct one another not in anger but in peace, as you find in the gospel. And anyone committing a wrong against another, let no one speak to him neither let him hear from you until he repents. 4 But your prayers and your charitable giving and all of your actions, do as follows: as you find in the gospel of our Lord.

SIGNS OF THE LORD'S RETURN

16.1 Be on the alert for your life, do not let your lamps be extinguished and ⌊do not be unprepared⌋[d] but be ready, for you do not know the hour in which our Lord comes.[e] 2 And be assembled together frequently,[f] seeking what is fitting for your souls. For the full time of your faith will be of no benefit

---

a. Literally "whatever your opinion"

b. It is also possible to translate this as "hold the Eucharist," though with the specific mention of "break bread" associated, such a translation is less likely.

c. Mal 1:11, 14

d. Literally "do not let your loins be ungirded"

e. Luke 12:35

f. Heb 10:24–25

to you unless you are found perfect at the final moment. [3] For in the final days false prophets and corrupters shall be multiplied, and the sheep will be turned into wolves and love will be turned into hate. [4] For as lawlessness increases, they will hate and they will persecute and they will betray one another.[a] And then the deceiver of the world shall appear as a son of God and he will perform signs and wonders, and the earth will be handed over into his hands and he will do incessantly vile things which have never happened before ₍since time began₎.[b] [5] Then the creation of mankind shall come to the burning ordeal of testing. And many will be led astray and will be destroyed, but the ones enduring in their faith will be saved[c] by the accursed one[d] himself. [6] And then the signs of the truth shall appear: first, a sign of an opening in heaven; then, a sign of the sound of a trumpet; and the third sign, the resurrection of the dead. [7] Now, not all of the dead but as was said, the Lord shall come and all the holy ones with him.[e] [8] Then the world will see the Lord coming upon the clouds of heaven.[f]

---

a. Matt 24:10–12

b. Literally "from eternity"

c. Matt 24:10, 13

d. Here "the accursed one" is actually Christ, the one cursed by those led astray.

e. Zech 14:5

f. Some (e.g., Neiderwimmer 226) hold the original ending of the Didache is lost, positing reconstruction of the ending from related sources (the Apostolic Constitutions and the Georgian version).

— *Epistle of Barnabas*

GREETINGS AND INTRODUCTION

[1.1] Greetings, sons and daughters, in the name of the Lord who loved us, in peace. [2] Indeed, the righteous acts of God being so great and rich to you, I am exceedingly overjoyed beyond anything and with abundance because of your blessed and glorious spirit, so implanted is the grace of the spiritual[a] gift you have received. [3] Therefore I rejoice within myself even more, hoping for salvation, because truly I see in you the Spirit has been poured out upon you from the wealth of the Lord's well, so that I was astounded by your greatly desired appearance to me. [4] Therefore being persuaded of this and being inwardly conscious that having spoken many *things* among you I know that the Lord has traveled with me in the way of righteousness and I myself am also totally compelled by this, to love you beyond my own soul, because great faith and love dwell in you, in the hope of his life. [5] Therefore, having considered this, that if I care enough for you to share some portion of that which I have received, that it will be to me, having served such spirits as these for a reward. I hasten to send a small *letter* to you, so that with your faith you might have complete knowledge. [6] Therefore, there are three doctrines of the Lord:[b] the hope[c] of life *which is* the beginning and end of our faith; and righteousness *which is* the beginning and end of judgment; love of gladness and exultation, *which is* the testimony of the works of righteousness. [7] For the Master has made known to us through the prophets the things past and the things present and has given ₎a foretaste to us₎[d] of

---

a. 1 Cor 2:13

b. 1 Cor 13

c. It is possible to translate this in two ways: "Therefore, there are three doctrines of the Lord: the hope of life," (Lightfoot, Lake, and Holmes) and also as "Therefore, there are three doctrines of the Lord of life: hope" (Ehrman and Kraft).

d. Literally "the first fruits to us to a taste"

the things about to be; which, seeing *them* come to pass one after another, just as he said, we ought to make a richer and more sublime sacrifice in fear of him. [8] And I, not as a teacher but as one of you, will make known a few things by which you will rejoice in the present time.

THE NEW LAW

[2.1] Therefore, since the days are evil and the one who is at work[a] is himself in power, we ought, paying attention to ourselves, to seek out the regulations of the Lord. [2] Therefore our helpers of faith are fear and endurance, and our allies[b] patience and self-control. [3] Therefore, while these things remain in holiness to the Lord, wisdom, understanding, insight, and knowledge rejoice together with them. [4] For he has made known to us through all the prophets that he requires neither sacrifices nor whole burnt offerings nor general offerings, saying ⌊in one place,⌋[c] [5] "'What is your multitude of your sacrifices to me?' says the Lord. 'I am full of whole burnt offerings and I do not desire the fat of lambs and the blood of bulls and goats, not even if you come to appear before me. For who has sought out these things from your hands? Do not continue to trample my court. If you bring fine wheat flour, it is futile. Incense is an abomination to me. Your new moons and Sabbaths I cannot put up with.'"[d] [6] Therefore he abolished these things in order that the new law of our Lord Jesus Christ, which is without the yoke of necessity,[e] should have its offering not made by a human. [7] And again he says to them, "Did I command your forefathers, when coming out of the land of Egypt, to offer me whole burnt offerings and sacrifices? [8] ⌊On the contrary,⌋[f] I commanded this to them: 'Each of you, do not bear an evil grudge against your neighbor, in your own heart, and do not love a false oath.'"[g] [9] Therefore we ought to understand, not being foolish, the purpose of the goodness of our Father, when he speaks to us,

---

a. 2 Thess 2:7; Luke 4:6; 12:5; 22:53; Acts 26:18; John 14:30; Col 1:13; Eph 2:2

b. The word συμμαχέω is literally "to fight with/alongside"; the sense in early Christian literature is that of helping someone in a task or situation. Here the translation "allies" alludes to the underlying literal meaning.

c. Literally "when"

d. Isa 1:11–13 (LXX)

e. Acts 15:10

f. Literally "But rather"

g. Jer 7:22–23; Zech 7:9

wanting us, not being led astray like those, to seek how we should come near to him. [10] Therefore he says to us as follows: "A sacrifice to the Lord is a broken heart; a fragrant odor to the Lord is a heart that glorifies the one who made it."[a] Therefore, brothers, we ought to pay close attention to our salvation, lest the Evil One cause deception to slip in among us and might hurl us away from our life.

EVERYTHING REVEALED IN ADVANCE

[3.1] Therefore, concerning these things again he says to them, "'Why do you fast for me,' says the Lord, 'so that today your voice is heard with shouting? This is not the fast I have chosen,' says the Lord, 'not a person who humbles his soul, [2] and not ⸢if you would bend your neck in a circle⸣[b] and put on sackcloth and spread out ashes, not even then will you call an acceptable fast.'"[c] [3] But he says to us, "'Behold,[d] this is the fast which I have chosen,' says the Lord, 'loose every bond of unrighteousness, untie the knots of forced agreements, send away the downtrodden in forgiveness, and tear apart every unjust contract. Break your bread with those who hunger, and if you see a naked man, clothe him. Bring the homeless into your house, and if you see someone of low status, do not disregard him, neither your descendants from your household. [4] Then your light will break forth early and your clothing[e] will rise quickly and righteousness will go on in front of you and the glory of God will clothe you. [5] Then you will cry out and God will hear you; while you are still speaking he will say, "Behold, here I am" if you put away from you bonds and threatening gestures and the word of complaint, and you should give to those who hunger your food from your soul, and have mercy on those of humble soul.'"[f] [6] For this reason, then, brothers, the ever-patient one foresaw that the people whom he had prepared

---

a. Ps 51:17

b. Literally "if you would bend your neck like a ring"

c. Isa 58:4–5

d. Isa 58:6–10

e. ιματια Lake, Ehrman] ιαματα Lightfoot, Holmes, Kraft. The difference is between "garments" and "healing." The same variation occurs in the LXX, the source this quotation is drawn from.

f. Isa 58:6–10

in his beloved one will believe in all purity; ₁he revealed everything to us in advance₁,[a] that we not be shattered to pieces as proselytes[b] by their law.

BE ON THE ALERT

4.1 Therefore, it is necessary for us, doing careful investigation concerning the present, to seek out the things which are able to save us. Therefore, let us flee completely from all the works of lawlessness, so that the works of lawlessness do not overcome us, and let us hate the deception of the present time, so that we may be loved in what is to come. 2 Let us give no freedom to our own soul, so that it has the ability to join with sinners and evildoers,[c] lest we become like them. 3 The final stumbling block is at hand, about which it was written, as Enoch[d] says, "For this reason, because the Master has cut short the times and the days, so that his beloved might make haste[e] and come to his inheritance." 4 And the prophet also says as follows: "Ten kingdoms will reign upon the earth and there will rise up after them a little king who will subdue three of the kings under one."[f] 5 Similarly, about the same one, Daniel says, "And I saw the fourth beast, wicked and powerful and more fierce than all the beasts of the sea, and that out of it sprang ten horns, and out of them a little horn offshoot and that it subdued three of the great horns under one."[g] 6 Therefore you ought to understand. And additionally I also ask you this, as one who is from you, and who also loves all of you in a special way more than my own soul; take heed to yourselves now, and do not become like some, heaping up your sins, saying that the covenant is of those and of us. 7 Now, it is ours, but those

---

a. Literally "he revealed beforehand to us concerning everything"

b. BDAG comments: "The point seems to be that Barnabas endeavors to provide correct understanding of the Sinaitic law so that his readers do not encounter it as newcomers or neophytes."

c. The idea here is that if we give freedom to our soul, it will pursue sinful things; so we should give ourselves no freedom.

d. Kraft notes: "The 'Enoch' allusion probably refers back to the general theme of the 'final scandal' ['final stumbling block' in the above translation — RB]. The style and content of *Barn* 4.3 strongly suggest that it is editorial comment, not an Enoch Text. If Pseudo-Barnabas had a precise Enoch passage in mind, it is apparently no longer preserved in extant Enoch literature (the best candidates are 1 *Enoch* 89:61-64; 90:17; 2 *Enoch* 34:1-3, but they are not very satisfactory."

e. Judg 13:10

f. Dan 7:24

g. Dan 7:7-8

people lost it in the end in this way, when Moses had already received it.[a] For the Scripture says, "And Moses was on the mountain fasting forty days and forty nights, and he received the covenant from the Lord, tablets made of stone inscribed by the finger of the hand of the Lord."[b] 8 But by turning to idols they lost it. For thus says the Lord, "Moses, Moses, go down quickly, because your people whom you led out of the land of Egypt broke the law."[c] And Moses understood and threw down the two tablets from his hands, and their covenant was broken[d] so that the covenant of the beloved Jesus might be sealed in our hearts in hope of his faith. 9 And wanting to write much, not as a teacher but as is fitting for one who loves not to leave off from that which we have, I hasten to write as your most humble servant. Therefore, let us be on the alert in the last days, for the whole time of our faith will benefit us nothing unless now, in the lawless time and the coming stumbling blocks, we resist as is fitting for the sons of God, that the Black One may not have an opportunity to sneak in. 10 Let us flee from all futility. Let us completely detest the works of the wicked path. Do not live alone, retiring to yourselves as if already being justified, but coming together, ₍seek out₎[e] ₍together₎[f] the common good. 11 For the Scripture says, "Woe to those who are intelligent to themselves and ₍wise in their own eyes₎."[gh] Let us be spiritual. Let us be a perfect temple to God, with as much as is in us, let us cultivate the fear of God and let us strive to keep his commandments, that we may rejoice in his regulations. 12 The Lord will judge the world impartially; each one will receive just as he has done. If he is good, his righteousness will go before him; if he is evil, the wages of his wickedness will go before him. 13 Never let us fall asleep in our sins, resting as if called, lest the evil ruler, having gained power over us, eject us from the kingdom of the Lord. 14 And in addition, my brothers, consider this as well: when you see after such great signs and wonders were done

---

a. Several versions (Lightfoot, Holmes, Kraft) end verse 6 here.
b. Deut 9:9–16; Exod 3:4; 24:18; 31:18; 32:7, 19; 34:28
c. Exod 32:7; Deut 9:12
d. Exod 32:19; Deut 9:17
e. Literally "discuss concerning"
f. Literally "to the same"
g. Literally "clever in their own opinion"
h. Isa 5:21

in Israel, and then they were abandoned; let us be on the alert lest we be found as it was written, "many called, but few chosen."[a]

THE SUFFERING OF THE LORD

5.1 For the Lord endured for this reason: to deliver his flesh to destruction, that we might be purified by the forgiveness of sins, that is, by his sprinkled blood.[b] **2** For it was written concerning him, some of which to Israel, others to us. And it says as follows: "He was wounded for our transgressions, and was made to suffer for our sins; by his wounds we were healed. As a sheep he was brought to slaughter, and as a lamb silent before its shearer."[c] **3** Therefore we ought to give heartiest thanks to the Lord, that he has made known also to us the things which have come to pass, and he has made us wise in the things of the present, and in the things to come we are not without understanding. **4** And the Scripture says, "Not unjustly are nets spread out for the birds."[d] This means that a person will justly perish who, having knowledge of the way of righteousness, ensnares[e] himself in the way of darkness. **5** And also, in addition to this, my brothers, if the Lord endured to suffer for our souls, being Lord of all the world, to whom God says since the foundation of the world, "Let us make humankind according to our image and likeness,"[f] how, therefore, did he endure to suffer under the hand of humanity? **6** Learn![g] The prophets, having grace from him, prophesied of him. And he, that he might abolish death and demonstrate the resurrection from the dead, because it was necessary for him to be manifested in the flesh, he endured **7** in order that he might fulfill the promise to the fathers and he, preparing for himself the new people, might demonstrate when he was upon the earth, that he, having brought about

---

a. Matt 22:14

b. 1 Pet 1:2; Heb 12:24

c. Isa 53:5, 7; 2 Pet 2:24–25

d. Prov 1:17

e. While the verb ἀποσυνέχω has the basic sense of "to keep" or "to hold," here the translation "to ensnare" (cf. Kraft, Holmes, BDAG) is preferred because of the earlier quotation of Prov 1:17 and the reference to nets being spread out (to trap) birds. Kraft notes: "The aptness of the proverb cited [here] for a Two Ways context is apparent not only from its original Old Testament setting but from the use of 'birds' elsewhere in Pseudo-Barnabas' tradition (10:4; 10) to symbolize pestilent plunderers like those 'sinners' described in Prov 1:10–19."

f. Gen 1:26

g. Some editions and translations have this word in verse 5.

the resurrection, will judge. **8** ₗFurthermoreₗ,ᵃ while teaching Israel and doing such great wonders and signs, he preached and dearly loved them.ᵇ **9** But when he chose his own apostles (who were going to preach his gospel, who were wicked above all sin) in order that he might demonstrate that "he came not to call the righteous, but sinners,"ᶜ then he revealed himself to be the Son of God. **10** For if he had not come in the flesh, people would not have been saved in any way by looking at him. When the sun, which is about to ₗcease existingₗ,ᵈ which is a work of his hands, looking intently at it they are not able to look directly at its rays.ᵉ **11** Therefore the Son of God came in the flesh for this *reason*: that he might complete the total of the sins of those who persecuted his prophets to death. **12** Therefore for this reason he endured. For God says of the wound of his flesh, that it comes from them: "When they strike down their own shepherd, then the sheep of the flock will be destroyed."ᶠ **13** And he was willing to suffer in this way, for it was necessary that he should suffer upon a tree. For the one who prophesies says concerning him, "Spare my soul from the sword"ᵍ and "Pierce my flesh with nails, because assemblies of evildoers have risen up against me."ʰ **14** And again he says, "Behold, I have put my back to whips and my cheeks to blows, but I set my face as a solid rock."ⁱ

BEING FORMED ANEW

6.1 When, therefore, he made the commandment, what did he say? "Who is the one who condemns me? Let him oppose me. Or who is the one who vindicates himself before me? Let him come close to the servant of the Lord. **2** Woe to you, because you all will become old like clothing, and the moth

---

a. Literally "Indeed surely"

b. As the pronoun (singular in Greek) refers to Israel, it seems best to translate as a plural ("them") in English.

c. Matt 9:13; Mark 2:17; Luke 5:32

d. Literally "not be"

e. While a bit convoluted in a literal translation, the idea of the verse is that, like we are unable to look into the rays of the sun and understand it, and the sun is just a work of his hands, how can we expect to be saved by only looking at him? He had to come and be with us in order to save us.

f. Zech 13:7; Matt 26:31

g. Ps 22:20

h. Ps 119:120; 22:16

i. Isa 50:6–7

will consume you!"[a] And again the prophet says, since he was placed as a strong stone for crushing,[b] "Behold, I will put into the foundations of Zion a costly stone, chosen, a cornerstone, valuable."[c] **3** Then what does he say? "And he who will hope upon it will live ₍forever₎."[de] Therefore is our hope upon a stone? May it never be! But the Lord has established his flesh in strength, for he says, "And he established me as a solid rock."[f] **4** And again the prophet says, "The stone which the ones building rejected, this became ₍the cornerstone₎."[gh] And again he says, "This is the great and wonderful day which the Lord has made."[i] **5** I write to you very simply that you may understand; I, the most humble servant of your love. **6** Therefore, what does the prophet again say?" "An assembly of evildoers surrounded me, they encircled me[j] like bees around a honeycomb"[k] and "They cast lots for my clothing."[l] **7** Therefore, he was about to be made manifest and to suffer in the flesh, he revealed his suffering beforehand. For the prophet says concerning Israel, "Woe to their souls, because they have plotted an evil plan against themselves, saying, 'Let us bind the righteous one because ₍he irritates us₎.'"[mn] **8** What does the other prophet, Moses, say to them? "Behold, the Lord God says this: 'Enter into the good land which the Lord swore to Abraham and Isaac and Jacob, and inherit it, a land flowing with milk and honey.'"[o] **9** But learn what knowledge says: "Hope," it says, "upon the one who is about to be made manifest to you in the flesh, Jesus. For a person the

---

a. Isa 50:8–9

b. Of this word, BDAG notes: "literally 'rubbing away,' crushing, destruction, of Christ, who is put in place like a firm stone εἰς συντριβήν to destroy those who dash against (=take offense at) him."

c. Isa 28:16

d. Literally "for the age"

e. Isa 28:16

f. Isa 50:7

g. Literally "the head of the corner"

h. Ps 118:22

i. Ps 118:23

j. Ps 22:16

k. Ps 118:12

l. Ps 22:18

m. Literally "he is inconvenient to us"

n. Isa 3:9–10; Wis 2:12

o. Exod 33:1, 3; Deut 6:18

earth is suffering. For the creation of Adam was from the face of the earth."[a]
[10] Therefore, what does he mean by "into the good land, land flowing with milk and honey"? Blessed is our Lord, brothers, who placed wisdom and understanding of his secrets in us. For the prophet speaks a parable of the Lord: "Who will understand (except) [b] the one who is wise and learned and who loves his Lord?"[c] [11] Therefore, since renewing us by the forgiveness of sins, he made us another type, as having the soul of children, as if he were forming us anew. [12] For the scripture speaks about us when he says to the Son, "Let us make humankind according to our image and according to our likeness, and let them rule the beasts of the earth and the birds of the sky and the fishes of the sea."[d] And the Lord said, upon seeing our good creation, "Increase and multiply and fill the earth."[e] He said these things to the Son. [13] Again I will show you how he speaks to us. In the last days he made a second creation. And the Lord says, "Behold, I make the last things as the first."[f] Therefore, for this reason the prophet proclaimed, "Enter into a land flowing with milk and honey, and rule over it."[g] [14] See, then, we have been formed anew, just as he says again in another prophet, "Behold," says the Lord, "I will take out from them (that is, those whom the Spirit of the Lord foresaw) the hearts made of stone and put into them hearts of flesh."[h] Because he himself was about to be made manifest in the flesh and to dwell among us. [15] For a holy temple to the Lord, my brothers, is the dwelling place of our heart. [16] For the Lord says again: "And with what shall I be seen before the Lord my God and be glorified?"[i] He says, "I will confess to you in the congregation of my fellow believers, and I will sing praise to you in the midst of the congregation of saints."[j] Therefore we are they

---

a. On this quotation, Kraft explains there is "a Semitic play on the words 'Adam' and 'land' (adama). Also in the background of that strange verse is the contrast between the ancient 'Jesus' (for that is the Greek form of the Hebrew 'Joshua') who led the older people into the land, and the eschatological Jesus who fulfills the promise."

b. Literally "if not"

c. The source of this quotation is unknown.

d. Gen 1:26

e. Gen 1:28

f. The source of this quotation is unknown.

g. Exod 33:3

h. Ezek 11:19

i. Ps 42:2

j. Ps 22:22

whom he brought into the good land. [17] Therefore, what are the milk and honey? Because first the child is nourished with honey, then with milk. Therefore we also, being nourished by the faith of the promise and by the word, will live, exercising dominion over the earth. [18] And we have already said above, "And let them increase and multiply and rule over the fishes." Therefore who is the one who is able now to rule over beasts or fishes or birds of the sky? For we ought to understand that to rule implies authority, so that the one who commands rules. [19] Therefore if this does not occur at present, then he has told us when it will occur: when we ourselves have also been made perfect to become heirs of the covenant of the Lord.

EVERYTHING REVEALED BEFOREHAND

[7.1] Understand therefore, children of gladness, that the good Lord revealed everything beforehand to us, so that we might know whom, giving thanks for everything, we ought to praise. [2] Therefore if the Son of God, being Lord and being destined to judge the living and the dead, suffered so that his wounds might make us live, let us believe that the Son of God could not suffer except for our sakes.[a] [3] But even when he was crucified, he was given vinegar and gall to drink. Listen how the priests of the temple made this known: The commandment was written, "Whoever does not fast the fast, he will be utterly destroyed by death."[b] The Lord commanded it because he was about to offer the vessel of his spirit as a sacrifice, he, on behalf of our sins, so that the type established by Isaac, who was offered upon the altar,[c] might be fulfilled. [4] Therefore, what does he say in the prophet? "And let them eat from the goat which is offered in the fast for all their sins"[d] (now pay attention carefully) "and let all the priests alone eat the entrails unwashed with vinegar." [5] Why?[e] "Since you are about to give to drink to me, being about to offer my flesh for the sins of my new people, gall with vinegar,[f] you alone shall eat while the people fast and mourn in sackcloth

---

a. Literally "on account of us"
b. Lev 23:29
c. Gen 22:9
d. Lev 16:9, 27
e. Literally "For what"
f. Ps 69:21

and ashes"[a] in order to show that he must suffer for them. [6] Pay attention to what was commanded: "Take two goats, good and similar, and offer them. And let the priest take the one for a whole burnt offering for sins."[b] [7] But what should they do with the other one? "The other one," he says, "is accursed."[c] Pay attention to how the type of Jesus is made known. [8] "And you all spit and poke at it and you tie scarlet wool around its head, and thus let it be expelled into the desert."[d] And when it happens thus, the one who bears the goat leads it into the desert and removes the wool and places it upon a bush, the kind called "rachel,"[e] of which also we are accustomed to eat the shoots in the country, so finding alone that of the "rachel" the fruit is sweet. [9] Therefore what does this represent? Pay attention! "The one is upon the altar, and the other is accursed." And that the accursed one is crowned, because they will see him then, on that day, having a scarlet robe to the feet,[f] around his body, and they will say, "Is this not he whom we once crucified, despising and piercing and spitting upon him? Truly this was then the one who said he was the Son of God!"[g] [10] For how is he like that goat? For this reason: "The goats are similar, beautiful and equal," so that when they see him, then upon coming, they will be greatly astounded by the likeness of the goat. See then the type of Jesus who was destined to suffer. [11] But why is it that the wool is put in the middle of the thorns? It is a type of Jesus placed in the church, because whoever desires to take away the scarlet wool, it is necessary for him to suffer many things because the thorns are terrible and can gain it only through affliction. Thus he says, "Those who desire to see me and to take hold of my kingdom must take hold of me through affliction and suffering."[h]

---

a. Lev 16:7, 9

b. Lev 16:7, 9

c. Lev 16:8

d. Lev 16:10

e. Kraft notes: "Apparently a thorny bush like the blackberry. The witnesses vary as to its exact name."

f. Rev 1:13

g. Matt 27:43; Mark 15:39

h. Acts 14:22

EXPLANATION OF THE TYPE

8.1 And what type do you think it is that he commanded Israel that people in whom sin is complete should offer a heifer and, having slaughtered it, burn it up and that then children should take away the ashes and put them in containers and tie the scarlet wool around a piece of wood (see again the type, the one of the cross and the scarlet wool) and the hyssop, and the children should sprinkle the people as follows, ₍one by one₎,[a] in order to purify them from their sins? **2** Understand how ₍plainly₎[b] he speaks to you: the calf is Jesus, the sinful men who offer it, those who brought him to the slaughter. Then they are no longer men; the glory of sinners is no more. **3** The children who sprinkle are those who proclaimed the good news to us of the forgiveness of sins and the purification of the heart, to whom he gave to proclaim the authority of the gospel (there were twelve as a testimony to the tribes because there were twelve tribes of Israel). **4** And why three children who sprinkle? As a testimony to Abraham, Isaac, and Jacob, because these men were great before God. **5** And why the wool upon the wood? Because the kingdom of Jesus is upon the wood, and because those who hope on him will live ₍forever₎.[c] **6** And why the wool and hyssop together? Because in his kingdom there will be evil and vile days, in which we will be saved, because even the one who feels pain in the flesh is healed through the foul juice of the hyssop. **7** And for this reason, things happening thus are evident to us but are obscure to them because they do not listen to the voice of the Lord.

CIRCUMCISION OF THE HEART

9.1 For he says again concerning the ears, how he circumcised our heart. The Lord says in the prophet, "₍When they heard₎,[d] they obeyed me."[e] And again he says, "Those who are far away will hear with the ear and will know what I have done,"[f] and "Circumcise, says the Lord, your heart."[g] **2** And again he

---

a. Literally "according to each"
b. Literally "in simplicity"
c. Literally "into the age"
d. Literally "Upon the hearing of the ear"
e. Ps 18:44; 2 Sam 22:45
f. Isa 33:13
g. Deut 10:16; Jer 4:4

says, "Hear, O Israel, for this is what the Lord your God says,"[a] and again the spirit of the Lord prophesies, "Who is the one who desires to live forever?[bc] With the ear let him hear the voice of my servant."[d] 3 And again he says, "Hear, O heaven, and give ear, O earth, because the Lord has spoken[e] these things as a testimony."[f] And again he says, "Hear the word of the Lord, rulers of this people."[g] And again he says, "Hear, O children, the voice of one crying out in the wilderness."[h] So then[i] he circumcised our ears so that upon hearing the word, we might believe, 4 but even the circumcision upon which they trust has been abolished. For he declared that circumcision is not of the flesh, but they disobeyed because an evil angel tricked them.[j] 5 He says to them, "The Lord your God says this" (here I find a commandment): "Do not sow among thorns; be circumcised to your Lord."[k] And what does he say? "Circumcise the hardness of your heart and do not stiffen your neck."[l] Take it again: "Behold, says the Lord, all the heathen have uncircumcised foreskins, but this people have an uncircumcised heart."[m] 6 But you will say, "And surely the people were circumcised as a seal,"[n] but so has[o] every Syrian and Arab and all the priests of the idols. Therefore, as a result, are those also from their covenant? But even the Egyptians practice circumcision![p] 7 Therefore, children of love, learn abundantly about everything, that Abraham, who first gave circumcision, circumcised in the spirit looking forward to Jesus, having received the doctrines of the three letters. 8 For it says, "And Abraham circumcised three hundred and

---

a. Jer 7:2-3; Ps 34:12-13
b. Literally "into the age"
c. Ps 34:12
d. Ps 50:10
e. Isa 1:2
f. Deut 4:26
g. Isa 1:10; 28:14
h. Isa 40:3
i. Some editions begin verse 4 here.
j. Literally "made them wise"
k. Jer 4:3-4
l. Deut 10:16
m. Jer 9:26
n. Gen 17:11
o. Literally "also"
p. Literally "are in circumcision"

eighteen men from his house."[a] Therefore what is the knowledge which was given to him? Learn that first he mentions the eighteen and after an interval he mentions the three hundred. The eighteen equals "I" (ten) and "H" (eight); you have Jesus.[b] And because the cross was destined to have grace in the "T" he says "and the three hundred."[c] Therefore he reveals Jesus in the two letters and the cross in the one. 9 He knows, the one who placed the implanted gift of his teaching in us. No one has learned a more genuine word from me, but I know that you are worthy.

INTERPRETATION OF FOOD LAWS

10.1 And that Moses said, "You will not eat pig or eagle or hawk or crow or any fish which does not have scales on itself,"[d] he included three doctrines in his understanding. 2 [Moreover,][e] he says to them in Deuteronomy, "And I will make a covenant of my regulations with this people."[f] Therefore, as a result the commandment of God is not [to refrain from eating,][g] but Moses spoke in the Spirit.[h] 3 Therefore, he mentioned the pig for this reason: you will not be joined, he says, with people such as these, who are like pigs. That is, when they live luxuriously, they forget the Lord, but when they have need, they acknowledge the Lord, as also the pig when it eats it does not know its owner, but when it is hungry it cries out, and after receiving food, it is silent again. 4 "And you shall not eat the eagle or the hawk or the kite or the crow."[i] He means you must not join with or [resemble][j] people such as these, who do not know how, by toil and sweat, to provide food for themselves, but they plunder what belongs to another in their lawlessness,

---

a. Gen 17:23; 14:14

b. The common abbreviation (*nomina sacra*) for "Jesus" ('Iησοῦς) is the first two letters, IH, thus Barnabas equates the numeric value of IH (10 + 8) to Jesus through the first two letters of his name.

c. The numeric value of the T is 300.

d. Lev 11:7–15; Deut 14:8–14

e. Literally "Indeed, surely concluding"

f. Deut 4:10, 13

g. Literally "not to eat"

h. Because Moses spoke in the Spirit, the application of the commandment is not literal (to not eat certain things) but spiritual. Barnabas will explain this next.

i. Lev 11:14; Deut 14:13

j. Literally "even seem like"

and they lie in wait,[a] as if conducting themselves in purity, and they look around to see whom they may plunder through their greediness, as also these birds alone do not provide food for themselves, but sitting idle, seek out how they may devour the flesh of another, having become a public nuisance in their wickedness. [5] And "You shall not eat," he says, "the sea eel or the octopus or the cuttlefish." He means you shall not become like such animals, joining with people such as these, who are ungodly to the end and who are condemned already to death, as also these cursed little fish swim alone in the deep water, not swimming as the rest, but they dwell in the mud beneath the deep water. [6] But also "You shall not eat the rabbit."[b] For what reason? You shall not become, he means, a child molester, or even seem like such as these, because the rabbit multiplies its anus each year, for as many years as it lives, so many holes it has.[c] [7] But "You shall not eat the hyena." He means do not become an adulterer or a corrupter, and do not even seem like such as these. For what reason? Because this animal changes its nature[d] each year, and it becomes ₍one year male₎,[e] ₍the next year female₎.[f] [8] But he also hated the weasel rightly. Do not become, he means, such as this, of the sort we hear committing transgression with the mouth[g] through impurity, and do not be joined with the unclean women, those who commit transgression with the mouth, for this animal conceives

---

a. Jdt 13:3

b. Lev 11:5; Deut 14:7

c. While the Greek is fairly plain, its meaning is not immediately evident to us, so long after this was written. Kraft provides the following background: "Despite the attempts of Aristotle and others to correct some of these stories, it was fairly common knowledge that the hare (1) adds a new anal opening each year to accommodate its excessive defecation; (2) is hermaphroditic; (3) simultaneously carries different sets of young in different stages of development in its womb ('superfetation') and thus can conceive when it already is pregnant; and (4) has many exits to its home." Kraft later continues, "In short, the special background to Barn 10.6–8 is popular Hellenistic natural history which has been transformed into moral lessons in association with Mosaic food prohibitions."

d. Kraft provides some background: "The foremost popular story that circulated concerning the hyena was that it had both male and female genital organs by which it reproduced (denied by Aristotle, the elder Pliny, Clement, etc.)—thus it became a symbol of adultery and homosexuality."

e. Literally "now male"

f. Literally "now female"

g. Kraft provides background: "The weasel was listed by many natural historians among the several creatures that conceive through the ears or mouth. Although the lesson which was sometimes drawn from this belief concerned minding one's tongue, [Barnabas] applies it to 'fellatores' and 'fellatrices' who induce sexual orgasm with the mouth."

with the mouth. ⁹ About food, Moses, having received three doctrines thus spoke ₗspirituallyₗ,ᵃ but they, because of the lust of the flesh, received them as about food. ¹⁰ And David received knowledge of the same three doctrines and says, "Blessed is the man who has not gone in the counsel of the ungodly," as also the fishes went in darkness into the deep waters, "and has not stood in the way of sinners," as those who seem to fear the Lord but sin like the pig, "and do not sit upon the seat of troublemakers,"ᵇ as the birds, sitting in wait for their plunder. ₗYou have received full enlightenmentₗᶜ about food. ¹¹ Again Moses says, "Eat from any animal which has a divided hoof and chews the cud."ᵈ What does he mean? That he who receives food knows the one who feeds him, and being relieved by him seems to rejoice. He spoke well with regard to the commandment. What then does he mean? Join with those who fear the Lord, with those who meditate in their heart upon what distinguishing word has been received, with those who speak of the regulations of the Lord and observe them, with those who know that meditation is a work of gladness and who ruminate on the word of the Lord. But why the one with a divided hoof? Because the righteous one both walks in this world and looks forward to the holy age. See how well Moses legislated! ¹² But how did those people understand or comprehend these things? But we, having rightly understood the commandments, we speak as the Lord wished. Because of this he circumcised our ears and hearts, that we might understand these things.

THE WATER AND THE CROSS

¹¹·¹ But let us inquire if the Lord took care to reveal beforehand about the water and about the cross. And about the water it has been written concerning Israel how they will not receive the baptism that brings forgiveness of sin, but they will build it for themselves. ² For the prophet says, "Be astonished, heaven, and let the earth shudder greatly at this, that these people have done two evil things: they have abandoned me, the spring of life, and have dug for themselves a pit of death."ᵉ ³ "Is my holy mountain

---

a. Literally "in the spirit"
b. Ps 1:1
c. Literally "You have complete information"
d. Lev 11:3; Deut 14:6
e. Jer 2:12–13

Sinai a desert rock? For you shall be as the fledglings of a bird fluttering
about when taken away from the nest."ᵃ 4 And again the prophet says, "I
will go in front of you and I will make mountains level, and I will shatter
brass gates, and I will break iron bars, and I will give to you treasures of
darkness, hidden and invisible, so that they will know that I am the Lord
God."ᵇ 5 And, "You shall dwell in a lofty cave of strong rock." And, "His
water is trustworthy, you shall see the King with glory, and your soul will
meditate on the fear of the Lord."ᶜ 6 And again, in another prophet, he
says: "And he who does these things shall be like the tree which is planted
at the ₎fork of the river₎,ᵈ which will give its fruit in its season, and will
not shed its leaf, and all things whatsoever he might do, will prosper. 7
Not so are the ungodly, not so; but rather they are like the dust which the
wind drives out from the face of the earth. Because of this, the ungodly
will not rise up in judgment, nor sinners in righteous counsel, because the
Lord knows the way of the righteous, and the way of the ungodly will perish."ᵉ 8 Notice how he explained the water and the cross ₎together₎.ᶠ For he
means this: blessed are they who, having hoped upon the cross, descended
into the water, because he speaks of the reward "in its season," then he
says, "I will repay." But now what does he say? "The leaf will not be shed."
He means this, that every word which will ever go out from you by your
mouth in faith and love will be for the conversion and hope of many. 9 And
again another prophet says, "And the land of Jacob was praised beyond any
land."ᵍ He means this: he is glorifying the vessel of his spirit. 10 Then what
does he say? "And a river was flowing on the right hand, and a beautiful
tree was growing out of it, and whoever eats from it will live ₎forever₎."ʰⁱ
11 He means this: that we indeed go down into the water being full of sin
and uncleanness, and we come up bearing fruit, the fear in the heart, and

a. Isa 16:1-2
b. Isa 45:2-3
c. Isa 33:16-18
d. Literally "partings of the water"
e. Ps 1:3-6
f. Literally "at the same"
g. Ezek 20:6, 15; Zeph 2:19
h. Literally "into the age"
i. Ezek 47:1-12

having hope on Jesus in the spirit. "And whoever eats of these things shall live ₁forever₁."[a] He means this: whoever, he says, hears these things being spoken and believes, he shall live ₁forever₁.[b]

MORE EXPLANATION OF THE CROSS

[12.1] Likewise again, about the cross he explains in another prophet, saying, "And when shall these things be accomplished? The Lord says, 'When the tree falls down and rises up, and when blood trickles from the tree.'"[c] Here again you have a reference about the cross and the one who would inevitably be crucified. [2] And he says again to Moses, when Israel was warred upon by foreigners, and in order that he might remind them, being warred upon, that because of their sins they were delivered to death; the Spirit says to the heart of Moses, that he should make a type of the cross and the one about to suffer, because he says unless they place their hope upon him, they will be warred upon ₁forever₁.[d] Therefore Moses put one shield upon another in the midst of the fight and being stood up higher than them all, he stretched out his hands and thus again Israel was victorious. Then whenever he lowered them, they began to perish.[e] [3] Why? So that they might know that they are not able to be saved unless they place their hope upon him. [4] And again, in another prophet he says, "The whole day I stretched out my hands to a disobedient people who oppose my righteous way."[f] [5] Again Moses makes a type of Jesus because it is necessary for him to suffer and he himself will give life, he whom they will suppose to have perished, by the sign when Israel was falling (for the Lord made every snake to bite them and they were dying because the transgression happened through the snake with Eve), in order that he might correct them so that because of their transgression they will be handed over to the affliction of death. [6] Finally, surely Moses himself commanded, "Neither a graven nor a carved image will be to you for your God."[g] He himself makes one in order to

a. Literally "into the age"
b. Literally "into the age"
c. The reference is unknown in the OT; Kraft notes Job 14:7 and Hab 2:11.
d. Literally "into the age"
e. Exod 17:8–15
f. Isa 65:2; Rom 10:21
g. Lev 26:1; Deut 27:15

show a type of Jesus. Therefore Moses makes a brass snake and puts it in a place of honor and calls the people by proclamation. 7 Therefore, coming [together][a] they pleaded with Moses, that he should offer up prayer about them, with regard to their healing. But Moses said to them, "Whenever," he said, "one of you is bitten, he may come to the snake, the one which is set upon the tree, and he may hope, believing that it, being dead, is able to give life, and immediately he will be saved." And thus they did.[b] You have again in these things the glory of Jesus, because all things are in him and for him.[c] 8 Again, what does Moses say to "Jesus" son of Nun when he gives him this name, being a prophet, that all the people should listen to him alone, because the Father was revealing everything about his Son Jesus. 9 Therefore Moses says to "Jesus" son of Nun, having given him this name, when he sends him as a spy of the land, "Take a book in your hands and write what the Lord says, because the Son of God will cut off the whole house of Amalek from its root in the last days."[d] 10 See again Jesus, not as son of man but as Son of God, and being made manifest in the flesh as a type. Since, therefore, they are about to say that the Christ is the son of David, David himself prophesies, fearing and understanding the error of the sinners, "The Lord says to my Lord, 'Sit at my right hand until I make your enemies a footstool for your feet.'"[e] 11 And again, Isaiah says thus, "The Lord said to the Messiah my Lord, of whom I held his right hand, nations [should obey][f] him, and I will shatter the strength of kings."[g] See how David calls him "Lord" and does not call him "Son"?

INHERITANCE

13.1 And let us consider if this people inherits or the former people, and if the covenant is for us or for them. 2 Hear, therefore, what the Scripture says about the people: "And Isaac prayed about Rebecca his wife, because she was barren, and she conceived. Then Rebecca went out to inquire from

---

a. Literally "to the same"
b. Num 21:6–9
c. Rom 11:36
d. Exod 17:14
e. Ps 110:1; Heb 1:13
f. Literally "should listen before"
g. Isa 45:1

the Lord, and the Lord said to her, 'Two nations are in your belly and two peoples are in your womb. And one people will dominate the other people, and the greater will serve the lesser.'"[a] 3 You ought to understand who is Isaac and who is Rebecca, and for whom it was shown that this people is greater than that people. 4 And in another prophecy Jacob says more plainly to Joseph his son, saying, "Behold, the Lord has not deprived me of your presence; bring me your sons so that I may bless them."[b] 5 And he brought Ephraim and Manasseh wishing that Manasseh should be blessed because he was older, for Joseph brought him to the right hand of his father Jacob. But Jacob saw in the Spirit a type ₁of the people to come₁.[c] And what does he say? "And Jacob made his hands ₁into a cross₁[d] and placed his right hand onto the head of Ephraim, the second and younger, and blessed him. And said Joseph to Jacob, 'Change your right hand onto the head of Manasseh, because he is my firstborn son.' And Jacob said to Joseph, 'I know, child, I know; but the greater will serve the lesser, and this one indeed shall be blessed.'"[e] 6 See upon whom he placed his right hand. This people is the first and heir of the covenant. 7 Therefore if in addition, he also remembered we received through Abraham the completion of our knowledge. Therefore what does he say to Abraham when, the only one believing, he was appointed for righteousness?[f] "Behold, I have made you, Abraham, the father of the nations who believe in God while being uncircumcised."[g]

WORTHINESS OF THE COVENANT

14.1 Yes. But let us consider if the covenant, which he swore to the forefathers to give to the people, if he has given it. He has given it. But they were not worthy to receive it because of their sins. 2 For the prophet says: "And Moses was fasting on Mount Sinai, to receive the covenant of the Lord for the people, forty days and forty nights. And Moses received from the Lord the two tablets, the ones inscribed by the finger of the hand of the Lord in

a. Gen 25:21–23
b. Gen 48:11, 9
c. Literally "of the next people"
d. Literally "crosswise"
e. Gen 48:14–15, 18–20
f. Gen 15:6
g. Gen 17:4–5; Rom 4:11

the spirit."[a] And having received them, Moses brought them down to give to the people. [3] And the Lord said to Moses, "Moses, Moses, go down quickly, because your people whom you led out of the land of Egypt have broken the law." And Moses understood that they cast for themselves again molten images, and he threw the tablets out of his hands and the tablets of the covenant of the Lord were broken into pieces.[b] [4] Moses indeed received it, but they were not worthy. But how did we receive it? Learn! Moses, being a servant, received it, but the Lord himself gave it to us, to the people of inheritance, by suffering for us. [5] And it was made known that both they might complete their sins and we might receive the covenant of the Lord Jesus through the one who inherited it, who was prepared for this reason, that by making known himself what had already been paid over to death, our heart, and had been given over to the lawlessness of deception, redeeming from the darkness, that he might make a covenant with us, a covenant in word. [6] For it is written how the Father commands him having redeemed us from the darkness to prepare for himself a holy people. [7] Therefore, the prophet says: "I, the Lord your God, have called you in righteousness and I will hold on to your hand and I will strengthen you and I have given you for a covenant of the people, for a light to the nations, to open the eyes of the blind and to lead out those who are shackled from their chains and those who sit in darkness from the prison house."[c] Therefore we know whence we have been redeemed. [8] Again, the prophet says, "Behold, I have made you for a light to the nations, that you may be for salvation as far as the end of the earth, thus says the Lord God who redeemed you."[9] And again the prophet says: "The Spirit of the Lord is upon me, who, because he has anointed me to proclaim the gospel of grace to the humble, he has sent me to heal ⌊the brokenhearted,⌋[d] to proclaim freedom to the captives and recovery of sight to the blind, to announce a year acceptable to the Lord and a day of recompense, to comfort all who mourn."[e]

---

a. Exod 24:18; 13:18
b. Exod 32:7-8, 19
c. Isa 42:6-7
d. Literally "those broken in heart"
e. Isa 61:1-2

ABOUT THE SABBATH

[15.1] Therefore, in addition it is also written about the Sabbath in the ten words[a] by which he spoke on Mount Sinai to Moses ⸢face to face⸣:[bc] "And sanctify the Sabbath of the Lord[d] with clean hands and with a pure heart."[e] [2] And in another place he says: "If my sons will keep the Sabbath,[f] then I will place my mercy upon them."[g] [3] He speaks of the Sabbath at the beginning of the creation: "And God made in six days the works of his hands and he finished on the seventh day and he rested on it and made it holy."[h] [4] Pay attention, children, to what is meant by "he finished in six days." It means this: that in six thousand years, the Lord will finish everything. For a day with him signifies a thousand years. And he himself testifies to me, saying, "Behold, the day of the Lord shall be as a thousand years."[i] So then, children, in six days (in six thousand years) the whole shall be completed. [5] "And he rested on the seventh day." This means upon coming his Son will abolish the time of the lawless one and will judge the ungodly and will change the sun and the moon and the stars. Then he will truly rest on the seventh day. [6] Finally, indeed, surely he says, "You will sanctify it with clean hands and with a pure heart." Therefore, if what God sanctifies that day now anyone can sanctify by being pure in heart, we have been completely deceived. [7] See that as a result, then, rightly resting, we will keep it holy when we ourselves are able, having been made righteous and having received the promise, when lawlessness exists no longer, but all things have been made new by the Lord, then we will be able to keep the Sabbath holy, ourselves having first been made holy. [8] Finally, indeed, surely he says to them: "Your new moons and sabbaths I cannot put up with."[j] Do you see what he means? The present sabbaths are not acceptable to me, but the one I have made in which, having given rest to all things, I will make the beginning of the

---

a. Here the "ten words" are a reference to the Ten Commandments.
b. Literally "according to the face"
c. Exod 33:11; Deut 5:4; 34:10
d. Exod 20:8; Deut 5:12; Jer 17:22
e. Ps 24:4; 51:10
f. Exod 31:16
g. Isa 56:1-8
h. Gen 2:2-3; Exod 20:11
i. Ps 90:4; 2 Pet 3:8
j. Isa 1:13

eighth day which is the beginning of another world. ⁹ Therefore, we also spend the eighth day in gladness, the day on which also Jesus rose up from the dead and, being made manifest, ascended into heaven."

ABOUT THE TEMPLE

¹⁶·¹ And in addition I will also speak to you about the temple, how the wretched ones having gone astray hoped on the building and not upon their God who made them, as if God were a house. ² For, almost like the heathen, they consecrated him in the temple, but learn how the Lord speaks, invalidating it: "Who has measured heaven with a span or the earth with a spread out hand? Have not I, says the Lord? The heaven is my throne, and the earth a footstool for my feet. What house will you build for me? or what place for my rest?"ᵃ You know that their hope is futile. ³ Finally, indeed, surely again he says, "Behold, those who destroyed this temple, they themselves will rebuild it."ᵇ ⁴ It is happening. For because of the war they waged, it was destroyed by the enemy; now even they, the servants of the enemies, will build it up again. ⁵ Again, when the city and the temple and the people of Israel were about to be delivered, it was made known, for the Scripture says: "And it will happen during the last days, and the Lord will deliver the sheep of his pasture, and the sheep-fold, and their tower to destruction." And it took place according to what the Lord said. ⁶ But let us inquire if the temple of God exists. It exists where he himself says he made and prepared it. For it is written: "And it will happen, ₁when the week is completed,₁ᶜ The temple of God shall be built in splendor upon the name of the Lord."ᵈ ⁷ Therefore I find that a temple exists. Therefore learn how it will be built upon the name of the Lord. Before we believed in God, the dwelling place of our heart was corruptible and weak, like a temple really built by hand, because it was indeed full of idol worship and it was a house of demons through doing what was against God. ⁸ "But it will be built upon the name of the Lord." And pay attention, in order that the temple of the Lord might be built in splendor. Learn how. Having received the

a. Isa 40:12; 66:1

b. Tob 14:4–6; Isa 49:17

c. Literally "the week having been completed"

d. Dan 9:24

forgiveness of sins, and having hoped upon the name, we have become new again, being created from the beginning. Therefore in our dwelling place God truly dwells in us. ⁹ How? His word of faith, the calling of his promise, the wisdom of the requirements, the commandments of the teaching, himself in us prophesying, himself in us dwelling, opening to us who had been enslaved to death the door of the temple (which is the mouth), giving repentance to us, he brings us into the incorruptible temple. ¹⁰ For he who desires to be saved looks not to man but to the one who dwells in him and who speaks to him, being amazed by never either having heard the one who speaks the words from his mouth, nor when he desired to hear them. This is a spiritual temple being built for the Lord.

WRITING WHAT IS FITTING

¹⁷·¹ ₍So far as₎ᵃ it can be possibly and simply made clear to you, my soul hopes with my deep desire not to leave out anything which is fitting for salvation. ² For if I write to you about things present or to come, you would never understand because they exist in parables. These things indeed are thus.

THE TWO WAYS

¹⁸·¹ And let us depart also to another knowledge and teaching.ᵇ There are two ways of teaching and authority, one of light and one of darkness, and there is a great difference between the two ways. For over the one are appointed light-bringing angels of God, but over the other angels of Satan. ² And the one is Lord from eternity and for the ages, but the other is the ruler of the present time of lawlessness.

THE WAY OF LIGHT

¹⁹·¹ Therefore, the way of light is this: if anyone desires to travel along the way to the appointed place, let him be diligent in his works. Therefore the knowledge which was given to us to walk in it is as follows:² You shall love the one who made you, fear the one who created you, and glorify the one

---

a. Literally "To as much as"

b. Here Barnabas proceeds to use portions of teaching that is known as "the two ways"; the Didache also uses this teaching as basis. There are several parallels between Barnabas and the Didache; see the studies/commentaries by Kraft (Barnabas and Didache) and Niederwimmer (Didache).

who redeemed you from death. You shall be sincere in heart and rich in spirit. You shall not be joined with those who walk in the way of death. You shall hate everyone who is not pleasing to God. You shall hate all hypocrisy. You shall never forsake the commandments of the Lord. ³ You shall not exalt yourself, but shall be humble in all things. You shall not take glory upon yourself. You shall not plot an evil plan against your neighbor. You shall not permit arrogance in your soul. ⁴ You shall not commit sexual immorality, you shall not commit adultery,ᵃ ₗyou shall not corrupt children,.ᵇ The word of God shall not go out from you with anyone impure. ₗYou shall not show favoritismₗᶜ when correcting someone concerning sin. You shall be gentle. You shall be quiet. You shall tremble at the words which you have heard. You shall not bear a grudge against your brother. ⁵ Do not be double minded, whether it will happen or not. Do not take the name of the Lord in vain.ᵈ You shall love your neighbor more than your own life. You shall not murder a child by ₗabortion,ₗᵉ and again, you shall not kill the just-born one. Do not withhold your hand from your son or from your daughter, but you shall teach them from youth the fear of God. ⁶ You shall not yearn after the things of your neighbor. You shall not be greedy, you shall not be joined by your soul with the haughty, but be associated with the humble and righteous. The activity that happens to you accept it as good, knowing that nothing takes place without God. ⁷ You will be neither double-minded nor glib of tongue. You will be subject to your master as a copy of God, in modesty and fear. Do not command your male slaveᶠ or female slave in bitterness, who are hoping in the same God, ₗlestₗᵍ ₗthey cease to fear,ʰ the God over you both, because he does not come to call ₗwith partiality,ⁱ but to whom the Spirit prepares. ⁸ You shall share in all things with your neighbor and you shall not say they are your own. For if you are sharers in the

---

a. Exod 20:14
b. Literally "Do not sodomize"
c. Literally "You shall not receive the presence"
d. Exod 20:7
e. Literally "destroying"
f. Normally δουλος would not merit the translation "male slave," but as the context includes a comparison to female slave/servant (παιδικη), "male" is included in the translation of δουλος.
g. Literally "not when"
h. Literally "they will not fear"
i. Literally "according to person"

incorruptible, how much more in the corruptible? You shall not be quick to speak, for the mouth is a snare of death. To the degree that you are able, you shall be pure for the sake of your soul. ⁹ Do not reach out your hand first to receive, only to pull back from giving. You shall love as ₗthe appleₗ[a] of your eye everyone who speaks the word of the Lord to you. ¹⁰ You shall remember the day of judgment night and day, and you shall seek out ₗevery dayₗ[b] the presence of the saints, either by laboring in word and going out to encourage and striving to save a soul by the word, or with your hands doing work as a ransom for your sins. ¹¹ You shall not hesitate to give nor grumble while giving, but you will come to know who is the good paymaster of the reward. You shall guard what you have received, neither adding to nor taking away from. ₗYou shall utterly detestₗ[c] the evil one. You shall judge justly. ¹² You shall not cause division, but make peace by bringing together those who fight. You shall make confession for your sins. You shall not come to prayer with an evil conscience. This is the way of light.

THE WAY OF DARKNESS

²⁰·¹ But the way of the Black One is crooked and filled with cursing, for it is the way of eternal death with punishment, in which are the things which destroy their soul: idolatry, arrogance, ₗarrogance in an influential positionₗ,[d] hypocrisy, acts of duplicity, adultery, murder, robbery, pride, transgression, deceit, malice, stubbornness, use of potions, magic, greediness, lack of fear of God; ² persecutors of the good, hating the truth, loving the lie, not knowing the reward of righteousness, not joining the good, not judging righteously, not being concerned about the widow and orphan, not caring in the fear of God but for what is evil, from whom ₗgentleness and endurance are inseparably removedₗ,[e] loving what is worthless, pursuing reward, not having mercy on the poor, not toiling for the downtrodden, prone to slander, not knowing the one who made them, murderers of children, corrupters of the creatures of God, rejectors of the needy ones,

---

a. Literally "the pupil"
b. Literally "according to each the day"
c. Literally "You shall completely hate"
d. Literally "haughtiness of power"
e. Literally "far and farther away [are] gentleness and endurance"

oppressors of the afflicted, defenders of the rich, lawless judges of the poor, people steeped in sin.

CONCLUSION AND BENEDICTION

21.1 Therefore it is good, having learned the regulations of the Lord, as many as have been written, to walk in them. For the one who does these things will be glorified in the kingdom of God. The one who chooses other things will be destroyed along with his works. Because of this there is a resurrection; because of this there is recompense. **2** I implore those who are in authority, if you will receive any of my well-intentioned counsel: You have among you those to whom you might do good. Do not fail in this. **3** The day is near in which all things will be destroyed with the Evil One. The Lord and his reward are near.[a] **4** Again and again I implore you: be good lawgivers to each other; remain trustworthy counselors to each other; remove all hypocrisy from yourselves. **5** And the God who rules over the whole world, may he give you wisdom, understanding, insight, knowledge of his commandments, and patience. **6** And be taught by God, seeking out what the Lord seeks from you. And you do it in order that you might be found faithful in the day of judgment. **7** But if there is any remembrance of good, remember me when thinking about these things, that even my desire and watchfulness might come to some good. I implore you, asking your kindness. **8** While the good vessel is still with you, do not fail in any of them but unremittingly seek out these things and fulfill every commandment, for these things are worthy. **9** Therefore I was eager all the more to write ₍from my ability₎[b] to make you glad. May you be saved, children of love and peace. The Lord of glory and all grace be with your spirit.

---

a. Isa 40:10; Rev 22:12
b. Literally "from that which I am able"

— *The Shepherd of Hermas*

THE VISIONS

VISION 1

1.1. Hermas and Rhoda

1.1 The one who brought me up sold me to a certain Rhoda in Rome. After many years, I became reacquainted with her and I began to love her as a sister. **2** After some time, I saw *her* bathing in the river Tiber, and I gave her my hand and helped her out of this river. Therefore, upon seeing her beauty, I considered in my heart, saying, "I would be fortunate if I had a wife such as this, even with her beauty and her character." I considered only this, and not even one other *thought*. **3** After some time, I was traveling around the countryside and glorifying the creatures of God because they are great and remarkable and mighty. Walking, I fell asleep and a spirit took hold of me and carried me away through a certain place with no paths, through which a person could not travel. And the place was steep and broken up by the waters. Therefore, crossing over that river, I came to the level ground and ⌊knelt down⌋[a] and began to pray to the Lord and to confess my sin. **4** And while I was praying, heaven opened and I saw that woman whom I had desired greeting me from heaven, saying, "Hermas, greetings!" **5** And looking at her, I said to her, "Lady, what are you doing here?" And she answered me, "I was taken up so that I might expose your sins against the Lord." **6** I said to her, "Now you are accusing me?" "No," she said, "but listen to the words which I am about to say to you. God, the one who dwells in the heavens and who created ⌊the things that exist out of

---

a. Literally "put down my knee"

nothing,[a] and who multiplied and increased *them* for the sake of his holy church, is angry with you because you sinned against me." 7 Answering, I said to her: "I sinned against you? In which place? Or when did I speak a shameful word to you? Did I not always regard you as a goddess? Did I not always respect you as a sister? Why do *you* falsely charge me, O woman, with these evil and impure things?" 8 Laughing at me she said, "The desire of wickedness came up in your heart. Or do you not think it is an evil deed for a righteous man if the evil desire comes up in his heart? Indeed, it is a sin, and a great one," she said. "For the righteous man has righteous plans. Therefore, while his plans are righteous, his glory is set straight in heaven, and the Lord is favorable in ₁whatever he does₁.[b] But those who plan evil things in their hearts, they bring upon themselves death and captivity, especially those who gain this world for themselves and who exult in their riches, and who do not hold fast to the good things which are to come. 9 Their souls will repent, whichever do not have hope but have given up themselves and their life as hopeless, but you, you pray to God and he will heal your sins and your whole house, and all of the saints."

1.2. Hermas' Gloom and the Elderly Lady

2.1 After she had spoken these words, the heavens were shut and I was completely shuddering and grieving. And ₁my inner self₁[c] began to speak: "If this sin is recorded against me, how can I be saved? Or how can I appease God regarding my completed sins? Or with which words can I question the Lord that he act with grace toward me? 2 While I was considering and evaluating these things in my heart, I saw in front of me a great white chair being made of snow-white wool, and there came a woman, an elderly woman, in shining clothing, holding on to a book in her hand, and she sat down alone and greeted me: "Hermas, greetings!" And I, grieving and weeping, said, "Lady, greetings." 3 And she said to me, "Why so gloomy, Hermas, who *is* ever-patient and not easily angered, who always laughs? Why so downcast in appearance and not cheerful?" And I said to her, "Because of a most excellent woman, who says that I sinned against her." 4 And she said, "By

---

a. Literally "out of the not existing the existing"
b. Literally "all his deeds"
c. Literally "I"

no means *let* this thing happen to the slave of God, but by all means it has entered into your heart, with regard to her. And it is a plan such as this which brings sin on the slaves of God. For *it is* an evil and shocking plan against a greatly revered and already approved spirit if someone desires an evil deed, and especially *if it is* Hermas the self-controlled, who abstains from every evil desire and is full of all simplicity and great innocence."

1.3. God's Anger and Healing

3.1 "But God is angry with you not on account of this, but in order that your family, which has sinned against the Lord and against you, their parents, you may turn back. But, being indulgent, you do not correct your family but permit it to be corrupted. Because of this, the Lord is angry with you, but he will heal you, all the past evils in your family. For because of those sins and iniquities, you have been corrupted by the things of daily life. 2 But the great compassion of the Lord has mercy on you and your family, and will strengthen you and will establish you in his glory, you only do not be idle but have courage and strengthen your family. For as the metalworker hammering his work achieves the task which he desires, so also the daily righteous word overcomes all wickedness. Therefore do not stop instructing your children, for I know that if they will repent with their whole heart, they will be inscribed in the book of life with the saints." 3 After she had ceased, she said these words to me: "Do you want to hear me read aloud?" and I said, "I want to, lady." She said to me, "Be a hearer and hear the glory of God." I heard great and wonderful *things* which I cannot remember, for all the words *were* frightening, which a person is not able to bear. So I remembered the last words, for they were advantageous to us and gentle: 4 "Behold, the God of the powers, whom I love,[a] by *his* mighty power and his great wisdom created the world, and by *his* glorious counsel surrounded his creation with beauty, and by *his* powerful word fixed the heaven and laid the foundation of the earth upon the waters, and by his own wisdom and foresight created his holy church, which he also blessed; behold, he changes the heavens and the mountains and the hills and the seas, and all things are becoming level ground for his elect, that he might

---

a. ὃν ἀγαπῶ Lake] ὁ ἀοράτῳ Holmes, Ehrman. The translation difference is "whom I love" (Lake) with "who is invisible" (Holmes, Ehrman).

give to them the promise which he promised with great glory and joy, if they keep the lawful ways of God, which they received with great faith."

1.4. *The First Vision Ends*

4.1 Therefore, when she finished her reading and rose from the chair, there came four young men, and they took up the chair and departed to the east. **2** And she called to me and touched my breast and said to me, "Did my reading please you?" And I said to her, "Lady, these last things are pleasing to me, but the first things *are* difficult and hard." And speaking she said to me, "These last things *are* for the righteous, but the first things *are* for the heathen and the apostates." **3** While she was speaking with me, two men appeared and took her by the arms, and departed where the chair *had gone*, to the east. And she departed cheerfully, and as she went away she said to me, "₁Be a man₁,ᵃ Hermas!"

VISION 2

2.1 *The Elderly Lady Returns*

5.1 While I was traveling around the countryside, about the same time ₁as last year₁,ᵇ walking I remembered the vision of last year, and again the spirit took me away and carried *me* to the same place ₁as last year₁.ᶜ **2** Therefore, having come to the place, ₁I knelt down₁ᵈ and began to pray to the Lord and to glorify his name because he considered me worthy and revealed to me my former sins. **3** And after I rose from prayer, I saw in front of me the elderly woman, whom I had also seen last year, walking and reading a little book. And she said to me, "Can you report these things to the elect of God?" I said to her, "Lady, I am not able to remember so much, but give me the small book, so that I may copy it." "Take it," she said, "and return it to me." **4** I took *it* and, going away to a certain place in the countryside, I copied all of it ₁letter by letter₁,ᵉ because I could not distinguish the syllables. Therefore, having finished *writing down* the letters of the small book,

---

a. Literally "Be courageous"
b. Literally "which [I] also [was] last year"
c. Literally "where [I] also [was] last year"
d. Literally "I put down my knee"
e. Literally "to the letter"

the small book was suddenly snatched out of my hand, but I did not see by whom.

2.2 The Little Book's Meaning Revealed

6.1 But after ₗfifteenₗ[a] days of my fasting and asking many questions to the Lord, the knowledge of the writing was revealed to me and these things were written: **2** "Your seed, Hermas, ₗhave declared God's irrelevanceₗ[b] and have blasphemed the Lord and have betrayed their parents in great wickedness, and they have been called betrayers of parents and having betrayed, they have not benefited but in addition they have added to their sins licentiousness and orgies of wickedness, and thus their trespasses have been completed. **3** But make these words known to all your children, and to your spouse who is about to become a sister, for even she does not hold back her tongue with which she does wrong, but hearing these words she will hold back and will obtain mercy. **4** After you have made these words known to them, which the Master commanded me to reveal to you, then all the sins which they had previously sinned will be forgiven them, and all the saints who have sinned up to this day, if they turn in repentance with their whole heart and take away double-mindedness from their heart. **5** For the Master has sworn by his own glory to his elect if, having appointed this day, sin is still there they shall not have salvation, for the repentance for the righteous has an end. The days of repentance have been completed for all the saints, but even the heathen have repentance until the last day. **6** Therefore you will speak to those who preside over the church, that they might set their ways straight in righteousness, that they receive in full the promises with great glory. **7** Remain, therefore, workers of righteousness, and be not double-minded, that your passing may be with the holy angels. Blessed *are* you, as many who endure the great tribulation which is coming, and as many who will not deny their life. **8** For the Lord has sworn by his Son that those who have denied their Christ have been dispossessed from their life, those who now are going to deny in the coming days. But those who previously denied, through his great compassion mercy has been given to them."

---

a. Literally "ten and five"
b. Literally "have declared God irrelevant"

2.3 The Application for Hermas

7.1 "But you, Hermas, no longer bear a grudge against your children and do not leave your sister alone,[a] that they might be cleansed from their former sins. For they will be disciplined with righteous discipline if you do not bear a grudge against them. The bearing of grudges brings about death, but you, Hermas, had great troubles of your own because of the transgressions of your family, because you did not pay attention to them but neglected *them* and you became entangled in their evil actions. **2** But it saves you, that you have not fallen away from the God of the living, and your simplicity and great self-control. These things have saved you, if you continue *to do them*, and they will save all those who do things such as these and who behave in innocence and simplicity. These will overcome all wickedness and will continue into life eternal. **3** Blessed *are* all those who practice righteousness; ₁they will never, ever be destroyed.₁[b] **4** But you will say to Maximus, 'Behold, tribulation is coming; if it seems good to you, deny again.' 'The Lord *is* near those who turn back *to him*,' as it is written in the *book of* Eldad and Modat,[c] who prophesied in the desert to the people."

2.4 Further Revelation for Hermas

8.1 And it was revealed to me, brothers, while sleeping, by a very handsome young man who said to me, "The elderly woman, from whom you received the small book, who do you think she was?" I said, "The Sibyl." "You are deceived," he said. "She is not." "Then who is she?" I said. "The church," he said. I said to him, "Then why *is* she old?" "Because," he said, "she was created first of all things. Because of this she *is* old, and on account of her the world was created." **2** And afterwards I saw a vision in my house. The elderly lady came and asked me if I had already given the book to the elders. I denied that *I* had given *it*. "You have done well," she said, "for I have words to add. Therefore, when I have finished all of the words, it shall be made

---

a. This is a reference to Hermas' wife.

b. Literally "not they will be destroyed until eternity"

c. The "Book of Eldad and Modat" is a reference to a pseudepigraphal book apparently based on Eldad and Modad, mentioned in Num 11:26-29. This citation/reference in Hermas is the only known reference to it, though the stichometry of Nicephorus indicates the original work is 400 lines.

known by you ₗto all the electₗ. ᵃ ³ Therefore you are to write two little books
and you will send one to Clement and one to Grapte. Then Clement will
send his to the outer cities, for that is his duty. And Grapte will instruct
the widows and the orphans. But you, *Hermas*, you will read *yours* in this
city with the elders who lead the church."

VISION 3

3.1 *The Elderly Lady Gives Another Vision*

⁹·¹ What I saw, brothers, was as follows: ² Having fasted many times and
having begged of the Lord that he reveal to me the revelation which he
had promised to show to me through the elderly lady, that very night the
elderly lady appeared to me and said to me, "Since you are so needy and
eager to know all things, come to the farm where you make grain, ᵇ and at
about the fifth hour I will appear to you and will show you what is necessary for you to see." ³ I asked her, saying, "Lady, to what part of the farm?"
"Wherever," she said, "you wish." I chose a beautiful secluded place, but
before *I* could speak to her and tell *her* the place, she said to me, "I will
be there, where you wish." ⁴ Therefore, brothers, I went to the farm and
I counted the hours and I came to the place where I had arranged for her
to come, and I saw a couch of ivory being placed *there* and upon the couch
there lay a linen pillow, and spread out over *it* a covering of fine linen.
⁵ Having seen these things sitting there and no one being in the place, I was
utterly astonished and, as it were, trembling seized me and my hair ₗstood
on edgeₗ ᶜ and, as it were, a panic came over me; I was alone. Therefore after
becoming myself, and remembering the glory of God and after taking courage, ₗkneeling downₗ ᵈ I confessed my sins again to the Lord, as also before.
⁶ And she came with six young men whom I had also seen before. And she
stood by me and listened attentively while *I* was praying and confessing to
the Lord my sins. And touching me she said, "Hermas, stop asking all these
questions about your sins. Also ask about righteousness, so that you may

---

a. Literally "to the elect, all of [them]"

b. BDAG further clarifies: "Probably means a field in which was located an apparatus for
preparing groats [coarsely crushed grain], where Hermas works."

c. Literally "straightened"

d. Literally "putting down my knee"

take some part of it to your family." ⁷ And she raised me up ª by the hand and brought me to the couch and said to the young men, "Go and build." ⁸ And after the young men went away and we were alone, she said to me, "Sit down here." I said to her, "Lady, let the elders sit down first." "Do what I tell you," she said, "and sit down." ⁹ Therefore I wanted to sit down at her right side. She would not allow me but gestured to me with her hand that I should sit down at her left side. Therefore, as I considered this and was grieved because she would not allow me to sit down at her right side, she said to me, "Are you sad, Hermas? The place at my right side is for others, those who have already pleased God and have suffered on account of the Name. But you ₍fall short₎ ᵇ in order to sit down with them but, as you continue, remain in your simplicity and you will sit down with them, and as will all if they do their deeds and they endure what those also endured."

3.2 The Tower and the Stones

¹⁰·¹ "What," I said, "have they endured?" "Listen," she said. "Whips, imprisonments, great afflictions, crosses, wild beasts, for the sake of the name. Because of this, theirs is the right side of holiness, and to whomever suffers because of the name. Now for the remaining, there is the left side, but for both, both those who sit on the right and those on the left *have* the same gifts and the same promises, only those on the right sit and have a certain glory. ² And you are very eager to sit down on the right *side* with them, but you *have* many failings. But you will be cleansed from your failings, and all who are not double-minded will be cleansed from all their sins to this day." ³ Having said these things, she wished to go away. But throwing myself at her feet, I implored her by the Lord that she show me what she had promised, a vision. ⁴ And again she took hold of my hand and stood me up and sat *me* down upon the couch on the left. And she herself also sat down on the right. And lifting up a certain shining rod, she said to me, "Do you see a great undertaking?" I said to her, "Lady, I see nothing." She said to me, "Behold, you do not see in front of you a great tower being built upon the waters with shining square stones?" ⁵ And the tower was being built in a

---

a. The NT appears to use ἐξεγείρω exclusively in raising up to life from death, or in waking up someone who was sleeping. In this present instance, the use is to simply represent vertical motion from a sitting position to a standing position, "to raise up."

b. Literally "much lack"

square by the six young men who had come with her, but myriads of other men were bringing up stones, some from the deep water, and others from the land. And they were giving *them* to the six young men, and they were taking *them* and building. **6** And all the stones which were dragged from the deep water thus were placed in the building, for they were shaped and matched by the joint with the other, and thus were joined to one another so that their joints could not be seen. But the building of the tower appeared as having been built from one stone. **7** But the other stones, those brought from the dry ground, some were thrown away, and others were placed in the building, and others were broken up and thrown far away from the tower. **8** And many other stones were lying around the tower, and they did not use them for the building, for some of them were ₗnot smooth enough₎, [a] and others had cracks, and others were too short, and others *were* white and round, not fitting into the building. **9** And I saw other stones being thrown far from the tower, and coming onto the road and not staying on the road, but rolling from the road into the wayless area. And others were falling into the fire and were being burned, and others were falling near the waters and could not be rolled into the water, although they wanted *them* to be rolled and to come into the water.

3.3 The Explanation of the Tower

11.1 Having shown these things to me, she wished to hurry away. I said to her, "Lady, what *does it* benefit me having seen these things and not understanding what matters they represent?" Answering me, she said, "You are a sly one, wanting to know the things about the tower." "Yes," I said, "Lady, that I may report to the brothers and they may become more cheerful, and upon hearing these things may know the Lord in great glory." **2** And she said, "Many indeed will hear, but upon hearing some of them will rejoice, and some will weep, but even these, if they hear and repent, even they themselves will rejoice. Therefore listen to the parable of the tower, for I will reveal all things to you and ₗyou no longer give me grief₎ [b] about revelation, for these revelations are complete, for they have been fulfilled. But you will not stop asking for revelations, for you are shameless. **3** And I myself

---

a. Literally "roughly surfaced"
b. Literally "you cause me trouble no longer"

am the tower which you see being built, the church who appeared to you, both now and the previous *time*. Therefore ask whatever you want about the tower and I will reveal *it* to you, that you may rejoice with the saints." ⁴ I said to her, "Lady, since you once considered me worthy to reveal everything to me, reveal it." And she said to me, "Whatever is possible to reveal to you, it will be revealed. Only let your heart be with God and do not be of two minds, whatever you may see." ⁵ I asked her, "Why has the tower been built upon the waters, Lady?" "I have told you," she said, "also previously, and you are seeking diligently. Therefore, by seeking you are finding the truth. Why, therefore, has the tower been built upon the waters? Listen. *It is* because your life was saved and will be saved through water, and the tower has been founded by the word of the almighty and glorious Name, and is kept by the invisible power of the Master."

3.4 The Six Men

¹²·¹ Answering, I said to her, "Lady, this thing is great and wonderful. But the young men, the six who are building, who are they, Lady?" "These are the holy angels of God, who were first created, to whom the Lord handed over all of his creation to increase and to build up and to be master of all of the creation. Therefore, through them the construction of the tower will be completed." ² "But the others, who are bringing up the stones, who are they?" "These too *are* holy angels of God, but these, the six, they are superior to them. Therefore the construction of the tower will be completed, and all will rejoice together around the tower and will glorify God because the construction of the tower has been completed." ³ I asked her, saying, "Lady, I want to know the fate of the stones and their power. What kind of *power* is it?" Answering me, she said, "*It is* not because you are more worthy than all others that it has been revealed to you. For there are others before you and better than you to whom these visions should be revealed, but in order that the name of God might be glorified, it has been revealed to you and will be revealed for the sake of the double-minded who argue in their hearts whether these things are possible or are not *possible*. Tell them that all these things are true and nothing is outside of the truth, but everything is strong and reliable and established."

3.5 About the Stones in the Tower

[13.1] "Now hear about the stones which go into the building. Therefore the stones, square and white and matched at their joints, these are the apostles and bishops and teachers and deacons who have walked according to the holiness of God and to the elect of God have served as bishops and teachers and deacons, in holiness and in honor. Some have fallen asleep while others are still alive. And they always agreed in themselves and they had peace among themselves and they listened to one another. Because of this, their joints are matched in the building of the tower." [2] "Now, those which are dragged from the deep water and added into the building and matched in their joints with the other stones, those which have already been built, who are they?" "These are those who have suffered for the sake of the name of the Lord." [3] "But the other stones, those carried from the dry ground, I want to know who they are, Lady." She said, "Those who go into the building without being hewn, these the Lord approved because they walked in the uprightness of the Lord and have carried out his commandments." [4] "But those who are being brought and being placed into the building, who are they?" "They are young in the faith and faithful, but they are warned by the angels to do good because wickedness has been found in them." [5] "But the ones they rejected and threw away, who are they?" "These are those who have sinned and who desire to repent. Because of this they have not been thrown far away from the tower because they will be useful for the building if they repent. Therefore those who are about to repent, if they repent, will be strong in the faith if they repent now while the tower is being built. But if the building is completed they will have a place no longer, but they will be rejects, and they will have only this: to lie at the tower."

3.6 About the Stones Away From the Tower

[14.1] "And those who are broken up and thrown far away from the tower, do you want to know about them? These are the sons of lawlessness. And they believed with hypocrisy, and ⌊all their wickedness remained with them⌋.[a] Because of this they do not have salvation, because they are not useful for the building because of their wickedness. Because of this, they were broken into pieces and thrown far away because of the anger of the Lord, because

---

a. Literally "all wickedness not did depart from them"

they made him angry. [2] But you have seen the others, many who were lying about *and* not going into the building, these who had a rough surface are those who have known the truth but are not remaining in it." [3] "And those who have the cracks, who are they?" "These are those who have *something* against one another in their hearts and who are not at peace with themselves but have the appearance of peace. But when they depart from one another, their wickedness remains in their hearts. Therefore these are the cracks which the stones have. [4] And those who are too short? These are they who have believed and they live the greater part in righteousness, but they have some portion of lawlessness. Because of this they are broken apart and not perfect." [5] "And the white and round *stones* which do not fit into the building, who are they, Lady?" Answering me she said, "ₗHow longₗ [a] will you be stupid and foolish, and ask all things and understand nothing? These are they who have faith but also have the riches of this world. When tribulation comes, because of their riches and because of their business affairs, they deny their Lord." [6] And answering her, I said, "Lady, then when will they be useful for the building?" "Whenever," she said, "the riches that beguile [b] them may be cut away from them, then they will be useful to God. For just as the round stone, unless it is hewn and ₗthe rubbleₗ [c] is thrown away from it, is not able to become square, so also those who are rich in this world, unless their riches are hewn away, they are not able to be useful to the Lord. [7] Understand first from yourself: when you were rich you were useless, but now you are useful and beneficial for life. [d] Be useful to God, for you yourself also are taken from the same stones."

3.7 About The Remaining Stones

[15.1] "But the other stones, which you saw being thrown far from the tower and falling on the road and rolling from the road into the place with no paths, these are those who have believed, but because of their double-mindedness they abandoned their road, the true *one*. Therefore thinking it possible to

---

a. Literally "Until when"

b. BDAG offers the definition of "to lead someone's soul astray."

c. Literally "something"

d. Lake translates this as a dative of purpose with reference to God ("for the Life"); others (Holmes, Ehrman) translate as a simple dative. Osiek translates generically as a dative of purpose ("for life").

find a better road, they have been deceived and are miserable, walking about in the place with no paths. ² But those who are falling into the fire and being burned, these are those who completely revolted against the living God and it has entered no longer into their heart to repent because of the lust of their licentiousness and the wicked deeds which they have done. ³ But the others which are falling near the waters and are not able to be rolled into the water, do you want to know who they are? These are those who heard the word and want to be baptized into the name of the Lord. Then, when the purity of the truth ₗcomes to mind₎, ᵃ ₗthey change their minds and again pursue₎ ᵇ their evil lusts." ⁴ Therefore she finished the explanation of the tower. ⁵ Still being shameless, I asked her whether all these stones which had been thrown off and did not fit into the building of the tower, whether ₗthey could repent₎ ᶜ and have a place in this tower. "They have," she said, "repentance, but they are not able to be fit into this tower. ⁶ But they will fit into another much inferior place, and this when they have been tortured and have fulfilled the days of their sins, and for this reason they will be taken away because they took part in the righteous word. And then it will happen to them to be taken away from their torments because of the evil deeds which they have done. But if it does not come upon their heart, they will not be saved because of their hardness of heart."

3.8 About the Seven Women

¹⁶·¹ Therefore when I stopped asking her about all of these things, she said to me, "Do you want to see something different?" Being very eager to see, I was very happy to look. ² Looking at me, she smiled and said to me, "Do you see seven women around the tower?" "I see, Lady." I said. "This tower is being supported by them, according to the command of the Lord. ³ Hear now their functions. The first of them, the one clasping her hands, is called 'Faith'; through her the elect of God are saved. ⁴ But the next one, who wears a belt and acts like a man, is called 'Self-control.' She is a daughter of Faith. Therefore whoever may follow her becomes blessed in his life, because he will hold back from all evil deeds, believing that if he holds back from every

---

a. Literally "comes into their remembrance"
b. Literally "changing their minds and they again go after"
c. Literally "is to them repentance"

evil lust he will inherit eternal life." [5] "But the others, Lady, who are they?" "They are daughters of one another, and they are called 'Simplicity' and 'Knowledge' and 'Innocence' and 'Reverence' and 'Love.' Therefore when you do all the works of their mother, you will be able to live." [6] "I want," I said, "to know, Lady, which of them has which power?" "Listen," she said, "to the powers which they have. [7] And their powers are controlled by one another, and they follow one another ₁in the order of their birth₁:[a] from Faith is born Self-control, from Self-control Simplicity, from Simplicity Innocence, from Innocence Reverence, from Reverence Knowledge, from Knowledge Love. Therefore these works are pure and reverent and divine. [8] Therefore whoever serves these and is strong enough to accomplish their works will have his dwelling in the tower with the saints of God." [9] And I began to ask her about the times, if it is already the end. But she shouted with a loud voice, saying, "Foolish man! Do you not see the tower still being built? Therefore, whenever the building of the tower is completed, the end comes, but it will be built up quickly. No longer ask me anything. This reminder and the renewal of your spirits is sufficient for you and for the saints. [10] But this was revealed not for you alone, but for you to make it known to them all [11] after three days, for you must first understand it. But I charge you first, Hermas, with these words which I am about to say to you, to speak them all into the ears of the saints, that by hearing and doing them they may be cleansed from their wicked deeds and you also with them."

3.9 Share from Your Abundance

[17.1] "Listen, my children, I brought you up in great simplicity and innocence and reverence through the mercy of the Lord, who instilled righteousness into you that you might be justified and sanctified from all wickedness and from all crookedness. But you did not want to cease from your wickedness. [2] Now, therefore, listen to me and if you are at peace among yourselves and take care of one another and help one another and not only do you partake of the creatures of God ₁from your abundance₁,[b] but you also share with the needy. [3] For some are contracting illness in their flesh from too much food and are injuring their flesh, but others who do not have food, their

---

a. Literally "just as also they were born"
b. Literally "from the soup"

flesh is being injured by not having sufficient food, and their flesh is wasting away. ⁴ Therefore this lack of sharing is harmful to you who have and do not share with those who are in need. ⁵ Consider the judgment which is coming. Therefore those who have an overabundance, let them seek out those who hunger while the tower is not yet completed, for with the completion of the tower, you will want to do good and you will not have opportunity. ⁶ Watch out, therefore, you who rejoice in your riches, lest those who are needy groan and their groaning goes up to the Lord, and you will be excluded, with your possessions, outside the door of the tower. ⁷ Now, therefore, I say to you, to those who preside over the church and to those who occupy seats of honor, do not be like the sorcerers. For the sorcerers carry their charms inside a box, but you *carry* your charm and poison in your heart. ⁸ You are calloused and do not want to cleanse your heart and join your wisdom ₍together₎ ᵃ in a clean heart that you may have mercy from the great King. ⁹ Therefore watch out, child, that this dissension does not rob your life. ¹⁰ How do you plan to instruct the elect of the Lord, yourselves not having instruction? Therefore teach one another and be at peace among yourselves, that I also, standing joyfully in front of the Father, may give an account about you all to the Lord."

3.10 *The Departure of the Lady*

¹⁸·¹ Therefore, when she stopped speaking with me, the six young men who were building came and they carried her away to the tower. And four others took away the couch and also carried it away to the tower. I did not see their faces because they were turned away. ² But as *she* was leaving I asked her that she might reveal to me about the three forms in which she appeared to me. Answering me she said, "About these things, it is necessary for you to ask another, in order that it may be revealed to you." ³ And she appeared to me, brothers, in the first vision in the previous year, very old and sitting in a chair. ⁴ But in the second vision, her face was younger and her body and her hair *were* older. And standing with me, she spoke, and was more joyful than the first time. ⁵ But in the third vision *she was* very much younger and breathtakingly beautiful, and only her hair was old.

---

a. Literally "upon the same"

And she was ₍completely₎ ᵃ joyful, and was sitting on a couch. ⁶ Being very deeply grieved about these things, I wanted to understand this revelation, and I saw the elderly woman in a vision of the night saying to me, "Every request needs humility; so fast and you will receive what you ask from the Lord." ⁷ So I fasted one day and that same night a young man appeared to me and he said to me, "Why do you ₍continually₎ ᵇ ask for revelations in prayer? Watch out, lest by making many requests you injure your flesh. ⁸ These revelations are sufficient for you. Are you able to see more powerful revelations than you have seen?" ⁹ Answering, I said to him, "Sir, this alone I ask, about the three forms of the elderly lady, that there may be a complete revelation." Answering, he said to me, "₍How long₎ ᶜ are you foolish? But your double-mindedness makes you foolish and you have not inclined your heart to the Lord." ¹⁰ Answering, I said again to him, "But from you, sir, we will know them more accurately."

3.11 *About the Lady in the First Vision*

¹⁹·¹ "Listen," he said, "about the forms which you seek after. ² In the first vision, why did an elderly lady appear to you, being seated upon a chair? Because your spirit is old and already fading away, and does not have power from your weakness and double-mindedness. ³ For just as old people, who no longer have hope of being made new, anticipate nothing else except their sleep, so also you, being weakened by the events of daily life, hand yourselves over to apathy, and do not cast your anxieties upon the Lord,ᵈ but your mind was broken and you became old in your grief." ⁴ "Why, then, I want to know, sir, did she sit in a chair?" "Because every weak person sits in a chair because of his illness, that the illness of his body may be supported. You have the example of the first vision."

3.12 *About the Lady in the Second Vision*

²⁰·¹ "But in the second vision, you saw her standing and having a younger face and more joyful than the first time, but her body and her hair *were*

---

a. Literally "to the utmost"
b. Literally "by the hand"
c. Literally "Until when"
d. Ps 55:22, 1 Pet 5:7

older. Listen," he said, "also to this parable. ² When someone is older, already he despairs of himself because of his weakness and poverty, he expects nothing else except the last day of his life. Then suddenly an inheritance was left to him, and having heard, he got up and being very happy he put on his strength and no longer lies down but stands up and his spirit is renewed, which was already destroyed by his former deeds, and no longer sits, but acts courageously. So also did you, upon hearing the revelation which the Lord revealed to you. ³ For he had compassion upon you and renewed your spirits, and you put away your weaknesses and inner strength came to you and you were strengthened in the faith; and the Lord, having seen your strengthening, rejoiced. And because of this, he made known to you the building of the tower and he will show *you* other things if you are at peace among yourselves with *your* whole heart."

3.13 About the Lady in the Third Vision

²¹·¹ "But in the third vision, you saw her younger and beautiful and joyful and her form *was* beautiful. ² For *it is* as if a good message comes to someone who is grieving, he immediately forgets his previous grieving and he expects nothing else except the message which he has heard, and is strengthened for the good left *to do*. And his spirit is renewed because of the joy which he has received, so also you have received renewal of your spirits, by seeing these good things. ³ And because you saw her sitting upon a couch, the position is secure because the couch has four feet and stands securely, for even the world is controlled by four elements. ⁴ Therefore those who have completely repented will be young and firmly established; they have repented with the whole heart. You have fully received the complete revelation, no longer ask anything about revelation; but if anything is necessary it will be revealed to you."

VISION 4

4.1 Hermas and the Beast

²²·¹ What I saw, brothers, twenty days after the previous vision, was a type of the tribulation which was coming. ² I was going into the country by

the Campanian Way. It is ₍just over a mile₎ [a][b] from the public road and the place is easily reached. [3] Therefore, walking by myself, I desired that the Lord complete the revelations and the visions which he made known to me through his holy church, that he might strengthen me and give repentance to his servants who had stumbled, that his great and glorious name might be glorified, because he considered me worthy to show to me his wonderful things. [4] And I was glorifying and giving thanks to him when the sound of a voice answered me, "Do not be of two minds, Hermas." I began to reason with myself and say, "How can I be of two minds having been so firmly established by the Lord and having seen *his* glorious deeds?" [5] And I approached a little further, brothers, and behold, I saw dust like into heaven, and I began to say to myself, "Maybe cattle are coming and raising dust?" And it was about ₍an eighth of a mile₎ [c][d] from me. [6] As the dust grew greater and greater, I suspected it was something supernatural. The sun shone a little, and behold, I saw a large beast like some sea monster and fiery locusts were coming out of its mouth. And the beast was about one hundred feet [e] in length and its head was like a ceramic jar. [7] And I began to weep and to ask the Lord that he rescue me from it, and I remembered the word which I had heard, "Do not be of two minds, Hermas." [8] Therefore brothers, having put on the faith of the Lord and remembering what great things he taught me, taking courage I gave myself over to the beast. And thus the beast came with a whoosh as though it was able to destroy a city. [9] I came near it, and the enormous sea monster stretched itself out on the ground. And ₍it only stuck out its tongue₎, [f][g] and did not move at all until I had passed it by. [10] And the beast had four colors upon its head: black, then red as fire and blood, then gold, then white.

---

a. Literally "about ten stades"

b. A "stade" is about one-eighth of a mile, or 200 yards.

c. Literally "a stade"

d. A "stade" is about one-eighth of a mile, or 200 yards.

e. The Greek word here is literally "feet," the body part. This is not a unit conversion: "about the length of one hundred feet."

f. Literally "it put nothing forward if not its tongue"

g. On the idiom, Osiek notes: "In his fear of the beast heading straight for him, he remembers the directive given him in advance by the mysterious voice, and realizes that faith in the Lord protects him like armor and is the source of his courage to face the beast head-on. The encounter turns out to be nothing dangerous, for the beast behaves more like a pet dog than a monster."

4.2 *Hermas Tells of His Encounter*

23.1 And after I passed the beast and went on ahead about thirty feet, [a] behold, a young woman [b] met me, adorned as if coming out from a bridal chamber, completely in white and white sandals, veiled [c] to the forehead, and her head covering was with a turban, and her hair was white. **2** I knew from the previous visions that she was the church and I became more cheerful. She greeted me saying, "Greetings, my man!" and I greeted her in return, "Lady, greetings!" **3** Answering me she said, "Did nothing meet you?" I said to her, "Lady, an enormous beast able to destroy nations, but by the power of the Lord and his great compassion I escaped it!" **4** "You escaped well," she said, "because you cast your anxiety upon God [d] and opened your heart to the Lord, believing that you are able to be saved by nothing except by the great and glorious name. Because of this, the Lord sent his angel who is over the beasts, whose name is Thegri, and he shut its mouth that it might not destroy you. You have escaped great tribulation because of your faith, and because having seen such an enormous beast, you were not double-minded. **5** Therefore go and make known his great acts to the elect of the Lord, and tell them that this beast is a type of the great tribulation which is coming. Therefore if you prepare ahead of time and repent with your whole heart to the Lord, you will be able to escape it, if your heart becomes pure and blameless, and the remaining days of your life you serve the Lord blamelessly. Cast your anxieties upon the Lord, and he will set them straight. [e] **6** Trust in the Lord, you double-minded ones, because he is able to do all things. He turns his wrath away from you and sends out torments to you who are double-minded. Woe to those who hear these words and who disobey! It would be more desirable for them to not have been born."

---

a. The Greek here is literally "feet," the body part, this is not a unit conversion. The idea is "the length of thirty feet."

b. This word (παρθένος) can be translated either "young woman" or "virgin" and has even been used to refer to widows who remained unmarried. It seems best to translate with the most general meaning ("young woman") which leaves the specific meaning of "virgin" available if the context dictates.

c. Sus 32 (Theodotion)

d. Ps 55:22, I Pet 5:7

e. 1 Pet 5:7

4.2 About the Four Colors

24.1 I asked her about the four colors which the beast had on its head. And answering me she said, "Again you are meddlesome about such things?" "Yes," I said, "Lady, explain to me what these things are." **2** "Listen," she said, "the black, this represents the world in which you dwell. **3** And the color of fire and blood *means* that it is necessary for this world to be destroyed by blood and fire. **4** And the gold part represents you, who have escaped this world, for just as the gold is tested by the fire and becomes useful, so also you who dwell among them are tested. Therefore those who stay and ₗpass through the flamesⱼ[a] will be purified by the flames, just as the gold throws off its slag, so also you will throw off all sorrow and distress and you will be purified and will be made useful for the construction of the tower. **5** And the white part is the age which is coming, in which the elect of God will dwell because those chosen by God for eternal life are without fault and pure. **6** Therefore you do not stop speaking to the ears of the saints. You also have the example of the great tribulation which is coming, but if you so desire, nothing will happen. Remember what was written beforehand." **7** Saying these things, she departed and I did not see to what place she departed, because a cloud came and I turned ₗaround in fearⱼ[b] thinking that the beast was coming.

VISION 5

5.1 The Shepherd

25.1 After I prayed at my house and sat down on my bed, a man entered, someone glorious in appearance, in the clothes of a shepherd, wearing a white goat skin and having a leather bag on his shoulders and a staff in his hand. And he greeted me, and I greeted him in return. **2** And immediately he sat down beside me and said to me, "I have been sent by the most holy angel that I should live with you for the rest of the days of your life." **3** I thought that he was here tempting me, and I said to him, "Who are you? For I," I said, "I know to whom I have been handed over." He said to me, "Do you not recognize me?" "No," I said. "I," he said, "I am the shepherd to

---

a. Literally "who burn"
b. Literally "to the back fearing"

whom you were handed over." [4] While he was still speaking, his appearance changed and I recognized him, that he was to whom I was handed over. And I was immediately confused and fear took hold of me and I was completely overcome by sorrow because I had answered him so wickedly and foolishly. [5] But answering me he said, "Do not be confused, but be strengthened in my commandments which I am about to command you. For I was sent," he said, "that I might show you again all the things which you previously saw; they *are* the main points which are advantageous to you. First of all, write my commandments and parables[a] and the other things just as I show to you. Thus you are to write for this *reason*," he said: "I am commanding you first to write the commandments and parables, that you may read them ₍continually₎[b] and be able to keep them." [6] Therefore I wrote the commandments and parables just as he commanded me. [7] Then if, upon hearing, you keep them, and walk in them and do them with a pure heart, you will receive from the Lord as much as he promised to you, but if upon hearing you do not repent but still add to your sins, you will receive the opposite from the Lord. The shepherd, the angel of repentance, thus commanded me to write all these things.

THE COMMANDMENTS

COMMANDMENT 1

1.1 *God is One*

[26.1] "First of all, believe that God is one,[c] who created all things and completed *them* and made all things from what did not exist into what does exist, and who contains all things, but alone is uncontained. [2] Therefore believe in him and fear him. And fearing *him*, exercise self-control. Observe these things and cast off all wickedness from yourself and put on every virtue of righteousness, and you shall live to God if you observe this commandment."

---

a. A reference to the next sections of the work.
b. Literally "by the hand"
c. Deut 6:4

COMMANDMENT 2

2.1 Simplicity and Innocence

[27.1] He said to me: "Hold on to simplicity and be innocent and you will be like the children who do not know the wickedness which destroys ₍human life₎.[a] [2] First, slander no one; do not even gladly listen to the one who slanders. ₍Otherwise₎[b] even you who listen will be guilty of the sin of the one who slanders, if you believe in the slander which you hear. For by believing you yourself also will hold a grudge against your brother; therefore in this way you will be guilty of the sin of the one who slanders. [3] Slander is evil, it is a restless demon, never at peace but always dwelling in dissension. Therefore abstain from it and you will always have well-being with everyone. [4] And put on reverence, in which there is no evil cause for stumbling, but everything is smooth and cheerful. Do good, and out of your labor, which God gives you, give generously to all who are in need, not doubting to whom you should give or to whom you should not give; give to all, for God wants to give to all from his own gifts. [5] Therefore those who receive will make an account to God why they received and for what *reason*. For those who receive while suffering hardship will not be judged, but those who receive in hypocrisy will pay the penalty. [6] Therefore the one who gives is innocent, for as he has received from the Lord a ministry to fulfill, he fulfilled it sincerely, not making a distinction to whom he should give or not give. Therefore this ministry, being sincerely fulfilled, was glorious before God. Therefore the one who serves so sincerely shall live to God. [7] Therefore keep this commandment as I have told you, that the repentance of you and your family may be found in sincerity and innocent, pure and undefiled."

COMMANDMENT 3

3.1 Love Truth and Speak Truthfully

[28.1] Again he said to me, "Love truth, and let all truth proceed from your mouth, that the spirit which God caused to dwell in this flesh may be found

---

a. Literally "the life of people"
b. Literally "But if not"

true in the sight of all people and thus the Lord who dwells in you will be glorified, for the Lord is true in every word and nothing from him is a lie. ² Therefore those who lie reject the Lord and become defrauders of the Lord, not returning to him the deposit which they received. For they received from him a spirit free from lies. If they return this as a false spirit they have defiled the commandment of the Lord and have become defrauders." ³ Therefore having heard these things, I wept very much, and upon seeing me weeping, he said "Why do you weep?" "Because," I said, "sir, I do not know if I am able to be saved." "Why?" he said. "Because not yet," I said, "sir, in my life have I spoken a true word, but I have always spoken deceitfully with everyone, and represented my lie as truth among all people, and nobody ever contradicted me but believed my word. Therefore how," I said, "sir, am I able to live having done these things?" ⁴ "You," he said, "are thinking good and true. For it is necessary that you, like a slave of God, walk in truth, and an evil conscience must not dwell with the spirit of truth, nor grief be brought upon the honorable and true spirit." "Never," I said, "sir, have I accurately heard words such as these." ⁵ "Therefore now," he said, "you understand them. Keep them so that the lies which you also previously spoke in your business, these may become true now that those have become trustworthy. For it is possible now that those have become trustworthy, if you keep these things, and ⌜speak nothing but truth⌝ᵃ from now on, you will be able to obtain life for yourself, and whoever hears this commandment and abstains from lying, that most evil sin, will live to God."

COMMANDMENT 4

4.1 Desire, Sin and Adultery

²⁹·¹ "I command you," he said, "to guard purity. And ⌜do not let any thoughts enter⌝ᵇ into your heart about the wife of another, or about any sexual immorality or about any such likeness of evil, for by doing this you commit great sin. But by always remembering your own wife, you will never go wrong. ² For if this desire enters into your heart, you will go wrong, and if other such evils enter your heart, you commit sin. For this desire is a great sin

---

a. Literally "speak all truth"
b. Literally "do not let [it] enter"

for the servant of God, and if anyone does this evil deed, he brings about death for himself. [3] Therefore see to it that you abstain from this desire, for where holiness dwells, there lawlessness must not enter into the heart of the righteous one." [4] I said to him, "Sir, allow me to ask you a few things." "Speak," he said. "Sir," I said, "if someone has a wife faithful in the Lord and he learns she is in some adultery, then does the husband sin by living with her?" [5] "As long as *he is* ignorant," he said, "he does not sin, but if the husband knows her sin, and the wife does not repent but continues in her sexual immorality and the husband still lives with her, he becomes guilty of her sin and a partner in her adultery." [6] "What then," I said, "sir, should the husband do if the wife continues in this lustful passion?" "Let him divorce her," he said, "and let the husband remain by himself. But if having divorced his wife he marries another, he himself also commits adultery." [7] "Therefore if," I said, "sir, after the wife is divorced, the wife repents and wants to return to her own husband, will she not be received?" [8] "And surely," he said, "if the husband does not receive her, he sins and he brings great sin upon himself, but it is necessary to receive the one who sins and who repents, but not ₍repeatedly₎[a] because there is one repentance for the servant of God. Therefore, because of repentance, the husband ought not to marry. This practice is given for wife and husband. [9] Not only," he said, "is it adultery if someone defiles his flesh, but ₍whoever does anything even like what the heathen do₎[b] commits adultery. So if anyone continues in deeds such as these and does not repent, stay away from him and do not live with him. ₍Otherwise₎[c] you are also a sharer in his sin. [10] Because of this, you are commanded to remain to yourselves, whether husband or wife, for to repent is possible in cases such as these. [11] Therefore I," he said, "do not give an opportunity that this business thus be completed, but for he who sins to sin no longer. And because of his former sin, there is one who is able to give healing, for he is the one who has all authority."

---

a. Literally "too often"
b. Literally "even who ever does like the heathen"
c. Literally "But if not"

4.2 Repentance

30.1 And I asked him again, saying, "Since the Lord considered me worthy that you should always dwell with me, bear with yet a few of my words since I do not understand anything and my heart has been hardened by my former deeds. Help me to understand, because I am very foolish and I understand nothing at all." **2** Answering me he said, "I," he said, "have *authority* over repentance, and I give understanding to all who repent. Or do you not think," he said, "this very repentance is understanding? To repent," he said, "is great understanding, for the sinner understands that he has done evil before the Lord, and the deed which he did enters into his heart, and he repents and no longer does the evil but lavishly does the good, and humbles his own soul and torments *it* because he sinned. Therefore you see that repentance is great understanding." **3** "Because of this, then," I said, "sir, I make careful inquiry *about* all things from you. First, because I am a sinner, that I may know by doing what deeds I will live, because my sins are many and various." **4** "You will live," he said, "if you keep my commandments and walk in them. And whoever upon hearing the commandments keeps them, he will live to God."

4.3 Second Repentance

31.1 "Still," I said, "sir, I will continue to ask." "Speak," he said. "I have heard," I said, "sir, from some teachers that a second repentance is not possible ₗbeyondₗ [a] that one, when we went down into the water and received forgiveness of our previous sins." **2** He said to me, "You have heard correctly for so it is. For it is necessary for the one who has received forgiveness of sins to sin no longer, but to dwell in purity. **3** But since you inquire exactly about all things, I will also make this known to you, not giving an excuse to those ₗwho will believe in the futureₗ [b] or those who already believe in the Lord. For those who already believe or ₗwho will believe in the futureₗ, [c] they do not have repentance for sins, but they do have forgiveness of their former sins. **4** Therefore those who were called before these days, the Lord

---

a. Literally "if not".
b. Literally "who are about to believe"
c. Literally "who are about to believe"

has appointed repentance. For being a knower of hearts,[a] the Lord also knows all things beforehand, the weakness of people and the cunning of the devil, that he will do some evil to the servants of God, and he will do wrong to them. [5] Therefore being full of compassion, the Lord had compassion upon his creation and established this repentance, and he gave the control of this repentance to me. [6] But I say to you," he said, "after the calling, that great and honorable *one*, if someone, being tempted by the devil, might sin, he has one repentance. But if he should sin and repent ₁repeatedly₁[b] it is harmful to the person such as this, for he will live with difficulty." [7] I said to him, "I was given life upon hearing these things from you so accurately, for I know that if I will no longer add to my sins I will be saved." "You will be saved," he said, "and all whoever may do these things."

4.4 Death and Remarriage

[32.1] I asked him again, saying, "Sir, since you have endured me once, in addition also make this known to me." "Speak," he said. "If a wife," I said, "sir, or on the other hand a husband passes away and ₁the survivor₁[c] marries, does not the one who marries sin?" [2] "He does not sin," he said, "but if he remains by himself he acquires an abundant honor for himself and great glory with the Lord. But even if he marries, he does not sin. [3] Therefore preserve purity and holiness, and you will live to God. These things, whatever I say and am about to say to you, keep *them* from now on, from the day which you were handed over to me, and I will dwell in your house. [4] But for your former sins there will be forgiveness if you keep my commandments. And everyone also will have forgiveness if they keep these commandments of mine and walk in this purity."

COMMANDMENT 5

5.1 Patience and Bitterness

[33.1] "Be even-tempered," he said, "and intelligent, and you will exercise dominion over all evil deeds, and will do all righteousness. [2] For if you are

---

a. Acts 1:24
b. Literally "by the hand"
c. Literally "one of them"

ever-patient, the Holy Spirit who dwells in you will be pure, not being obscured[a] by another evil spirit but dwelling in a roomy place it will rejoice greatly and will be glad with the body in which it dwells and will serve God with great cheerfulness having well-being in itself. [3] But if any bad temper comes, immediately the Holy Spirit, being delicate, is distressed, not having a pure place. And it seeks to depart out of the place, for it is choked out[b] by the evil spirit, not having a place to serve the Lord as it desires, being defiled by the bad temper. For the Lord lives in patience, but the devil in bad temper. [4] Therefore both spirits dwelling in the same *place* is harmful and evil to that person in whom they dwell. [5] For if you take a very little bit of wormwood and pour *it* into a jar of honey, is not the honey completely ruined? And so much honey is destroyed by so little wormwood. And it destroys[c] the sweetness of the honey and it no longer has the same favor with the master, because it has been made bitter and its use is lost. But if the wormwood is not poured into the honey, the honey is found to be sweet and it becomes useful to its master. [6] You see that patience is sweet beyond the honey, and it is useful to the Lord and he dwells in it. But the bad temper is bitter and useless. Therefore if bad temper is mixed with patience, patience is defiled and its intercession is no longer useful to God." [7] "I would like," I said, "sir, to know ⌊how bad temper works⌋,[d] that I may be kept from it." "And indeed," he said, "if you and your house do not keep from it, you have destroyed all of your hope. But keep from it, for I will be with you. And all also will refrain from it, whoever repents from their whole heart, for I will be with them and will preserve them, for all *of them* have been justified by the most holy angel."

5.2 The Importance of Refraining from Bad Temper

[34.1] "Hear now," he said, "⌊how bad temper works⌋,[e] how evil it is and how it overturns my servants with its working, and how it leads them astray from righteousness. But it does not lead astray those who are filled with

---

a. BDAG notes that in this verse, "The imagery is one of contrast between a bright and open [καθαρόν] spirit and a base spirit that darkens."

b. Matt 13:7; Mark 4:7; Luke 8:7

c. The referent is wormwood.

d. Literally "the working of bad temper"

e. Literally "the working of bad temper"

faith, nor is it able to work *evil* to them because my power is with them.
But it does lead astray those who are quite empty and double-minded.
² And when it sees such as these people being tranquil, it insinuates itself
into the heart of that person, and out of nothing the man or the woman
becomes bitter because of the matters of daily life, or because of food or
some trifle, or because of some friend, or because of giving or receiving, or
because of foolish matters such as these. For all these things are foolish and
vain and ignorant and harmful to the slave of God. ³ But patience is great
and strong, and has power and sturdiness, and thrives with broad application, it is cheerful, rejoicing greatly, free from care, glorifying the Lord
at every event, having nothing bitter in itself, continuing through everything gentle and quiet. Therefore this patience dwells with those who have
undiminished faith. ⁴ But bad temper is indeed first stupid, both frivolous
and foolish, then from the foolishness comes bitterness, and from the bitterness rage, and from the rage wrath, and from the wrath vengefulness.
Then this vengefulness, being established by so much evil, becomes a great
and incurable sin. ⁵ For when these spirits dwell in one vessel where the
Holy Spirit also dwells, that vessel does not contain them, but overflows. ᵃ
⁶ Therefore the delicate Spirit does not have a habit to dwell with an evil
spirit or with hardness; it departs from the person such as this, and it seeks
to dwell with gentleness and quietness. ⁷ Then, when it departs from that
person where it dwells, that person becomes empty of the righteous Spirit
and the rest is filled with the evil spirits. He is unsettled in his every deed,
being distracted here and there by the evil spirits and he is altogether
blinded from the good way of thinking. Thus it happens with all the bad
tempered. ⁸ Therefore refrain from bad temper, that most evil spirit, and
put on patience and resist bad temper and bitterness, and you will be found
with the holiness which is loved by the Lord. See to it, then, that you never
disregard this commandment, for if you master this commandment you
will be able to keep the remaining commandments also, which I am about
to command to you. Be strong in them and be empowered, and let all be
empowered, whoever wants to walk in them."

---

a. 1 Tim 1:14

COMMANDMENT 6

6.1 Walk the Straight Path

35.1 "I commanded you," he said, "in the first commandment that you keep the faith and the fear and the self-control." "Yes, sir," I said. "But now I want you," he said, "to also make known their abilities so that you might understand which of them has which ability and function, for their functions are two-fold. Therefore they relate to righteousness and unrighteousness. 2 Therefore you, you trust the righteous, but do not trust the unrighteous, for the righteous one has a straight path but the unrighteous one a crooked *path*. But you, you walk the straight and level path and leave the crooked path alone. 3 For the crooked path does not have a trail but *is* a place with no paths and many stumbling blocks and is rough and thorny. Therefore it is harmful to those who walk in it. 4 But those who go on the straight path walk smoothly and without stumbling, for it is neither rough or thorny. Therefore you see that it is most advantageous to walk this road." 5 "It pleases me," I said, "sir, to walk in this path." "You will walk," he said, "and whoever turns to the Lord with the whole heart will walk in it."

36.1 "Hear now," he said, "about faith. There are two angels with each person, one of righteousness and one of wickedness." 2 "How then," I said, "sir, will I know their workings, because both angels dwell with me?" 3 "Listen," he said, "and understand them. Indeed the angel of righteousness is delicate and modest and gentle and quiet. Therefore when this one enters into your heart, immediately he speaks with you about righteousness, about purity, about holiness, and about contentment, and about every righteous deed, and about all glorious virtue. When all these things enter into your heart, you know that the angel of righteousness is with you. Therefore these things are the works of the angel of righteousness. So believe in this one and in his works. 4 Therefore also see the works of the angel of wickedness. First of all, he is irritable and bitter and foolish and his evil works are tearing down the servants of God. Therefore when this one enters into your heart, you know him by his works." 5 "How," I said, "sir, will I perceive him? I do not know." "Listen," he said, "when some bad temper or bitterness comes upon you, know that he himself is in you. Then the desire of many deeds and the luxuries of many foods and intoxicating drinks and many drinking bouts and various and unnecessary foods and lust of women and greediness and some great arrogance and boastfulness and whatever resembles and is like these things. Therefore when these things enter into your heart, know that the angel of wickedness is in you. [6] Therefore you, having learned his works, keep away from him, believe him in no way, because his works are evil and harmful to the servant of God. Therefore you have the workings of both of the angels. Understand them and believe the angel of righteousness. [7] But stay away from the angel of wickedness because his teaching is evil in every way. For if a man is faithful and the thought of this angel enters into his heart, that man or woman must commit some sin. [8] But again if some man or woman be most evil and the works of the angel of righteousness enter into his heart, out of necessity he must do something good. [9] Therefore you see," he said, "that it is good to follow the angel of righteousness, but to renounce the angel of wickedness. [10] This commandment makes known the things about the faith, that you may trust in the works of the angel of righteousness and by doing them you will live to God. But believe that the works of the angel of wickedness are dangerous; therefore by not doing them you will live to God."

COMMANDMENT 7

7.1 Fear the Lord

[37.1] "Fear," he said, "the Lord and keep his commandments. Therefore, by keeping the commandments of God, you will be competent in every action and your actions will be beyond compare. For by fearing the Lord you will do everything well. And this is the fear which is necessary for you to fear and to be saved. [2] But do not fear the devil, for by fearing the Lord, you will exercise dominion over the devil because power is not in him. And where there is no power, there is neither fear, but where there is glorious power,[a] there is also fear. For everyone who has power has fear, but the one who does not have power is despised by all. [3] But fear the works of the devil because they are evil. Therefore, by fearing the Lord, you will not do them,

---

a. δύναμις ἡ ἔνδοξος Lake, Ehrman] δύναμις ᾖ ἔνδοξος Lightfoot, Holmes. The difference is between an article (Lake/Ehrman) and a subjunctive verb (Lightfoot/Holmes); however, respective translations are relatively uniform as the verb would be implied when reading as English.

but will stay away from them. 4 Therefore the fears are ₁of two kinds₁. ᵃ For
if you want to do evil, fear the Lord and you will not do it. But if however
you want to do good, fear the Lord and you will do it. So then, the fear of
the Lord is powerful and great and glorious. Therefore fear the Lord and
you will live to him. And whoever fears him and keeps his commandments
will live to God." 5 "Why," I said, "sir, did you say about those who keep his
commandments, 'They will live to God'?" "Because," he said, "all the creation fears the Lord, but it does not keep his commandments. Therefore
those who fear him and who keep his commandments, for those life is with
God. But those who do not keep his commandments *have* no life in him."

COMMANDMENT 8

8.1 Self Control

³⁸·¹ "I said to you," he said, "that the creatures of God are two-fold, because
self-control is also two-fold. For concerning some things it is necessary to
exercise self-control, but concerning others it is not necessary." ² "Make
known to me," I said, "sir, about which things it is necessary to exercise
self-control and about which things it is not necessary." "Listen," he said,
"exercise self-control over evil, and do not do it, but do not exercise self-control over good, but do it. For if you exercise self-control, not doing good,
you commit great sin. But if you exercise self-control, not doing evil, you
do great righteousness. Therefore exercise self-control over all wickedness,
doing what is good." ³ "What kinds," I said, "sir, are the wickednesses from
which it is necessary for us to exercise self-control over?" "Listen," he said,
"from adultery and sexual immorality, from lawless drunkenness, from evil
luxury, from many foods and extravagance of riches and of boasting and
of haughtiness and of arrogance, and from lying and slander and hypocrisy, bearing a grudge and all blasphemy. 4 These are the most evil works
of all in the life of people. Therefore it is necessary for the servant of God
to exercise self-control over these works. For the one who does not exercise self-control over these things is not able to live to God. Therefore also
listen to what follows these things." 5 "For sir," I said, "are there yet *other*

---

a. Literally "double"

evil deeds?" "₁Yes₁," ᵃ he said, "there are many over which it is necessary for
the servant of God to exercise self-control: stealing, lying, fraud, false testimony, greediness, evil lust, deceit, vanity, boastfulness, and whatever is like
these things. ⁶ Does it not seem to you these things are evil?" "Exceedingly
evil," I said, "to the servants of God." "It is necessary for the one who serves
God to exercise self-control over all of these things. Exercise self-control
over all of them so that you will live to God and you will be written down
with those who exercise self-control over them. Therefore *the things* over
which it is necessary for you to exercise self-control are these things. ⁷ But
what is necessary for you to not exercise self-control over," he said, "but
listen to the good to do: do not exercise self-control over *the good*, but do it."
⁸ "And of the good things, to me," I said, "sir, make known the power, that
I may walk in them and serve them, that by doing them I might be able to
be saved." "Listen," he said, "and do the deeds of the good things, which
are necessary for you to do and to not exercise self-control over. ⁹ First of
all, faith, fear of the Lord, love, harmony, words of righteousness, truth,
patience; there is nothing better than these things in the life of people. If
anyone observes these things and does not exercise self-control over them,
he becomes blessed in his life. ¹⁰ Next hear what follows these things: minister to widows, care for orphans and those in need, rescue the servants
of God from distress, be hospitable, for doing good is found in hospitality;
oppose no one, be quiet, become poorer than all of humanity, reverence the
aged, practice righteousness, preserve the community of believers, endure
mistreatment, be even-tempered, bear not a grudge, encourage those who
are sick in the soul, cast not aside those who have fallen away from the
faith but convert and ₁encourage them₁,ᵇ admonish those who sin, afflict
not debtors and the poor, and ₁whatever₁ᶜ is similar to these things. ¹¹ Does
it seem to you," he said, "these things are good?" "For what," I said, "sir, is
better than these things?" "Therefore walk," he said, "in them, and do not
exercise self-control over them, and you will live to God. ¹² Therefore keep
this commandment: If you do good and do not exercise self-control over it,
you will live to God, and all will live to God who so act. And again, if you

---

a. ¹ Literally "and indeed"
b. Literally "to bring about cheer"
c. Literally "if anything"

do not do evil and exercise self-control over it, you will live to God, and all will live to God, whoever keeps these commandments and walks in them."

COMMANDMENT 9

9.1 Double-Mindedness

[39.1] He said to me, "Remove double-mindedness from yourself and be not at all double-minded about asking anything from God, saying in yourself, namely, 'How am I able to ask from the Lord and receive, having sinned against him so much?' [2] Do not consider these things too carefully, but with your whole heart turn to the Lord and ask from him confidently and you will come to know his great tenderheartedness, that he may never forsake you but will fulfill the petition of your soul. [3] For God is not like people who bear malice, but ⌊he himself bears no malice⌋[a] and has compassion upon his creation. [4] You, therefore, purify your heart from all of the worthless things of this world, and the words which were previously spoken to you, and ask from the Lord and you will receive everything, and ⌊all of your requests will be granted⌋,[b] if you ask confidently from the Lord. [5] But if you doubt in your heart, you will never receive any of your requests, for those who doubt in God, these are double-minded ones, and ⌊they are never granted any⌋[c] of their requests. [6] But those who are perfect in the faith, they ask for everything trusting upon the Lord, and they receive it because they ask confidently, being double-minded in nothing. For every double-minded man, if he does not repent, will be saved with difficulty. [7] Therefore purify your heart from double-mindedness and put on faith, because it is powerful, and believe God, that all of your requests which you ask you will receive, and if when making a request of the Lord you receive it more slowly *than you expect*, do not be double-minded because you did not quickly receive the request of your soul, by all means for *it is* because of some temptation or some sin which you yourself are ignorant of *that* you receive your request more slowly *than you expect*. [8] Therefore you do not stop making the request of your soul, and you will receive it, but if you

---

a. Literally "he himself is without malice"
b. Literally "from all of your petitions you will not be lacking"
c. Literally "they never obtain any"

become discouraged and double-minded when asking, blame yourself and not the one who gives to you. [9] Watch out for this double-mindedness, for it is evil and senseless, and it uproots many from the faith, yes, even *the* very faithful and powerful *ones*. For this double-mindedness is also a daughter of the devil and it does great wrong to the servant of God. [10] Therefore despise double-mindedness and exercise dominion over it in every way, putting on the faith which *is* strong and powerful. For faith promises all things *and* perfects all things, but double-mindedness, not trusting itself, fails in all of the deeds which it attempts. [11] So you see," he said, "that faith is from above, from the Lord, and it has great power, but double-mindedness is an earthly spirit, from the devil, having no power. [12] Therefore you serve the faith which has power, and abstain from double-mindedness which has no power, and you will live to God and everyone who thinks these things will live to God."

COMMANDMENT 10

10.1 *The Evil of Grief*

[40.1] "Take away from yourself," he said, "grief, for this is also a sister of double-mindedness and of bad temper." [2] "How," I said, "sir, is it a sister of these? For it seems to me bad temper is one thing, and double-mindedness another and grief another." "You are foolish, man!" he said, "and you do not understand that grief is more evil than all of the spirits, and most terrible to the servants of God, and beyond all the spirits corrupts a person and exhausts the holy spirit[a] and saves again?" [3] "I," I said, "sir, am foolish and do not understand these parables. For how it is possible to exhaust and again to be saved? I do not understand." [4] "Listen," he said, "those who have never inquired concerning the truth and who do not search about the deity but who have only believed, and who are mixed up with business affairs and riches and heathen friendships and with many other occupations of this world. Therefore, as many as are involved in these things, they do not understand the parables of the deity, for they are obscured by these deeds and are corrupted and have become barren. [5] Just as the good vineyards,

---

a. Here the spirit is "holy" in contrast to the evil spirits; this is not an explicit reference to the Holy Spirit.

when they experience neglect, become barren by the thorns and various weeds, so too people who have believed and who have fallen into these many deeds which have been previously mentioned are misled by their way of thinking and they really understand nothing about righteousness, but even when they hear about deity and truth, their understanding has been busied with their deed and they really understand nothing. ⁶ But those who have fear of God and who investigate into deity and truth and who have a heart to the Lord, everything that is said to them they quickly understand and perceive, because they have the fear of the Lord in themselves, for where the Lord dwells, there also is much understanding. Therefore cling to the Lord and you will understand and perceive everything."

10.1 The Evil of Grief

⁴¹·¹ "Therefore listen," he said, "foolish man, how grief exhausts the Holy Spirit and saves again. ² When the double-minded one undertakes some work and this work fails because of his double-mindedness, this grief enters into the person and grieves the Holy Spirit and exhausts it. ³ Then again, when bad temper clings to a person regarding some matter, and he becomes very bitter, again grief enters into the heart of the person who is irritable, and he is grieved by his deed which he did, and he repents because he committed evil. ⁴ Therefore this grief seems to bring salvation because, having done evil, he repented. So both deeds grieve the Spirit: double-mindedness because it did not achieve its purpose, and bad temper grieves the Spirit because it did evil. So both are distressing to the Holy Spirit, double-mindedness and bad temper. ⁵ Therefore remove grief from yourself and do not oppress the Holy Spirit which is dwelling in you, lest it appeal to God and depart from you. ⁶ For the Spirit of God that was given to this flesh grief does not endure or distress."

⁴²·¹ "Therefore put on cheerfulness, which always has favor with God and which is acceptable to him, and indulge in it. For every cheerful person does good things and thinks good things and despises grief. ² But the mournful one always does wrong. First, he does wrong because he grieves the Holy Spirit, the cheerful one, which was given to him. And second, grieving the Holy Spirit he works lawlessness, not interceding or confessing to the

Lord. For the intercession of the mournful one ⌊never has the power⌋[a] to ascend to the altar of God." 3 "Why," I said, "does the intercession of the mournful one not ascend to the altar?" "Because," he said, "grief resides in his heart. Therefore grief, having been mixed with intercession, does not permit the intercession to ascend upon the altar in purity. For just as vinegar and wine, having been mixed ⌊together⌋,[b] do not have the same pleasant taste, so also grief, having been mixed with the Holy Spirit, does not have the same intercession. 4 Therefore purify yourself from this evil grief and you will live to God, and everyone will live to God, whoever casts off grief from themselves and puts on all cheerfulness."

COMMANDMENT 11

11.1 True and False Prophets

43.1 He showed me people sitting upon a bench and another person sitting upon a chair. And he said to me, "Do you see the people sitting upon the bench?" "I see," I said, "sir." "These," he said, "are faithful, and the one who sits upon the chair is a false prophet who destroys the mind of the servants of God. But he destroys the double-minded, not the faithful. 2 Therefore these double-minded ones, like to a soothsayer, they come and ask him what possibly will happen to them, and that false prophet, having no power of the divine spirit in himself, speaks with them according to their questions and according to the lust of their wickedness, and he fulfills their souls, just as they themselves desire. 3 For he, being empty, also gives empty answers to empty *people*, for whatever he is asked, according to the emptiness of man he answers. But he also speaks some true words, for the devil fills him with his spirit, *to see* if he will be able to rip apart any of the righteous. 4 Therefore as many as are strong in the faith of the Lord, having put on the truth, do not cling to spirits such as these, but remove yourself from them. But as many as are double-minded and change their minds constantly, they also prophesy like the heathen and bring great sin upon themselves, being idolaters. For the one who asks a false prophet about any deed is an idolater and empty of the truth and foolish. 5 For every spirit

---

a. Literally "always has no power"
b. Literally "into the same [vessel]"

which is given from God does not ask questions but having the power of the deity speaks all things from itself, because it is from above, from the power of the divine spirit. [6] But the spirit which is questioned and speaks according to the lusts of humanity is earthly and frivolous, having no power, and does not speak at all unless it is asked." [7] "How then," I said, "sir, will a person know which of them is a prophet and which a false prophet?" "Listen," he said, "regarding both of the prophets, and as I am about to tell you, so you will test the prophet and the false prophet. Test the person who has the divine spirit by his life. [8] First, the one who has the spirit from above is gentle and quiet and humble, and abstains from all wickedness and futile lusts of this age, and makes himself poorer than all of humanity, and he answers nothing to anyone when asked, and he does not speak by himself (nor does the holy spirit speak when a person wants to speak), but he speaks at that time when God wants him to speak. [9] Therefore when the person who has the divine spirit comes into the assembly of righteous men who have the faith of the divine spirit, and intercession is made to God by the assembly of those men, then the angel of the prophetic spirit who rests with him, he fills the person, and being filled, the person with the Holy Spirit speaks to the group just as the Lord desires. [10] Therefore thus will the divine spirit be evident. Such, then, is this power regarding the divine spirit of the Lord. [11] Listen now," he said, "about the earthly and empty spirit, which does not have power but is foolish. [12] First, that person who seems to have a spirit exalts himself and desires to have the best seat, and he is immediately bold and shameless and talkative, and conducting himself in many luxuries and in many other deceits, and receiving wages for his prophecy, but if he does not receive *wages*, he does not prophesy. Therefore is it possible for a divine spirit to receive wages and prophesy? It is not possible for the prophet of God to do this, but the spirit of prophets such as these is earthly. [13] Then he does not come near at all to the assembly of righteous men, but he escapes from them and joins himself with the double-minded and empty, and he prophesies them into a corner and deceives them, speaking all things in vain according to their lusts, for he also answers the empty ones. For the empty vessel placed with the empties is not broken, but they match one another. [14] But when he comes into an assembly full of righteous men who have a divine spirit and intercession is made by them, that person is emptied and the earthly spirit flees from him in fear and that person is rendered speechless and is altogether broken,[a] not able to say anything. [15] For if you store wine or olive oil in a cellar and put an empty jar among them, and you want to make the storehouse empty again, that jar which you put in empty you will find still empty. Thus also the empty prophets, when they come to the spirits of the righteous, they also are found *to be* such as those *were* when they came. [16] You have the life of both of the prophets. Therefore test by deeds and life the person who declares himself to be a spirit-bearer. [17] But you, you believe in the spirit which comes from God and has power, but believe in no way the earthly and empty spirit, because there is no power in it, for it comes from the devil. [18] Therefore hear the parable which I am about to tell you. Take a stone and throw *it* into the sky. See if you are able to touch it.[b] Or again, take a pump of water and squirt *it* into the sky. See if you are able to make a hole in the sky." [19] "How," I said, "sir, it is possible for these things to be? For both of these things you have spoken *are* impossible." "Therefore like these things," he said, "are impossible, so also the earthly spirits are incapable and powerless. [20] Therefore take the power which comes from above. The hail is a very small, tiny grain and when it falls upon someone's head, how much pain it causes! Or again, take a drop which falls from the roof tile on the ground and makes a hole in the stone. [21] You see, then, that the smallest things which fall down upon the earth from above have great power. So also the divine spirit which comes from above is powerful. Therefore believe in this spirit, but stay away from the other."

COMMANDMENT 12

12.1 *Evil Desire Destroys*

[44.1] He said to me, "Remove from yourself all evil desire and put on the good and honorable desire, for putting on this desire you will hate the evil desire and will curb it, just as you wish. [2] For the evil desire is savage, and is tamed with difficulty, for it is fearful and utterly destroys people with its savagery, but especially if a servant of God fall into it and not be

---

a. BDAG comments on the usage of this word in Hermas: "[Used] in imagery of a wine jug that when empty can bang against others similarly empty without breaking, but in encounter w[ith] a full one is broken: of a false prophet encountering spirit-filled Christians."

b. The reference is to the sky.

sensible, ₁he is dreadfully ruined by it₁.ᵃ But it destroys those such as this, who do not have the garment of good desire but are mixed up with this world. These, then, it hands over to death." ³ "What," I said, "sir, are the deeds of the evil desire which hand over people to death? Explain *them* to me that I may abstain from them." "Listen," he said, "by what deeds the evil desire destroys the servants of God."

12.2 The Deeds of Evil Desire

⁴⁵˙¹ "Above all is the desire for a wife or husband belonging to another, and for the extravagance of riches, and many worthless foods and intoxicating drinks, and for many other foolish luxuries. For all luxury is foolish and vain for the servants of God. ² Therefore these desires are evil, bringing death to the servants of God. For this evil desire is a daughter of the devil. Therefore it is necessary to abstain from the evil desires, that by abstaining, you may live to God. ³ But as many as are overcome by them and are not resistant to them, ₁they will utterly perish₁,ᵇ for these desires are fatal. ⁴ But you, you put on the desire of righteousness, and being armed with the fear of the Lord, resist them. For the fear of God dwells in the good desire. If the evil desire sees you armed with the fear of God and resisting it, it will flee far away from you and it will no longer be seen by you, fearing your weaponry. ⁵ Therefore you, having conquered *it* and being crowned over it, you come to the desire of righteousness, and delivering to it the victory which you have won, serve it just as it wishes. If you serve the good desire and are under submission to it, you will be able to overcome the evil desire and bring it under control, just as you wish.

12.3 Difficulty of Doing the Good Desire

⁴⁶˙¹ "I would like," I said, "sir, to know in what ways it is necessary for me to serve the good desire." "Listen," he said, "practice righteousness and virtue, truth and fear of the Lord, faith and gentleness and whatever good things are like these things. By practicing these things you will be a pleasing servant of God and will live to him. And all who serve the good desire will live to God." ² Therefore he finished the twelve commandments and he

---

a. Literally "he is terribly destroyed by it"
b. Literally "they will perish to the end"

said to me, "You have these commandments; walk in them. And earnestly plead with those who hear, that their repentance may be pure the rest of the days of their life. ³ This ministry which I give to you, carefully complete it and you will accomplish much, for you will find favor in those who are about to repent. And they will obey your words, for I will be with you and will compel them to obey you." ⁴ I said to him, "Sir, these commandments are great and good and glorious, and are able to cheer up the heart of the one who is able to keep them. But I do not know if these commandments are able to be kept by anyone because they are very hard." ⁵ Answering, he said to me, "If you plan with yourself that they are able to be kept, you will easily keep them and they will not be hard. But if it has already entered into your heart that they are not able to be kept by anyone, you will not keep them. ⁶ But now I say to you, if these you do not keep but you disregard them, you will not have salvation, neither your children nor your household, since you have already judged for yourself these commandments are not able to be kept by anyone."

12.4 Put the Lord into Your Heart

⁴⁷·¹ And he spoke these things to me very angrily, so that I was confused and feared him very much, for his form changed so that a person could not endure his anger. ² But upon seeing me completely disturbed and confused, he began to speak to me more gently and cheerfully, and he said, "Foolish, senseless, and double-minded one! Do you not understand the glory of God, how great and strong and wonderful it is, because he created the world for the sake of humanity, and he subjected all of his creation to humanity, and he gave all authority to him, to exercise dominion over all things under heaven? ³ Therefore if," he said, "man is lord of all creatures of God, and becomes master of all, is it not also possible to master these commandments? He is able," he said, "to master all things and all of these commandments, the one who has the Lord in his heart. ⁴ But those who have the Lord upon their lips, but their heart is hardened and they are far away from the Lord, to these people these commandments are demanding and difficult to walk in. ⁵ Therefore, you who are empty and frivolous in the faith, put the Lord into your heart, and you will know that nothing is easier than or sweeter than or more kind than these commandments. ⁶ Be converted, you who walk in the commandments of the devil, which

are difficult and bitter and savage and licentious, and do not be afraid of the devil, because in him there is no power against you. [7] For I, the angel of repentance who masters him, will be with you. The devil only causes fear, but fear of him has no force. Therefore do not fear him and he will flee from you."

12.5 Be Strengthened in the Lord

[48.1] I said to him, "Sir, listen to a few words from me." "Say," he said, "what you wish." "Indeed, a person," I said, "sir, is eager to keep the commandments of God, and there is no one who does not ask from the Lord that he be strengthened in his commandments and submit to them, but the devil is demanding and he oppresses them." [2] "He is not able," he said, "to oppress the servants of God who hope in him with *their* whole heart. The devil is able to wrestle, but he is not able to win the match. Therefore, if you resist him, being conquered he will flee from you, having been put to shame. But whoever," he said, "is empty is afraid of the devil, as if *he* had power. [3] When a person fills many jars of good wine and in those jars a few are quite empty, he comes to the jars and does not consider the full ones, for he knows that they are full. But he notices the empty ones, fearing that |they turn into vinegar|,[a] for the mostly empty jars |turn into vinegar|[b] quickly and the taste[c] of the wine is ruined. [4] So also the devil comes to all the servants of God, tempting them. Therefore as many as are filled with the faith, they resist him powerfully, and he departs from them, not having a place where he may enter. Therefore he comes then, to the nearly empty ones, and having a place he also enters into them and what he wants in them he does, and they become enslaved to him."

12.6 Do Not Be Afraid of the Devil

[49.1] "But I, the angel of repentance, I say to you: do not be afraid of the devil, for I was sent," he said, "to be with you who repent with your whole heart, and to strengthen you[d] in the faith. [2] Therefore believe in God, you who

---

a. Literally "they have turned sour"

b. Literally "turn sour"

c. Num 11:8; Wis 16:20

d. The "you" here is plural, and the reference is to "you who repent with with your whole heart."

have given up your life as hopeless because of your sin, and have added to *your* sins and have weighed down your life, because if you turn to the Lord with your whole heart and do righteousness the remaining days of your life and serve him rightly, according to his will, he will heal your former sins and you will have power to master the deeds of the devil. But do not be at all afraid of the threat of the devil, for he is powerless, just like the sinews of a dead man. ³ So listen to me and fear the one who is able *to do* all things, to save and to destroy. And keep these commandments and you will live to God." ⁴ I said to him, "Sir, now I have been strengthened in all the commandments of the Lord because you are with me. And I know that you will overcome all the power of the devil, and we shall master him and will win the victory over all of his deeds. And I hope, sir, I am able to keep these commandments which you have commanded, the Lord giving strength." ⁵ "You will keep *them*," he said, "if your heart is also pure to the Lord. And everyone will keep *them*, whoever might purify their hearts from the worthless lusts of this world, and they will live to God."

THE PARABLES

PARABLE 1

1.1 *Christians Are Strangers in This World*

⁵⁰·¹ He said to me, "You know that you dwell in a foreign country, you, the servants of God, for your city is far from this city. If, then, you know," he said, "your city in which you are about to dwell, why do you prepare fields and costly furnishings and worthless buildings and rooms here? ² Therefore the one who prepares these things for this city is not able to return to his own city. ³ Foolish and double-minded and wretched man! Do you not understand that these things are all foreign and are under the power of another? For the ruler of this city will say, 'I do not want you to dwell in my city, but go out of this city because you do not use my laws.' ⁴ You, then, having fields and houses and many other possessions, being cast out by him, what will you do with your field and house and all the rest *of the things* you prepared for yourself? For the ruler of this region says to you rightly, 'Either use my laws or get out of my region!' ⁵ Therefore what are you about to do, having a law in your city? Because of your fields and

remaining possessions, will you totally deny your law and will you walk in the law of this city? Take care that it is not [against your best interest] [a] to deny your law, for if you want to return to your city, you will not ever be welcome because you have denied the law of your city and will be banished from it. [6] Therefore you take care, as if dwelling in a foreign country. Prepare for yourself nothing extra, only your sufficient contentment, and be ready that when the master of this city wants to expel you, being in opposition to his law, you may go out of his city and depart into your city, and use your law without insolence, rejoicing greatly. [7] Therefore watch out, you who serve the Lord and who have him in your heart. Do the deeds of God, remembering his commandments and his promises which he promised, and believe him, that he will do them if his commandments are kept. [8] Instead of fields, then, purchase afflicted souls as each is able, and care for [b] widows and orphans and do not overlook them, and spend all your riches and furnishings for fields and houses such as these, which you have received from God. [9] For [this is why] [c] the Master made you rich, that you might fulfill these ministries for him. It is much better to buy fields and properties and houses such as these, which you will find in your city when you return to it. [10] This extravagance is beautiful and holy, not having grief or fear but having joy. Therefore have nothing to do with the extravagance of the heathen, for it is harmful to you, the servants of God. [11] But accomplish your own extravagance in which you are able to rejoice and not counterfeit or touch what belongs to another, or lust after it, for it is evil to lust after what belongs to another, but do your own work and you will be saved."

PARABLE 2

2.1 *The Elm Tree and the Vine*

[51.1] I was walking in the country and noticed an elm tree and a vine, and was thinking about them and their fruit. The shepherd appeared to me and

---

a. Literally "disadvantageous"
b. Jas 1:27
c. Literally "for this"

said, "What ₁are you asking yourself₁ ᵃ about the elm tree and the vine?" "I am
considering," I said, "sir, that they are well suited to one another." ² "These
two trees," he said, "are given as a type for the servants of God." "I would
like," I said, "to know the type of these trees of which you speak." "Do you
see," he said, "the elm tree and the vine?" "I see," I said, "sir." ³ "The vine,"
he said, "this *vine* bears fruit, but the elm tree is unfruitful. But this vine,
₁unless it climbs₁ ᵇ the elm, it is not able to bear much fruit, being spread
on the ground, and what fruit it bears, it bears rotten, not hanging upon
the elm. Therefore when the vine is attached to the elm, it bears fruit
from itself and from the elm. ⁴ Therefore you see that the elm tree also
gives much fruit, not less than the vine but instead even more." "How," I
said, "sir, even more?" "Because," he said, "the vine, hanging upon the elm,
gives abundant and beautiful fruit, but being spread on the ground it bears
sparse and rotten *fruit*. Therefore this parable is applicable to the servants
of God, to the poor and the rich." ⁵ "How," I said, "sir? Make it known to me."
"Listen," he said. "The rich person has wealth, but he is poor to the Lord,
being distracted with his own riches, and he has very little intercession and
praise ᶜ to the Lord, and what he has *is* feeble and small and has no other
power. Therefore when the rich person relies upon the poor and supplies
to him what is necessary, he believes that if he does *something* for the poor,
he will be able to find a reward with God because the poor person is rich
in intercession and in praise, and his intercession has great power with
God. Therefore the rich person provides all things without hesitation to
the poor. ⁶ But the poor person, being provided for by the rich, intercedes
to God, giving thanks to him ᵈ for the one who gives to him, ᵉ and that one ᶠ
₁is even more zealous₁ ᵍ for the poor, that ₁he may lack nothing₁ ʰ in his life,
for he knows that the intercession of the poor is acceptable and rich to the
Lord. ⁷ Therefore both *of them* complete the work: the poor person works in

---

a. Literally "do you seek in yourself"

b. Literally "if it does not grow upon"

c. According to BDAG, some (Dibelius, et. al.) see ἐξομολόγησις meaning "prayer of thanks-
giving" here due to its proximity with "intercession."

d. Here the referent is God.

e. Here the referent is the poor person.

f. Here "that one" refers to "the one who gives," who is the rich person.

g. Literally "still is more zealous"

h. Literally "he might be without failing"

intercession, in which he is rich, which he received from the Lord; this he pays back to the Lord who provides to him. And the rich person likewise supplies without hesitation the wealth which he received from the Lord to the poor. And this work is great and acceptable with God because the rich person understands about his wealth and works for the poor with the gifts of the Lord and completes the ministry rightly. [8] Therefore, among people the elm tree seems not to bear fruit, and they do not know or understand that when there is drought, the elm tree, having water, nourishes the vine, and the vine, continuously having water, gives double the fruit, both for itself and for the elm. So also the poor, interceding to the Lord for the rich, complement their wealth, and again the rich, providing to the poor what is necessary, complement their prayers. [9] Therefore they both become partners in the righteous work. Therefore the one who does these things will not be deserted by God, but will be recorded in the books of the living. [10] Blessed *are* those who have *wealth* and understand that they have been made wealthy by the Lord, for the one who understands this will also be able to do some good ministry."

PARABLE 3

3.1 *Trees in the Winter*

[52.1] He showed me many trees ˌwithoutˌ[a] leaves but seemed to me to be dried up, as it were, for they were all alike. And he said to me, "Do you see these trees?" "I see," I said, "sir, *them* being alike, and dried up." Answering me he said, "These trees which you see are those who dwell in this world." [2] "Therefore why," I said, "sir, are they dried up, as it were, and alike?" "Because," he said, "neither the righteous nor the sinners ˌare distinguishableˌ[b] in this world, but they are alike. For this world is winter to the righteous and ˌthey are indistinguishable,ˌ[c] living with the sinners. [3] For just as in the winter the trees, having shed their leaves, are alike and which are

---

a. Literally "not having"
b. Literally "are made apparent"
c. Literally "they are not made apparent"

dried up or alive ₍is indistinguishable₎, ͣ so in this world neither the righteous nor the sinners ₍are distinguished₎, ᵇᶜ but all are alike."

4.1 Budding and Dried-up Trees

⁵³·¹ He showed me again many trees, some of which were budding, others of which *were* dried up, and he said to me, "Do you see," he said, "these trees?" "I see *them*," I said, "sir, some budding, others dried up." ² "These trees," he said, "which are budding are the righteous who ₍are destined to live₎ ͩ in the age which is coming, for the age which is coming is summertime to the righteous but winter to the sinners. So when the mercy of the Lord shines forth, then those who serve God will be revealed, and everyone will be revealed. ³ For just as in the summer the fruit of each individual tree appears and they are recognized for what kind *of fruit* they are, so also the fruit of the righteous will be made plain and they all will be known, thriving in that age. ⁴ But the heathen and the sinners, the dried-up trees which you saw, such as these, will be found dried up and fruitless in that age, and will be burned up like wood and will be made evident because their deeds in their life have been evil. For the sinners will be burned because they sinned and did not repent, but the heathen will be burned because they did not know the one who created them. ⁵ You, therefore, bear fruit so that your fruit may be known in that summer. But avoid ₍many business activities₎ ͤ and you will in no way go wrong, for those ₍who always pursue business₎ ᶠ ₍also pursue sin₎, ᵍ being distracted by their deeds and in no way serving their Lord. ⁶ Therefore how," he said, "can such a person ask for anything from the Lord and receive *it*, not serving the Lord? The ones who serve him, those people will receive their requests, but the ones who do

---

a. Literally "is not made apparent"

b. Literally "are made apparent"

c. Due to the way negatives work in Greek, this verb+negator structure "are indistinguishable/not distinguished" is redundant in the English translation, which (given the neither/nor) has already negated the statement.

d. Literally "are about to dwell"

e. Literally "much business"

f. Literally "who does much"

g. Literally "also sin much"

not serve the Lord, those people will receive nothing. [7] But if ₁anyone is occupied with one business₁, [a] he is also able to serve the Lord, for his mind will not be corrupted away from the Lord, but he will serve him, having his mind pure. [8] Therefore if you do these things you are able to bear fruit into the coming age. And whoever does these things will bear fruit."

PARABLE 5

5.1 The Acceptable Fast

[54.1] While fasting and sitting on a certain mountain and giving thanks to the Lord for all that he did with me, I saw the shepherd sitting beside me and saying, "Why have you come here so early in the morning?" "Because," I said, "sir, I have a station." [2] "What," he said, "is a 'station'?" "I am fasting," I said, "sir." "But," he said, "what fast is this which you fast?" "As I have been accustomed," I said, "sir, so I fast." [3] "You do not know how," he said, "to fast to the Lord, and it is not a fast, this useless fast which you fast for him." "Why," I said, "sir, do you say this?" "I say to you," he said, "that it is not a fast, this fast which you think to fast, but I myself will teach you what an acceptable and complete fast to the Lord is. Listen," he said. [4] "God does not want such a worthless fast, for fasting in this way to God you will do nothing for righteousness. But fast to God a fast such as this: [5] Do no wrong in your life, but serve the Lord with a pure heart; keep his commandments, walking in his ordinances; and let no evil desire enter into your heart. And believe in God, that if you do these things and fear him and exercise self-control over every evil deed, you will live to God. And if you will do these things, you will accomplish a great and acceptable fast to God."

5.2 The Vineyard and the Slave

[55.1] "Listen to the parable which I am about to tell you which relates to fasting. [2] A certain man had a field and many slaves. And on a certain part of the field he planted a vineyard. And choosing a certain faithful, pleasing, and honored [b] slave, he called him and said to him, 'Take this vine-

---

a. Literally "anyone works one deed"

b. ἔντιμον Lake, Lightfoot] αὐτῷ ἀποδηῶν Holmes, Ehrman. The difference affects the whole phrase. Lake translates "in good esteem and honor," appending onto the phrase. The

yard which I planted and fence it until I come, and do not do otherwise to the vineyard. And keep this commandment of mine and you will gain freedom from me.' And the master of the slave went out on his journey. ³ And when he had gone, the servant took and fenced in the vineyard. And finishing the fencing in of the vineyard, he saw *that* the vineyard was full of weeds. ⁴ Therefore he reasoned to himself, saying, 'This commandment of the master I have accomplished; next I will cultivate this vineyard, and it will look even better after cultivation. And not having weeds, it will produce even more fruit, not being choked by the weeds.' After taking *it*, he cultivated the vineyard and all the weeds which were in the vineyard, he pulled *them* out. And that vineyard was looking its best and thriving, not having weeds choking it. ⁵ After some time, the master of the slave and of the field came. And he entered into the vineyard and upon seeing the vineyard attractively fenced in, and in addition also cultivated and all the weeds pulled out and the vines thriving, he rejoiced greatly because of the work of the servant. ⁶ Therefore calling his beloved son, who was *his* heir, and his friends who were counselors, he said to them what he commanded to his servant and what he found accomplished, and those people rejoiced with the servant because of the testimony which the master testified to him. ⁷ And he said to them, 'I promised freedom to this servant if he might keep my commandment which I commanded to him. And he kept my commandment and added good work to the vineyard, and I was exceedingly pleased. Therefore because of this work which he has done, I want to make him a fellow heir with my son, because the good which he thought *to do* he did not disregard but accomplished it.' ⁸ The son of the master agreed with this his intention, that the slave might become a fellow heir with the son. ⁹ After a few days, he made a feast and sent much food to him from the feast. But the servant, after receiving the food which was sent to him from the master, kept what was sufficient for him and distributed the rest to his fellow servants. ¹⁰ And his fellow servants, after receiving the food, rejoiced and began to pray for him, that he might find greater favor from the master because he had treated them in this way. ¹¹ All these things that happened, his master heard and again rejoiced exceedingly because of his

---

difference in Holmes and Ehrman is significant, adding "[pleasing] to him. When he was about to go on a journey."

action. The master, again summoning his friends and his son, reported to them his deed, what he did with his food which he received. And they were in even more agreement *that* the slave should become a fellow heir with his son."

5.3 Accomplishing the Acceptable Fast

56.1 I said, "Sir, I do not know these parables nor am I able to understand unless you explain them to me." **2** "I will explain everything to you," he said, "and whatever I talk *about* with you. **3** I will show his [a] commandments to you, and if you do anything good beyond the commandment of God, you will acquire even greater glory for yourself, and with God you will be even more honorable than what you were about to be. Therefore if, keeping the commandments of God, you also add these services, you will rejoice if you observe them according to my commandment." **4** I said to him, "Sir, whatever you command me I will keep it, for I know that you yourself are with me." "I will be," he said, "with you because you have such eagerness for doing good. And I will also be with everyone," he said, "who possesses this eagerness. **5** This fast," he said, "by keeping the commandments of the Lord, is very good. Therefore you will keep this fast which you are about to observe as follows: **6** First of all, abstain from every evil word and every evil lust and purify your heart from all of the worthless things of this world. If you observe these things, this will be to you the perfect fast. **7** And you will do as follows: after completing what has been written in that day on which you fast, you will taste nothing except bread and water, and of your food which you would have eaten, after calculating the amount of the cost of that day which you would have expended, you will give it to the widow or orphan or someone in need, and thus you will be humble-minded that the one who receives from your humility, may his own soul be filled and may he pray on your behalf to the Lord. **8** Therefore if thus you accomplish the fast as I commanded you, your sacrifice will be acceptable to God, and

---

a. δείξω σοι τὰς ἐντολὰς αὐτοῦ Lightfoot, Lake, Ehrman] δείξω σοι τὰς ἐντολὰς τοῦ κυρίου φύλασσε καὶ ἔσῃ εὐάρεστος αὐτῷ καὶ ἐγγραφήσῃ εἰς τὸν ἀριθμὸν τῶν τηρούντων τὰς ἐντολὰς αὐτοῦ Holmes. The difference in translation is from "I will show you his commandments" (Lightfoot, Lake, Ehrman) to "and will interpret for you whatever I say to you. Keep the Lord's commandm ments, and you will be pleasing to him and will be enrolled among the number of those who keep his commandments." Also note that Lake places the text in verse 3 while the others place the text in verse 2.

this fast will be recorded, and the service which you have thus worked will be good and cheerful and acceptable to the Lord. [9] These things thus you will observe, you with your children and your whole family. And observing them, you will be blessed, and whoever upon hearing observes them, he will be blessed, and whatever he asks from the Lord, he will receive."

5.4 Understanding the Parable

[57.1] I pleaded with him much, that he might make known to me the parable of the field and the master and the vineyard and the servant who fenced in the vineyard and the fence and the weeds which were pulled out from the vineyard and the son and the friends, the counselors. For I understood that all these things are a parable. [2] And the one who answered said to me, "You are very arrogant to ask. You ought not," he said, "to ask anything at all, for if it is necessary to explain to you, it will be explained." I said to him, "Sir, whatever you make known to me and do not explain I will have seen it in vain, and will not understand what it is. Likewise also, if you speak parables to me and do not explain them to me, I will have heard something from you in vain." [3] And he again answered me, saying, "Whoever," he said, "is a servant of God and has his Lord in his heart asks for understanding from him and receives it, and he explains every parable, and the sayings of the Lord which were spoken through parables, they become known to him. But as many as are feeble and idle in intercession, those hesitate to ask from the Lord. [4] But the Lord is rich in compassion and to all who ask from him he gives unceasingly. But you, having been strengthened by the holy angel and having received such intercession from him and are not idle, why do you not ask for understanding from the Lord and receive it from him?" [5] I said to him, "Sir, since I have you with me, I have necessity to ask you and to inquire of you, for you show all things to me and speak with me, but if I had seen or had heard them without you, I would have asked the Lord, that he might make it clear to me."

5.5 The Explanation of the Parable of the Field

[58.1] "I told you," he said, "even now, that you are crafty and arrogant, asking for the explanations of the parables. But since you are so persistent, I will explain to you the parable of the field and the rest of all that follows, that you may make them known to everyone. Listen now," he said, "and understand them. ² The field is this world, and the master of the field is the one who created all things and perfected and strengthened them. And the servant is the Son of God, and the vines are this people which he himself planted. ³ And the fences are the holy angels of the Lord who support his people. And the weeds which were pulled out from the vineyard are lawless deeds of the servants of God. And the food which was sent to him from the feast are the commandments which he gave to his people through his Son, and the friends and counselors *are* the holy angels who were first created. And the absence of the master is the time which remains until his coming." ⁴ I said to him, "Sir, all is great and wonderful, and all is glorious. How, then," I said, "could I have understood these things? Nor ₁anyone else₁, ᵃ even if extremely intelligent, ₁no one would₁ ᵇ be able to understand them. Yet," I said, "sir, explain to me what I am about to ask you." ⁵ "Speak," he said, "if you want something." "Why," I said, "sir, does the Son of God appear in the guise of a servant in the parable?"

5.6 The Son of God in the Parable

⁵⁹·¹ "Listen," he said, "the Son of God does not appear in the guise of a servant, but appears in great power and lordship." "How," I said, "sir? I do not understand." ² "Because," he said, "God planted the vineyard, that is, he created the people, and gave it over to his Son. And the Son appointed the angels over them to preserve them, and he himself purified their sin, laboring much and enduring ᶜ much toil. For no vineyard is able to be cultivated apart from toil or hardship. ³ Therefore he, having purified the sins of the people, he made known to them the well-worn paths of life, giving them the law which he received from his Father. ⁴ But why ᵈ did the Lord take his Son and the glorious angels as counselor concerning the inheritance of the

---

a. Literally "another of the people"

b. Literally "anyone might not"

c. The figurative sense of "endure" does not occur in the NT. BDAG notes the figurative sense "develops out of the idea of constantly drawing from a source, in this case, troubles."

d. ὅτι Lake] βλέπεις, φησίν, ὅτι αὐτὸς κύριός ἐστι τοῦ λαοῦ, ἐξουσίαν πᾶσαν λαβὼν παρὰ τοῦ πατρὸς αὐτοῦ. ὅτι Lightfoot, Ehrman, Holmes. Here Lake omits a conjecture from Gebhardt (based on the Latin) that others include, positing *homoioteleuton*. The difference is adding "'You see,' he said, 'that he is Lord of the people, having received all power from his Father.'" Note that Ehrman includes this text in verse three of his Greek text, but includes the text in verse four of his translation.

servant? Listen. [5] The Holy Spirit, which pre-exists, which created all creation, God caused to dwell in the flesh that he desired. Therefore this flesh
in which the Holy Spirit dwelled served the Spirit well, walking in holiness
and purity, in no way at all defiling the Spirit. [6] Therefore it, [a] having lived
commendably and purely, and having labored together with the Spirit and
having worked together in all deeds, behaving strongly and bravely, he took
it as partner with the Holy Spirit. For the conduct of this flesh pleased *him*
because it was not defiled upon the earth while possessing the Holy Spirit.
[7] Therefore he took the Son and the glorious angels as counselor, that this
flesh also, having served the Spirit blamelessly, might have some dwelling
place, and not seem to have lost the reward of its service. For all flesh will
receive a reward, the *flesh* found undefiled and without fault, in which
the Holy Spirit has dwelt. [8] You also have the explanation of this parable."

5.7 Flesh and Spirit

[60.1] "I am glad," I said, "sir, having heard this explanation." "Listen now," he
said, "guard this flesh of yours, pure and undefiled, that the spirit which
dwells in it may bear witness to it, and your flesh may be justified. [2] See
to it that it does not enter into your heart *that* this flesh of yours is mortal,
and that you might misuse it in some defilement. If you defile your flesh,
you will also defile the Holy Spirit, and if you defile the body, you will not
live." [3] "But if," I said, "sir, there was any previous ignorance before these
words were heard, how can the person who defiled his flesh be saved?"
"Because of the previous sins committed in ignorance," [b] he said, "God alone
is able to give healing, for all authority is his [4] if, [c] for the remaining *time*,
you defile neither your flesh nor your spirit, for both are in common and
apart from each other are not able to be defiled. Therefore keep both pure
and you will live to God."

---

a. This is a reference to "the flesh"

b. Heb 9.7; 1 Macc 13.39; Tob 3.3; Sir 23.2

c. ἐάν Lake] ἀλλὰ νῦν φύλασσε σεαυτόν, καὶ ὁ Κύριος ὁ παντοκράτωρ, πολύσπλαγχνος ὤν, περὶ
τῶν προτέρων ἀγνοημάτων ἴασιν δώσει. ἐάν. Lightfoot, Holmes, Ehrman. Lightfoot, Holmes, and
Ehrman add a conjecture. The difference is adding, "But now protect yourself, and the Lord,
who is exceedingly compassionate, will give healing for your previous acts of ignorance"
(Holmes). Lake adds: "The Editors (probably rightly) usually accept this addition."

PARABLE 6

6.1 *The Shepherd*

6.1.1 Sitting in my house and glorifying the Lord for all which I had seen, and inquiring about the commandments because *they were* beautiful and powerful and cheerful and glorious and able to save the soul of a person, I was saying to myself, "I will be blessed if I might walk in these commandments, and whoever might walk in these will be blessed." **2** While I said these things to myself, I suddenly saw him sitting beside me and saying these things: "Why are you double-minded about the commandments which I commanded you? They are beautiful. Do not be at all double-minded, but clothe yourself with the faith of the Lord and you will walk in them, for I will strengthen you in them. **3** These commandments are advantageous to those who are about to repent, for if they do not walk in them, their repentance is in vain. **4** Therefore, those who repent, you do away with the wickednesses of this world which destroy you, and having clothed yourselves with every virtue of righteousness you will be able to keep these commandments and no longer add to your sins. Therefore walk in these commandments of mine and you will live to God. All these things have been spoken to you by me." **5** And after he spoke these things with me, he said to me, "Let us go into the countryside and I will show you the shepherd of the sheep." "Let us go," I said, "sir." And we came to a field and he showed a young shepherd to me, wearing a suit of clothes, saffron-yellow in color. **6** And he was feeding very many sheep, and these sheep seemed well fed, were also very frisky, and were cheerful, leaping for joy here and there. And the shepherd himself was very cheerful over his flock, and ₁the very appearance of the shepherd₁ ª was very cheerful and he was running about among the sheep.

6.2 *The Sheep of the Shepherd*

6.2.1 And he said to me, "Do you see this shepherd?" "I see," I said, "Sir." "This," he said, "is the angel of luxury and deception. This one destroys the souls of the servants of God and turns them away from the truth, deceiving them with the evil lusts in which they are destroyed. **2** For they forget the

---

a. Literally "the appearance of the shepherd himself"

commandments of the living God and walk in deception and worthless luxury, and they are destroyed by this angel, some to death and others to destruction." ³ I said to him, "Sir, I do not know what is 'to death' and what is 'to destruction.'" "Listen," he said, "the sheep which you saw cheerful and leaping for joy, these are those which have been drawn away from God completely and have given over themselves to the lusts of this world. Among these, then, there is no repentance of life because they added to their sins and concerning the name of God, they blasphemed against it. Therefore death is for such as these. ⁴ But you saw the sheep which were not leaping for joy but were feeding in one place; these are the ones who have given themselves over to luxuries and deception, but concerning the Lord, they blasphemed against *him* in no way. Therefore these have been corrupted from the truth; in these there is hope of repentance, in which they are able to live. Corruption, then, has some hope of renewal, but death has eternal destruction." ⁵ Again I went on a little way, and he showed me a great shepherd, like a wild man in appearance, wearing a white goatskin, and he had a leather pouch upon his shoulder and a very gnarled and knotty ᵃ staff and a great whip. And he had a very bitter look, so *bitter* that I was afraid of him, *because* he had a look such as this. ⁶ Therefore this shepherd was taking the sheep from the young shepherd, those *sheep* which were frisky and well fed but were not leaping for joy, and he put them into someplace steep and thorny and full of thistles, so that the sheep could not disentangle *themselves* from the thorns and thistles, but were entangled in the thorns and thistles. ⁷ So these *sheep*, being entangled, were grazing in the thorns and thistles and they were very miserable, being beaten by him, and he was driving them about here and there, and he gave them no rest, and those sheep were not at all at peace.

6.3 The Angel of Punishment

⁶³·¹ Therefore upon seeing them so beaten and miserable, I began to grieve for them because they were so tormented and had no relief ᵇ at all. ² I said to the shepherd who was speaking with me, "Sir, who is this shepherd who *is* so merciless and bitter and has no compassion at all on these sheep?"

---

a. Wis 13:13
b. 1 Macc 12:25

"This," he said, "is the angel of punishment. But he is one of the righteous angels, and is appointed over punishment. ³ Therefore he takes those who have strayed from God and walked in the lusts and deceptions of this world and he punishes them, just as is proper, with severe and various kinds of punishments." ⁴ "I would like," I said, "sir, to know these various kinds of punishments, what kinds they are." "Listen," he said, "to the various kinds of torments and punishments. The torments are belonging to daily life, for some are punished with loss, and others with deprivations, and others with various illnesses, and others with every kind of disturbance, and others are insulted by worthless people and suffer many other things. ⁵ For many, being unsettled in their intentions, begin many *things* and nothing at all succeeds for them. And they say they do not prosper in their deeds, and it does not enter into their heart that they have done evil deeds, but they blame the Lord. ⁶ Therefore, when they are afflicted with every tribulation, then they are handed over to me for good instruction and are strengthened in the faith of the Lord. And the rest of the days of their life they serve the Lord with a pure heart. But if they repent, then it enters into their heart, those evil deeds which they did, and then they glorify God, saying that he is a righteous judge and they suffered righteously, each according to his deeds. And for the remaining *time* they serve the Lord with their pure heart, and they will prosper in ₍everything they do₎, ᵃ receiving from the Lord all things, whatever they ask for. And then they glorify the Lord that they were handed over to me, and no longer suffer evil in any way."

6.4 *Luxury and Punishment*

⁶⁴⋅¹ I said to him, "Sir, reveal this to me as well." "What," he said, "do you want to know?" "If as a result," I said, "sir, those who live in luxury and pleasure are tormented for the same time, as long as they live luxuriously and pleasurably?" He said to me, "They are tormented for the same amount of time." ² "Very little," I said, "sir, are they tormented, for those who live in such luxury and forget God ought to be tormented seven times over." ³ He said to me, "You are foolish and do not understand the power of torment." "For if I understood," I said, "sir, I would not have asked that you explain it to me." "Listen," he said, "to the power of both. ⁴ The time of luxury and

---

a. Literally "all of their deeds"

pleasure is one hour, but the hour of torment has the power of thirty days. Therefore if someone lives in luxury and pleasure one day, and is tormented for one day, the day of torment has the strength of a whole year. So as many days as one lived in luxury, he is tormented as many years. You see, then," he said, "that the time of luxury and pleasure is very short; *the time* of punishment and torment is long."

6.5 More About Luxury and Punishment

65.1 "Still," I said, "sir, I do not at all understand about the time of pleasure and luxury and torment. Explain *it* to me more clearly." 2 Answering, he said to me, "Your foolishness is constant, and you do not want to purify your heart and serve God. See to it," he said, "lest the time be fulfilled and you be found foolish. So listen," he said, "to what you want *to know*, that you may understand such things. 3 The one who lives in luxury and deception for one day and who does what he wants is clothed with great foolishness and does not understand ⌊what he does⌋. a For tomorrow he forgets what he did ⌊yesterday⌋. b For luxury and deception have no memories because of the foolishness with which they are clothed. But punishment and torment, when they cling to a person for one day, *it is as if* he is punished and tormented for a year, for punishment and torment have long memories. 4 Therefore, being tormented and punished for a whole year, then he remembers the luxury and deception and knows that he suffers evil because of them. Therefore all people who live in luxury and deception are tormented in this way because, possessing life, they hand themselves over to death." 5 "What sort," I said, "of luxuries, sir, are harmful?" He said, "Every deed is a luxury to the person who does *it* with pleasure. For even the irritable one, giving satisfaction to his own temper, lives luxuriously. And the adulterer and the drunkard and the slanderer and the liar and the greedy person and the defrauder and the one who does similar to these things gives satisfaction to his own sickness, so he lives in luxury from his deed. 6 All these luxuries are harmful to the servants of God. Therefore those who are punished and tormented suffer because of these deceptions. 7 But there are also luxuries that save people, for many who do good

---

a. Literally "the deed which he is doing"
b. Literally "the previous day"

live in luxury, carried away by their own pleasure. Therefore this luxury is advantageous to the servants of God, and brings life to such a person as this. But the harmful luxuries which were spoken of beforehand bring torments and punishments to them. But if they persist and do not repent, they will bring death upon themselves."

PARABLE 7

7.1 *The Affliction of Hermas*

66.1 After a few days I saw him in the same field where I had also seen the shepherds, and he said to me, "What do you want to know?" "I have come," I said, "sir, that you may command the punishing shepherd to leave from my house, because he afflicts me terribly." "It is necessary for you," he said, "to be afflicted. For thus," he said, "the glorious angel commanded concerning you, for he wants you to be put to the test." "For what," I said, "sir, have I done *that is* so evil that I should be handed over to this angel?" **2** "Listen," he said, "your sins *are* many, but not so many that *you* have been handed over to this angel; but your family has done great iniquities and sins, and the glorious angel is fed up [a] by their deeds. And because of this he commanded you to be afflicted for some amount of time, that those ones also might repent and purify themselves from every lust of this world. So when they repent and are purified, then the angel of punishment will depart." **3** I said to him, "Sir, if those ones have done such things that the glorious angel becomes enraged, what have I myself done?" "In some other way," he said, "those ones are not able to be afflicted unless you, the head of the household, are afflicted. For you, being afflicted, those ones also necessarily will be afflicted. But while you are at peace, they are not able to have any affliction." **4** "But look!" I said, "Sir, they have repented with their whole heart." "I myself also know," he said, "that they have repented with their whole heart. Therefore do you think the sins of those who repent immediately are forgiven? ⌞By no means⌟, [b] but it is necessary for the one who repents to torment his own soul and to be extremely humble-minded in

---

a. Osiek notes that the angel is "annoyed to the point of exasperation" and translates the verb as "fed up."

b. Literally "not completely"

all he does and to be afflicted with all kinds of various afflictions. And if he can endure the afflictions which come upon him, certainly the one who created and gave power to all things, will have compassion and will give some *measure of* healing to him. ⁵ And this certainly, when he sees that the heart of the one who repents *is* clean from every evil deed. But it is advantageous to you and to your family to be afflicted now. But why do I say so much to you? It is necessary for you to be afflicted, just as the angel of the Lord commanded, that one who handed you over to me. And you be thankful to the Lord for this, because he considered you worthy to reveal the affliction to you, that knowing beforehand, you might endure it with strength." ⁶ I said to him, "Sir, you be with me and I will be able to endure all affliction." "I," he said, "I will be with you. And I will also ask the punishing angel that he afflict you lightly. But you will be afflicted a short amount of time, and you will again be restored to your house.ᵃ Only continue being humble-minded and serving the Lord in all things with a pure heart, and your children and your household,ᵇ and walk in my commandments which to you I commanded, and your repentance will be able to be strong and pure. ⁷ And if you keep these commandments with your household, all affliction will depart from you, and also from everyone," he said, "affliction will depart whoever may walk in these commandments of mine."

PARABLE 8

8.1 *The Willow Tree*

⁶⁷·¹ He showed me a great willow tree covering fields and mountains, and under the shade of the willow tree all who were called by the name of the Lord had come. ² And there stood an angel of the Lord, glorious *and* very tall, at the willow tree, wielding a large sickle. And he was chopping off branches from the willow tree, and he gave *them* to the people, those covered by the willow tree. And he gave them little sticks, about ₗeighteen

---

a. οἶκόν Lake] τόπον Holmes, Ehrman. The difference is between "house/family/household" (Lake) and "place" (Holmes, Ehrman). The reading of Holmes and Ehrman (Osiek agrees as well) makes much more sense and seems more likely.

b. The thought here is that Hermas, his children, and his household must be humble-minded and continue to serve the Lord in all things.

inches in length_|.ᵃ ³ After all of them had received sticks, the angel put down his sickle, and that tree was healthy, like even as I had *first* seen it. ⁴ And I wondered in myself, saying, "How, having so many branches chopped off, is the tree healthy?" The shepherd said to me, "Do not wonder that this tree remains healthy, when so many branches were chopped off. But when," he said, "you have seen everything, *then* what it is will be explained to you." ⁵ The angel who had given the sticks to the people asked for them again, and just as they had received, so also they were called to him, and each one of them gave back the sticks. And the angel of the Lord took and considered them. ⁶ From some he received withered and ₁moth-eaten₁ᵇ sticks. The angel commanded those who had given such sticks to stand separately. ⁷ And others gave withered *sticks*, but they were not ₁moth-eaten₁.ᶜ And he commanded these to stand separately. ⁸ And others gave half-witheredᵈ *sticks*, and these stood separately. ⁹ And others gave their sticks, half-withered and having cracks, and these stood separately. ¹⁰ And others gave their sticks, green and having cracks, and these stood separately. ¹¹ And others gave sticks half withered and half green, and these stood separately. ¹² And others brought their sticks, ₁two-thirds₁ᵉ of the stick green and ₁one-third₁ᶠ withered, and these stood separately. ¹³ And others gave ₁two-thirds₁ᵍ withered ₁and one-third₁ʰ green, and these stood separately. ¹⁴ And others gave their sticks, a little less than completely green, but a very small portion of their sticks was withered *at* the tip. And they had cracks in them, and these stood separately. ¹⁵ And of others there was a very small portion of green and the rest of the stick *was* withered, and these stood separately. ¹⁶ And others came bringing green sticks, like they had received from the angel. And the greater part of the crowd gave such sticks. And the angel, because of this, rejoiced exceedingly, and these stood separately. ¹⁷ And others gave their sticks, green and having buds, and these stood separately,

---

a. Literally "a cubit in length"
b. Literally "eaten as if by a moth"
c. Literally "eaten by moths"
d. BDAG notes this is a compound of ἡμι-+ ξηρός (half + dried/withered).
e. Literally "two parts"
f. Literally "third"
g. Literally "two parts"
h. Literally "and the third"

and because of these the angel rejoiced exceedingly. [18] And others gave their sticks, green and having buds, and their buds had something like fruit. And those people whose sticks were found such as this were very cheerful, and the angel rejoiced greatly because of these people, and the shepherd was very cheerful because of these people.

8.2 Gathering and Planting the Sticks

[68.1] And the angel of the Lord commanded crowns to be brought, and they brought crowns, like being made of palm leaves, and he crowned the people who had given sticks which had buds and some fruit, and he sent them away into the tower. [2] And he sent away the others also into the tower, those who had given green sticks and having buds, but the buds not having fruit, giving them seals. [3] And all those who went into the tower had the same clothing, white like snow. [4] And those who had given sticks green like they had received *them*, he sent away, giving them clothing and seals. [5] After the angel had finished these things, he said to the shepherd, "I am going away, but will send you away these inside the walls, to the degree that any are worthy to dwell *there*. But consider their sticks carefully, and so send *them* away; but consider carefully. See to it that no one slips past you," he said, "but if anyone slips past you, I myself will test them at the altar." Upon saying this to the shepherd, he departed. [6] And after the angel departed, the shepherd said to me, "Let us take everyone's sticks and plant them, *to see* whether some of them will be able to live." I said to him, "Sir, these withered ones, how are they able to live?" [7] Answering me he said, "This tree is a willow tree, and the species *is* tenacious of life. So if they are planted and receive a little moisture, the sticks, many of them, will live. And then let us also try to pour water on them. If any of them can live, I will rejoice with them, but if it does not live, I will not be found negligent." [8] And the shepherd commanded me to call each of them as they stood. They came, group *by* group, and they gave their sticks to the shepherd. And the shepherd received their sticks and he planted them according to groups. And after planting, he poured much water on them, so *much* that because of the water, the sticks could not be seen. [9] And after he watered the sticks, he said to me, "Let us go, and after a few days let us return and examine all the sticks, for the one who created this tree wants everyone who received branches from this tree to live. And I myself also hope that the sticks, the greater part of them, which received this moisture and were irrigated with water, will live."

8.3 About the Tree and the Angel

[69.1] I said to him, "Sir, this tree, make known to me what it is, for I am perplexed about it because ₍even with so many branches chopped off₎,[a] the tree is healthy and nothing appears to have been chopped from it. Therefore in this I am perplexed." [2] "Listen," he said, "this great tree which covers fields and mountains and all the earth is the law of God which was given to the whole world. And this law is the Son of God being preached to the ends of the earth. And the people under the shade are those who have heard the preaching and believed in him. [3] And the angel, the great and glorious Michael, who has authority over this people and governs them, for this one is the one who puts the law into the heart of those who believe. Therefore he examines those to whom he gave *the law, to see* if, as a result, they have observed it. [4] But you see the sticks of each one; for the sticks are the law. You see, then, many sticks have been made useless, and you will know them all, those who do not observe the law, and you will see the dwelling place of each one." [5] I said to him, "Sir, why did he send some away into the tower, and leave others to you?" "As many as," he said, "have transgressed the law which they received from him, he left them to my authority for repentance. But as many as have already taken delight in the law and have observed it, he keeps them under his own authority." [6] "Therefore who," I said, "sir, are those who have been crowned and went into the tower?" "As many as," he said, "wrestled with the devil and conquered him, *these* have been crowned. These are the ones who have suffered for the law. [7] And the others also who gave their green sticks, and having buds, but not having fruit, who were afflicted for the law but who have not suffered and have not denied their law. [8] And those who gave green *sticks* like they received *are* honorable and righteous and have walked with an exceedingly pure heart, and have kept the commandments of the Lord. And the rest you will know when I consider these sticks which have been planted and watered."

---

a. Literally "when so many branches were chopped off"

8.4 Review of the Sticks (Part 1)

⁷⁰·¹ And after a few days we came to the place and the shepherd sat down in the place of the angel and I stood by him. And he said to me, "₍Put on a work apron₎ᵃ ᵇ and serve me." ₍I put on a clean work apron made of sackcloth₎.ᶜ ² And upon seeing me ₍with my work apron on₎ᵈ and ready to serve him, he said: "Summon the people whose sticks have been planted according to the group that each gave their sticks." And I went away into the field and I summoned all of them, and they all stood group by group. ³ He said to them, "Each of you pull out your own stick and bring it to me." ⁴ The first ones, those having withered and chopped-off *sticks*, returned *them* and like this they were found, withered and chopped off. He commanded them to stand separately. ⁵ Then those having the withered and not chopped-off *sticks* returned *them*. And some of them returned green sticks, and some withered and chopped off as if by moths. Therefore those who returned green *sticks* he commanded to stand separately and those who returned withered and chopped-off *sticks*, he commanded to stand with the first *group*. ⁶ Then those having half-withered and cracked *sticks* returned *them*. And many of them returned green *sticks* ₍without cracks₎,ᵉ and some green and having buds and fruit on the buds, such as the ones who went into the tower having been crowned had, and some returned *them* withered and eaten, and some withered and not eaten, and some such as they were, half-withered and having cracks. He commanded them, each one, to stand separately, some to their own group, and others separately.

8.5 Review of the Sticks (Part 2)

⁷¹·¹ Next the ones having the green sticks but having cracks gave. These all returned green *sticks* and stood in their own group. And the shepherd rejoiced because of these, that all were changed and had lost their cracks. ² And they also gave, the ones having the half-green and half-withered *sticks*. Then the sticks of some were found completely green, some half-withered,

---

a. Literally "Gird yourself with an apron"

b. BDAG provides details in its definition for the word translated as "apron": "a piece of cloth made of coarse linen for workers."

c. Literally "I girded myself with an apron made of clean sackcloth"

d. Literally "girded"

e. Literally "and not having cracks"

some withered and eaten, and some green and having buds. These all were sent away, each to its group. [3] Then they gave, the ones having ₗtwo-thirds₎ [a] green and ₗone-third₎ [b] withered. Many of them gave green *sticks*, but many half-withered, and others withered and eaten. These all stood in their own group. [4] Then they gave, the ones having ₗtwo-thirds₎ [c] withered and ₗone-third₎ [d] green. Many of them gave half-withered *sticks*, but some withered and eaten, and others half-withered and having cracks, and a few green. These all stood in their own group. [5] And they gave, those having their green sticks but a very small portion *were* withered and had cracks. Of these, some gave green *sticks*, and some green and with buds. These also went away into their group. [6] Then they gave, the ones having a very small portion green but the remaining parts withered. Of these, the sticks were found the greatest part green and having buds and fruit in the buds, and others completely green. Because of these sticks, the shepherd rejoiced very greatly because they were found in this way. And these went away, each into their own group.

8.6 *The Withered Sticks*

[72.1] After he had considered all the sticks, the shepherd said to me, "I told you that this tree is tenacious of life. Do you see," he said, "how many have repented and been saved?" "I see," I said, "sir." "You see then," he said, "the rich mercy of the Lord, that he is great and glorious and he gave *his* spirit to those who are worthy of repentance." [2] "So why," I said, "sir, did not all repent?" "The ones he saw," he said, "whose heart would become pure and *would* serve him with the whole heart, to these he gave repentance. But the ones in whom he saw deceit and wickedness would repent in hypocrisy, to those he did not give repentance, that they might not again profane his name." [e] [3] I said to him, "Now then, sir, explain to me the sticks which were returned, what kind *of person* each of them is, and ₗwhere they live₎, [f]

---

a. Literally "two parts"

b. Literally "the third"

c. Literally "two parts"

d. Literally "the third"

e. ὄνομα Lake Lightfoot, Holmes] νόμον Ehrman. The difference is between "profane his name" (Lake, Lightfoot, Holmes) and "blaspheme his law" (Ehrman).

f. °Literally "their dwelling place"

that upon hearing, those who believed and have received the seal and have broken it, not keeping *it* whole, understanding their own deeds, they might repent, receiving a seal from you and they might glorify the Lord, that he had mercy upon them and sent you to renew their spirits." ⁴ "Listen," he said, "those whose sticks were found withered and eaten by moths, these are the apostates and traitors of the church. And having blasphemed the Lord in their sins, and in addition also being ashamed of the name of the Lord which was called over them, these, then, have completely perished to God. And you see that not even one of them repented, although *they* heard the words which you spoke to them, which I commanded to you; from ones such as these life has departed. ⁵ And those who gave withered and not rotted *sticks*, these *are* also near them, for they were hypocrites and brought in strange doctrines and corrupted the servants of God, and especially those who have sinned, not permitting them to repent but per-suading them with foolish doctrines. Therefore these have hope of repen-tance. ⁶ And you see many of them also have repented, since I told[a] them my commandments, and they will still repent. But as many as will not repent have lost their life, and as many of them have repented become good and their dwelling was inside the first walls, and some also went up inside the tower. You see, then," he said, "that repentance from sin brings life, but to not repent *brings* death."

8.7 The Half-Withered and Cracked Sticks

⁷³·¹ "And as many as gave half-withered *sticks* and they had cracks in them, listen also about them. Those whose sticks were half-withered, they are double-minded, for they are neither alive nor dead. ² And those having half-withered *sticks* and cracks in them, these are also double-minded and slanderous and are never at peace among themselves but are always caus-ing dissension; but even for these, repentance is a possibility. You see," he said, "some of them have repented and still, the hope of repentance is in them. ³ And as many of them who have repented, they will have their dwell-ing place inside the tower. And as many of them who have repented more slowly, they will dwell inside the walls. And as many who do not repent

---

a. ἐλάλησα Lake] ἐλάλησας Holmes, Ehrman. The difference is between "I told/spoke" (Lake) and "you told/spoke" (Holmes and Ehrman).

but continue in their deeds, ₗthey will surely die₎.ᵃ 4 And those who gave their green sticks with cracks, these were always faithful and good, but had some jealousy among themselves about preeminence and about some greatness; but all of these are foolish among themselves, having jealousy about preeminence. 5 But even these, upon hearing my commandments *and* being good, they purified themselves and quickly repented. Therefore their dwelling is inside the tower. But if any of them would turn again to dissension, he will be thrown out from the tower and will lose his life. 6 Life is for all of those who keep the commandments of the Lord, but in the commandments there is nothing about preeminence or about greatness; but about a person's patience and humility. Among those such as these, then, is the life of the Lord, but among the causers of dissension and the lawless, *there* is death."

8.7 *The Mostly Green and Partly Withered Sticks*

74.1 But those who gave their sticks half green and half withered, these are those who are mixed up with business affairs and who do not cling to the saints; because of this half of them lives and half is dead. 2 Therefore many, upon hearing my commandments, repented. As many, then, as repented, have their dwelling in the tower. But some of them fell away completely. Therefore these have no repentance, for due to their business affairs they blasphemed the Lord and denied *him*. Therefore they have lost their life because of the wickedness which they did. 3 And many of them were double-minded. These still have repentance if they repent quickly, and their dwelling will be in the tower. But if they repent more slowly, they will dwell inside the walls, and if they do not repent they also have lost their life. 4 And those who gave *sticks* ₗtwo-thirds₎ᵇ green and ₗone-third₎ᶜ withered, these are those who have denied with various denials. 5 Therefore many of them repented and went away to dwell in the tower, but many completely fell away from God; these completely lost their lives. And some of them were double-minded and caused disagreement; these then have repentance

---

a. Literally "they will die the death"
b. Literally "two parts"
c. Literally "the third"

if they repent quickly and do not continue in their pleasures; but if they continue in their deeds, these also will accomplish death for themselves."

8.9 The Mostly Withered and Partly Green Sticks

75.1 And those who gave their sticks ₁two-thirds₁ ᵃ withered and ₁one-third₁ ᵇ green, these are *those* who were faithful but became rich and became honored among the heathen. They clothed themselves with great arrogance and became proud and abandoned the truth and did not join with the righteous but lived with the heathen, and this way of life was more pleasant to them. But they did not fall away from God but continued in the faith, ₁even though they did not do₁ ᶜ the works of the faith. ² Therefore many of them repented and their dwelling was in the tower. ³ But others lived with the heathen to the end and being corrupted with the worthless delusions of the heathen, they fell away from God and did the deeds of the heathen. These were counted with the heathen. ⁴ And others of them were double-minded, not hoping to be saved because of the deeds which they had done; and others were double-minded and made divisions among themselves. Therefore these who were double-minded because of their deeds, they still have repentance, but their repentance must be swift, so that their dwelling may be inside the tower. But for those who do not repent but continue with their pleasures, death is near."

8.10 The Green Sticks and the Withered Sticks

76.1 "But those who gave green sticks but their tips were withered and cracked, these were always good and faithful and glorious before God but they sinned a bit because of a few lusts and petty *quarrels* they held against one another, but upon hearing my words, the greater part quickly repented and their dwelling was inside the tower. ² But some of them were double-minded, and some, being double-minded, caused greater dissension. With regard to these, then, there is still hope of repentance because they were always good; only with difficulty will any of them die. ᵈ ³ But those

---

a. Literally "two parts"

b. Literally "third"

c. Literally "not doing"

d. While the Greek is relatively plain, its meaning in context is difficult to discern. Ehrman notes the Greek is "obscure" and translates "and none of them will easily die." Holmes

who gave their sticks withered but having a very small portion green, these are those who only believed, but who did the deeds of lawlessness. But they never fell away from God and they bore the name gladly and they gladly welcomed the servants of God into their households. Therefore upon hearing this repentance they repented without doubting and they are doing all virtue and righteousness. ⁴ But some of them are also afraid, knowing their deeds which they had done. Therefore the dwelling of all of these will be inside the tower."

8.11 The Mostly Green and Partly Withered Sticks

⁷⁷·¹ And after he finished the explanations of all of the sticks, he said to me, "Go and tell everyone that they may repent and live to God because the Lord, being compassionate, sent me to give repentance to everyone, although some are not worthy because of their deeds. But being patient, the Lord wants those who were called through his Son to be saved." ² I said to him, "Sir, I hope that all who hear them will repent. For I am persuaded that each one, recognizing his own deeds and fearing God, will repent." ³ Answering me, he said, "All those who," he said, "repent with their whole heart and purify themselves from their wickednesses which were previously mentioned, and no longer add anything to their sins, they will receive healing from the Lord for their previous sins, unless they are double-minded about these commandments, and they will live to God. But all those who," he said, "add to their sins and walk in the lusts of this world will condemn themselves to death. ⁴ But you, you walk in my commandments and you will live to God, and whoever walks in them and does rightly, they will live to God." ⁵ Having shown and spoken all these things to me, he said to me, "And I will show *you* the rest after a few days."

PARABLE 9

9.1 The Field and the Mountains

⁷⁸·¹ After I wrote the commandments and parables of the shepherd, the angel of repentance, he came to me and said to me, "I want to show you

---

translates "and scarcely one of them will die." This translation follows Osiek, "only with difficulty will any of them die."

what the Holy Spirit who spoke with you in the form of the church showed you, for that Spirit is the Son of God. [2] For since you were too weak in the flesh it was not shown to you by an angel. Therefore when you were strengthened by the spirit and made strong in your strength so that you could also see an angel, then, therefore, the construction of the tower was revealed to you by the church. You saw all things well and honorably, |as with virgin eyes|.[a]o But now you see by an angel, indeed by the same spirit. [3] But it is necessary for you to learn all things more accurately from me, because for this *reason* I was also given by the glorious angel to dwell in your house, that you might see all things keenly, being cowardly in nothing, like your former self." [4] And he led me away to Arcadia, to a certain rounded mountain, and sat me down upon the top of the mountain. And he showed me a great field, and around the field twelve mountains, the mountains each one having a different appearance. [5] The first was black as soot, and the second *was* bare, not having vegetation, and the third *was* full of thorns and thistles. [6] And the fourth had half-withered vegetation, the tops of the plants *were* green, but the *parts* by the roots *were* withered, and some vegetation became withered when the sun scorched *them*. [7] And the fifth mountain had green vegetation and was rough. And the sixth mountain was completely full of cracks; some of which *were* small, others of which *were* large, and the cracks had plants but the plants were not very healthy but instead were as if fading away. [8] And the seventh mountain had healthy plants and the whole mountain was thriving, and all kinds of cattle and birds were grazing on that mountain. And as many cattle and birds were feeding, the plants of that mountain flourished |even more|.[b] And the eighth mountain was full of springs, and every kind of the Lord's creatures drank from the springs of that mountain. [9] And the ninth mountain had no water at all and was completely desert-like, but it had in it wild beasts and deadly reptiles that were destroying people. And the tenth mountain had large trees and was completely shaded, and under the shade of the trees sheep were lying down, resting and chewing their cud. [10] And the eleventh mountain |was covered with trees|,[c] and those

---

a. Literally "as by a virgin"
b. Literally "more and more"
c. Literally "was very forested"

trees were very fruitful, with many and various fruits adorning *them*, so that anyone upon seeing *them*, they would desire to eat from their fruits. And the twelfth mountain was completely white and its appearance was cheerful. And the mountain was in itself incredibly beautiful.

79.1 And in the middle of the field he showed me a great white rock coming up out of the field. And the rock was higher than the mountains, square so that it could contain the whole world. **2** And that rock was old, having a door hewn out *of it*, and it seemed to me the chiseling out of the door was recent. And the door shone so much because of the sun that I wondered at the brightness of the door. **3** And around the door stood twelve virgins. ᵃ So the four who stood in the corners seemed to be more glorious to me, but the others were also glorious, and stood in the four parts of the door, between each of them two virgins. **4** And they were clothed in linen tunics and were girded appropriately, ᵇ having their right shoulders bare, as if being about to carry some load. Thus they were ready, for they were very cheerful and eager. **5** After I had seen these things I wondered to myself, because I was seeing great and glorious deeds. And again I was greatly perplexed at the virgins, that being so delicate they stood bravely, as if *they* were about to carry the whole heaven. **6** And the shepherd said to me, "Why do you argue with yourself and become greatly perplexed, and bring grief upon yourself? For whatever you are not able to understand do not try, having good sense; but ask the Lord that upon receiving understanding, you may comprehend such things. **7** What *is* behind you, ₗyou cannot seeₗ; ᶜ but what *is* in front of you, you see. Therefore, what ₗyou cannot seeₗ, ᵈ let go *of it* and do not torment ᵉ yourself. But what you see, master those things; and about the rest, do not concern yourself ᶠ⁶ and I

---

a. Lake translates generically as "maidens," but the specific translation "virgins" seems best in this context.

b. Lake and Ehrman both translate "beautifully"; Holmes translates "becomingly." BDAG, however, notes the sense of "appropriately" is more likely correct in this context.

c. Literally "you are not able to see"

d. Literally "you are not able to see"

e. While στρεβελόω occurs in the NT with the sense "to twist, distort" (2 Pet 3:16), it does not occur in the NT in the sense used here, "to torment."

f. Again, Hermas is to be concerned about taking action regarding the things he is able to see; the things he does not see are not to concern him.

myself will explain everything to you, whatever I will show you. Therefore look at the rest."[a]

9.3 The Six Men and the Tower

[80.1] I saw six men had come, tall and glorious and alike in appearance, and they called a multitude of men. And those who also came were tall men, and beautiful and powerful. And the six men commanded them to build a tower on the rock. And there was a great commotion among those men, who had come to build the tower, running here and there around the door. [2] And the virgins, standing around the door, were telling the men to hasten to build the tower. And the virgins spread out their hands, like *they were* about to receive something from the men. [3] And the six men commanded stones to come up from some deep place and to go into the construction of the tower. And ten square, bright, unhewn stones came up. [4] And the six men called the virgins and commanded them to carry all the stones which were going to go into the construction of the tower and to walk through the door and give *them* to the men who were going to build the tower. [5] And the virgins put the first ten stones which came up from the deep place upon one another and they carried *them* together like a single stone.[b]

9.4 Stones of Many Colors

[81.1] And just as they had stood together around the door, in this way those who seemed to be strong carried *them*. And they were getting under the corners of the stone, and the other *virgins* had got under the sides[c] of the stone, and in this way they carried all the stones. And they carried them through the door, just as they had been commanded, and gave *them* to the men inside the tower. And those men, taking the stones, were building. [2] And the construction of the tower was upon the great rock, and above the door. Therefore those ten stones were fit together and they filled the

---

a. Here the shepherd directs Hermas' attention to the rest of the vision, not "the rest" of what he cannot see (as this language was used previously in this verse).

b. Holmes translates "stone by stone," taking "together" to refer to the virgins acting together, not as referring to the stones being carried together.

c. NT usage of πλευρά is in relation to the human body (the side of the body); here usage is more generic.

whole rock. And those stones were the foundation of the construction of
the tower, and the rock and the door were supporting the whole tower.
3 And after the ten stones, another twenty a stones came up from the deep
place, and these were fit into the construction of the tower, carried by the
virgins [in the same way as] b the previous stones. And after these thirty-five came up, and these likewise were fit into the tower. And after these
another forty stones came up, and all these were put into the construction
of the tower. Therefore there were four rows in the foundation of the tower.
4 And they stopped coming up from the deep place, and the builders also
stopped for a little while. And again the six men commanded the multitude
of the crowd to bring up stones for the construction of the tower from the
mountains. 5 Therefore *stones* were brought up from all of the mountains,
with various colors, c having been hewn by the men, and they were given
to the virgins. And the virgins carried them through the door and gave
them for the construction of the tower. And when the various stones were
put into the building, they became like white and the various colors were
changed. 6 But some stones were given by the men for the construction and
they did not become bright but as they were placed so also they were found,
for they were not given over by the virgins and not brought in through the
door. Therefore these stones were unsuitable d for the construction of the
tower. 7 And the six men, upon seeing the unsuitable stones in the building,
commanded them to be taken away and brought down to their own place,
from where they had been brought. 8 And they said to the men who were
bringing in the stones, "You really must not hand over the stones inside
the building, but you must put them at the tower so that the virgins may
bring them through the door and may give *them* for the construction. For
if," they said, "they are not brought through the door by the hands of these
virgins, their colors cannot change. So do not labor," they said, "in vain."

---

a. Some sources have "twenty-five," others have "fifteen."
b. Literally "just as also"
c. 2 Macc 3:16
d. 4 Macc 6:17

9.5 A Pause in the Construction

[82.1] And the building was completed on that day, but the tower was not finished, for it was about to be built upon again and there was a pause in the construction. And the six men commanded all the builders to go away a little while and rest, but they commanded the virgins not to go away from the tower. And it seemed to me the virgins were left behind to guard the tower. [2] And after they all went away and were resting, I said to the shepherd, "Why," I said, "sir, was the construction of the tower not completed?" "Not yet," he said, "is the tower able to be completed, unless its ruler comes and tests this building, so that if some stones are found to be rotten, he can replace them, for according to the will of that one the tower is being built." [3] "I would like," I said, "sir, to know of this tower. What does this building represent? And about the rock and door, and the mountains, and the virgins, and the stones, those which came up from the deep and were not hewn, but thus went into the building. [4] And why first ten stones were placed on the foundation, then twenty, then thirty-five, then forty; and about the stones that went into the building and were taken away again and returned into their own place. About all of these things, give rest to my soul, sir, and make them known to me." [5] "If," he said, "you are not found to be concerning yourself about worthless things, you will know everything, for after a few days, we will come here and you will see the rest of what happens to this tower, and you will accurately understand all the parables." [6] And after a few days, we came to the place where we had sat, and he said to me, "Let us go to the tower, for the master[a] of the tower is coming to examine it." And we came to the tower and no one at all was ₁there₁[b] except the virgins alone. [7] And the shepherd asked the virgins if perhaps the master of the tower had come. And they said that he was about to come to examine the building.

9.6 The Master of the Tower

[83.1] And behold, after a little while I saw a procession of many men coming, and in the midst *of them was* a particular man, tall with such size that *he*

---

a. 1 Tim 2:12
b. Literally "at it"

rose above[a] the tower. ² And the six men who had been in charge[b] of the building were walking with him both on the right and the left. And all those who worked at the building were with him, and many other glorious ones *were* around him. And the virgins who guarded the tower ran up to kiss him and they began to walk around the tower, ₁staying close to₁[c] him. ³ And that man examined the building carefully, so that he touched ₁each individual₁[d] stone. And holding a staff in his hand, he struck ₁each individual₁[e] stone of ₁the building₁.[f] ⁴ And when he struck, some of them became black like soot, and some rough, and some having cracks, and some mutilated, and some neither white nor black, and some rough and not matching the other stones, and some having many spots. These were the varieties of the rotten stones which were found inside the building. ⁵ Therefore he commanded all of these *stones* to be carried out of the tower and to be put beside the tower, and other stones to be brought and to be put into their place. ⁶ And the builders asked him from which mountains he wanted stones to be brought and to be put into their place, and he commanded *them* not to be brought from the mountains but he commanded *them* to be brought from a field which was nearby. ⁷ And the field was quarried and bright, square stones were found, but also some round *stones*. ₁And however many₁[g] stones were in the field, those all were brought and carried through the door by the virgins. ⁸ And the square stones were hewn and put into the place of those taken away, but the round *stones* were not put into the building because they were difficult to hew and it happened slowly. But they were put beside the tower like they were about to be hewn and put into the building, for they were very splendid.

9.7 *Instructions for the Shepherd*

⁸⁴·¹ Therefore, having completed these things, the glorious man and ruler of the whole tower called the shepherd and handed all the stones over to him,

---

a. 1 Kgs 8:8
b. Jdt 8:10; 12:11
c. Literally "near"
d. Literally "according to one"
e. Literally "according to one"
f. Literally "what was built"
g. ⁷ Literally "and as many"

those lying beside the tower which had been removed from the building, and he said to him, ² "Carefully cleanse these stones and put them inside the building of the tower, the ones able to fit with the rest. But those which do not fit, throw *them* far away from the tower." ³ Having commanded these things to the shepherd, he went from the tower with all of them with whom he had come. But the virgins stood around the tower guarding it. ⁴ I said to the shepherd, "How can these stones come into the building of the tower, having been rejected?" Answering me he said, "Do you see," he said, "these stones?" "I see," I said, "sir." "I," he said, "will hew the greater part of these stones and will put *them* into the building and they will fit with the remaining stones." ⁵ "How," I said, "sir, can they, being hewn, fill the same place?" Answering, he said to me, "All those which will be found small, they will be put into the middle of the building, and all those which *are* larger will be put outside and they will support it." ⁶ Having spoken these things to me, he said to me, "Let us go, and after two days let us return and cleanse these stones and put them into the building, for everything around the tower must be cleansed lest the master suddenly return and find the things around the tower dirty and become angry, and these stones will not go into the building of the tower, and I will seem to be negligent before the master." ⁷ And after two days we came to the tower and he said to me, "Let us consider all the stones and let us see which are able to come into the building." I said to him, "Sir, let us consider *them*."

9.8 Reviewing the Stones

⁸⁵·¹ And having begun, first we considered the black stones, and they were also found the same as when they were put out of the building. And the shepherd commanded them to be carried away out of the tower and removed. ² Then he considered those having a rough surface, and taking *them* he hewed many of them and commanded the virgins to take them away and put *them* into the building. And the virgins took them away and put *them* into the building in the middle of the tower. And he commanded the remaining *stones* to be put with the black *stones*, for even these also were found to be black. ³ Then he considered the ones with cracks, and he hewed many of these. And he commanded *them* to be carried away by the virgins into the building. And they put *them* outside because they were found to be stronger. But the rest, because of the large number of cracks,

were not able to be hewn. Therefore, for this reason they were thrown away from the building of the tower. 4 Then he considered the mutilated *stones* and many black *stones* were found among them, and some had huge cracks. And he also commanded these to be put with those that had been thrown away. But having cleansed and hewn the majority of them, he commanded *them* to be put into the building. And the virgins, having taken them away, fit *them* into the middle of the building of the tower, for they were very weak. 5 Then he considered the half white and half black *stones*, and many of them were found to be black, and he also commanded these to be taken away with those that had been rejected. But the rest were all taken away by the virgins, for being white, they were fitted by the virgins themselves into the building. And they were put outside because they were found to be sound, so that they could support those put in the middle, for of these, not a one was too short. 6 Then he considered the rough and hard *stones*, and a few of them were thrown away because they could not be hewn, for they were found to be very hard. But the rest of them were hewn and taken away by the virgins and were fitted into the middle of the building of the tower, for they were very weak. 7 Then he considered the stones ₁with₁ [a] spots, and of these a trivial amount turned black, and they were thrown away with the rest. But the majority were found to be splendid and sound, and these were fitted by the virgins into the building, but were put outside because of their strength.

9.9 *The Round Stones*

86.1 Next he came to consider the white and round stones, and he said to me, "What do we do with these stones?" "How," I said, "₁would I know₁, [b] sir?" "So, you notice nothing about them?" 2 "I," I said, "sir, do not have this skill, and I am not a stonecutter, and I am not able to understand." "Do you not see," he said, "they are very round, and if I want to make them square, it is necessary for a great deal to be cut away from them? But it is necessary for some of them, out of necessity, to be put into the building." 3 "If then," I said, "sir, it is a necessity, why do you torment yourself and do not choose which *stones* you want for the building and fit *them* into it?" He chose

---

a. Literally "having"

b. Literally "do I know"

the larger and more splendid of them and hewed them. And the virgins, taking *them* away, fit *them* into the outer parts of the building. ⁴ And the rest, those which were left, were taken away and put back into the field from where they were brought. But they were not thrown away, "Because," he said, "the tower lacks, *there is* still a little to be built, and the master of the tower wants all these stones to be fitted into the building because they are very splendid." ⁵ And twelve women were called, incredibly beautiful in appearance, clothed in black, girded, and having the shoulders bare and their hair loose. And these women seemed to me to be wild. And the shepherd commanded them to take away the stones, those which had been removed from the building, and to carry them away to the mountains from where they were brought. ⁶ And they gladly took and carried away all the stones and put *them* back from where they were taken. And after all the stones were taken away and not a stone remained around the tower, the shepherd said to me, "Let us go around the tower and see if any defect is in it." And I went around with him. ⁷ And the shepherd, upon seeing the tower being very beautiful in its construction, was very cheerful, for the tower thus was built, so that upon seeing *it* I greatly desired its construction, for thus it was built, as if from one stone, not having a single joint in it. And the stone appeared as if chiseled out from one rock, for it seemed to me to be a single stone.

9.10 Final Preparations

⁸⁷·¹ And I, walking with him, was cheerful upon seeing such good *things*. And the shepherd said to me, "Go, and bring lime and small pottery shards so that I may fill the marks of the stones which were taken away and put inside the building. For everything around the tower must be level." ² And I did just as he commanded and brought *them* to him. "Serve me," he said, "and soon the work will be completed." Then he filled the marks of the stones, the ones that had gone inside the building, and he commanded the area around the tower to be swept and made clean. ³ And the virgins, taking brooms, swept. And ₗthey swept awayₗ ᵃ all the filth from the tower and sprinkled water, and the place of the tower became cheerful and very beautiful. ⁴ The shepherd said to me, "Everything," he said, "has been made

---

a. Literally "they took away"

clean. If the ruler comes to examine the tower, ₁he cannot blame us for anything₁."ᵃ Upon saying these things, he wanted to leave. ⁵ And I grabbed his traveler's bag and began to adjure him in the name of the Lord that he might explain to me what he had shown me. He said to me, "I am busy for a little while, then I will explain everything to you. Wait for me here until I come." ⁶ I said to him, "Sir, being alone here, what will I do?" "You are not," he said, "alone, for these virgins are with you." "Then commend," I said, "me to them." The shepherd called them and said to them, "I entrust this one to you until I come." And he went away. ⁷ And I was alone with the virgins, and they were cheerful and gracious to me, especially the four of them who were more glorious.

9.11 Hermas and the Virgins Wait

⁸⁸·¹ The virgins said to me, "The shepherd is not coming here today." "So what," I said, "will I do?" "Until evening," they said, "wait for him, and if he comes, he will speak with you. But if he does not come, you will stay with us here until he does come." ² I said to them, "I will wait for him until evening, and if he does not come, I will go away to my house and will come back again early in the morning." But answering they said to me, "You were handed over to us; you are not able to go away from us." ³ "Where then," I said, "will I stay?" "With us," they said. "You will sleep *with us* like a brother and not like a husband, for you are our brother, and from now on we are going to live with you, for we love you very much." But I was ashamed to stay with them. ⁴ And the one who seemed to be most prominent among them began to kiss and embrace me, and the others, upon seeing that one embracing me, they themselves also began to kiss me and to lead *me* around the tower, and to play with me. ⁵ And *it was* as if I had become younger, and I myself also began to play with them, for some were dancing in a chorus, and others were dancing, and others were singing. But I was silent, *and* I walked around the tower with them, and was cheerful with them. ⁶ And when it was evening, I wanted to go to my house, but they did not allow *me* but prevented me, and I stayed the night with them and slept beside the tower. ⁷ For the virgins spread out their linen tunics on the ground, and they had me lie down in the midst of them, and they did nothing else

---

a. Literally "he does not have anything to blame us for"

except they prayed, and I with them; I prayed unceasingly and not less than they did^m, and the virgins rejoiced thus when I was praying, and I stayed there until the next day, until the second hour, with the virgins. **8** Then the shepherd came and said to the virgins, "Have you done any mistreatment to him?" "Ask," they said, "him." I said to him, "Sir, I was made glad staying with them." "What," he said, "did you eat?" "I feasted," I said, "sir, on the words of the Lord all the night." He said, "Did they receive you well?" "Yes," I said, "sir." **9** "Now," he said, "what do you want to hear first?" "Just as," I said, "sir, you showed *me* from the beginning, I ask you, sir, that just as I would ask you, in this way you might also explain to me." "Just as you desire," he said, "in this way I will also explain to you, and I will hide nothing at all from you."

9.12 The Explanation of the Parable

89.1 "First of all," I said, "sir, explain this to me: Who is the rock and the door?" "This rock," he said, "and the door are the Son of God." "How," I said, "sir, *as* the rock is old but the door new?" "Listen," he said, "and understand, foolish one. **2** The Son of God is older than all of his creation, so that he was counselor to the Father of his creation; for this *reason* the rock *is* also old." "But the door, why is it new," I said, "sir?" **3** "Because," he said, "[he was revealed][a] at the end of the days of the consummation; the door is new for this *reason*: that those who are going to be saved may enter through it into the kingdom of God. **4** Do you see," he said, "the stones which entered through the door have been put into the construction of the tower, but those that did not enter have been put back again in their own place?" "I see," I said, "sir." "In the same way," he said, "no one will enter into the kingdom of God unless he takes his holy name. **5** For if you want to enter into some city, and that city [has been completely surrounded with a wall][b] and has one door, can you enter into that city, except through the door which it has?" "For how," I said, "sir, can it be otherwise?" "If, then, you are not able to enter into the city except through the door which it has, so," he said, "also into the kingdom of God a person is not able to enter otherwise, except through the name of his Son who was loved by him. **6** Do you

a. Literally "he became apparent"
b. Literally "has been walled around"

see," he said, "the crowd that was building the tower?" "I see," I said, "sir." "Those," he said, "are all glorious angels; by these, then, the Lord has been completely surrounded.[a] But the door is the Son of God. This is the only entrance to the Lord. Therefore no one will enter into it otherwise, except through his Son. [7] Do you see," he said, "the six men and the glorious and great man among them who walked around the tower and rejected the stones from the building?" "I see," I said, "sir." [8] "The glorious man," he said, "is the Son of God, and those are six glorious angels supporting him on the right and on the left." He said, "None of these glorious angels will enter into *the presence of* God without him. Whoever does not receive his name will not enter into the kingdom of God."

9.13 The Tower, the Virgins, and the Thrown-Away Stones

[90.1] "But the tower," I said, "what is it?" "The tower," he said, "this is the church." [2] "And these virgins, who are they?" "These," he said, "are holy spirits. And a person cannot be found inside the kingdom of God otherwise, unless these ones clothe him with their clothing. For if you receive only the name but do not receive the clothing from them you will not have any benefit, for these virgins are the powers of the Son of God. If you bear the name but do not bear his power, you will be bearing his name in vain. [3] And the stones," he said, "which you saw thrown off, these bear the name, but they are not clothed with the clothing of the virgins." "What," I said, "is their clothing, sir?" "The names themselves," he said, "are their clothing. Whoever bears the name of the Son of God also must bear these names, for even the Son himself bears the names of these virgins. [4] As many stones," he said, "that you saw enter inside the construction of the tower, given by their hands and remaining inside the building, are clothed with the power of these virgins. [5] For this *reason* you see the tower has become a single stone with the rock. So also those who believed in the Lord through his Son and who put on these spirits will be made into one spirit, one body and one color of their clothes. And the dwelling of such as those who bear the name of the virgins is inside the tower." [6] "Therefore," I said, "sir, the stones that were thrown away, why were they thrown away? For they went through the door and by the hands of the virgins they were put inside the

---

a. Literally "has been walled around"

construction of the tower." "Since everything to you," he said, "is a concern, and you inquire carefully, listen concerning the stones that were thrown away. ⁷ These," he said, "all received the name of the Son of God, and they also received the power of these virgins. Therefore, by receiving these spirits they were strengthened and were with the servants of God, and they had one spirit and one body and one clothing, For they thought the same things and did righteous deeds. ⁸ Therefore, after some time, they were persuaded by the women whom you saw clothed in black clothing, having their shoulders bare and their hair loose, and beautiful. Upon seeing these *women*, they desired them and clothed themselves with their power, and took off the clothing and the power of the virgins. ⁹ Therefore, these were thrown away from the house of God and were handed over to those *women*. But those who were not deceived by the beauty of these women, they remained in the house of God. You have," he said, "the explanation of those that were thrown away."

9.14 Repentance for Those Cast Out

⁹¹·¹ "What then," I said, "sir, if these men, being such as this, repent and cast off their lusts for these women and return to the virgins and walk in their power and in their deeds? Will they not enter into the house of God?" ² "They will enter," he said, "if they cast off the deeds of these women and take up the power of the virgins and walk in their deeds. For because of this also there was a pause in the construction, so that if they might repent, they themselves may go away into the construction of the tower. But if they do not repent, then others will enter and these ₗwill finally be thrown out.ₗ" ᵃ ³ For all these things I gave thanks to the Lord because he had mercy on all those who called upon his name, and he sent out the angel of repentance to us who had sinned against him and restored our spirit; even when we were already corrupt and had no hope of life, he renewed our life. ⁴ "Now," I said, "sir, explain to me why the tower was not built on the ground but upon the rock and upon the door." "Still," he said, "are you foolish and senseless?" "I have need," I said, "sir, to ask you everything because I am not able to understand anything at all, for everything great and glorious is also difficult for people to understand." ⁵ "Listen," he said, "the name of

---

a. Literally "will be thrown out at the end"

the Son of God is great and incomprehensible and it supports the whole world. If, then, all creation is supported by the Son of God, what do you think of those who are called by him and who bear the name of the Son of God and who walk in his commandments? [6] Do you see, then, what sort *of people* he supports? Those who bear his name with *their* whole heart. Therefore he himself was their foundation and he gladly supports them because they are not ashamed to bear his name."

9.15 *The Names of the Virgins and the Women in Black*

[92.1] "Explain to me," I said, "sir, the names of the virgins and of the women clothed in the black clothes." "Listen," he said, "to the names of the stronger virgins who stand in the corners. [2] And the first *is* Faith, and the second Self-Control, and the third Power, and the fourth Patience. And the others, each standing between these, have these names: Sincerity, Innocence, Purity, Cheerfulness, Truth, Understanding, Harmony, *and* Love. The one who bears these names and the names of the Son of God will be able to enter into the kingdom of God. [3] Hear also," he said, "the names of the women who who wear black clothes. And from these four are stronger. The first *is* Unbelief, the second Self-Indulgence, and the third Disobedience, and the fourth Deception. And their followers are called Grief, Wickedness, Licentiousness, Irritability, Falsehood, Foolishness, Slander, *and* Hate. The servant of God who bears these names will see the kingdom of God, but will not enter into it." [4] "But the stones," I said, "sir, the ones from the deep, that were fit into the construction, who are they?" "The first ones," he said, "the ten which were put into the foundation *are* the first generation, and the twenty-five *are* the second generation of righteous men, and the thirty-five *are* the prophets of God and his servants, and the forty *are* apostles and teachers of the preaching of the Son of God." [5] "Why then," I said, "sir, did the virgins also give these stones for the construction of the tower, after carrying *them* through the door?" [6] "For these first ones," he said, "bore these spirits and they did not depart at all from one another, not the spirits from the men or the men from the spirits, but the spirits remained with them until their slumber. And if they had not had these spirits with them, they would not have been useful to the construction of this tower."

9.16 The Stones from the Deep

93.1 "Even more to me," I said, "sir, explain." "What," he said, "do you want to know?" "Why," I said, "sir, did the stones come up from the deep, and *why* were they put inside the construction of the tower, after bearing these spirits?" **2** "They had need," he said, "to come up through the water, that they might be made alive, for they were not able to enter into the kingdom of God otherwise, unless they put away the deadness of their former life. **3** Therefore these who had fallen asleep also received the seal of the Son of God and entered into the kingdom of God, for before," he said, "a man bears the name of the Son of God, he is dead. But when he receives the seal, he lays aside deadness and takes up life. **4** Therefore the seal is the water. So the dead go down into the water and they come up living. Therefore this seal was preached to them also, and they made use of it, that they might enter into the kingdom of God." **5** "Why," I said, "sir, did the forty stones also come up with them from the deep already having the seal?" "Because," he said, "these apostles and teachers who preached the name of the Son of God, having fallen asleep in the power and faith of the Son of God, preached also to those who fell asleep before *them* and they themselves gave the seal of the preaching to them. **6** Therefore they went down with him into the water and came up again, but these went down living and came up living; but those who fell asleep before went down dead but came up living. **7** Therefore they were made alive through them and they came to know the name of the Son of God. For this *reason* they also came up with them and were fit together for the construction of the tower, and were built up together, unhewn. For they fell asleep in righteousness and in great purity, ₁but they were only missing this seal₁. **a** Therefore you also have the explanation of these things." "I have it," I said, "sir."

9.17 The Twelve Mountains

94.1 "Therefore now, sir, explain to me about the mountains, why their appearances are ₁so different₁ **b** and diverse?" "Listen," he said, "these mountains are the twelve tribes that inhabit the whole world. Therefore the Son of God was preached to these *tribes* through the apostles." **2** "But why is the mountains'

---

a. Literally "but only this seal they did not have"
b. Literally "different and different"

appearance diverse and ₁so different₁?ᵃ Explain it to me, sir." "Listen," he said,
"these twelve tribes that inhabit the whole world are twelve nations, and they
are diverse in wisdom and in understanding. Therefore just as you saw the
various mountains so there are also varieties of these, of the understanding
and the wisdom of the nations. And I will also make clear to you the function
of each one." ³ "First," I said, "sir, explain this: Why, the mountains being so
diverse, when their stones were put into the construction, they became one
color, bright ₁just like₁ᵇ the stones which came up from the deep?" ⁴ "Because,"
he said, "all the nations that dwell under heaven, upon hearing and believing,
were called by the name of the Son of God. Therefore upon receiving the seal,
they had one wisdom and one understanding and their faith became one, ₁as
did their love₁;ᶜ and they bore the spirits of the virgins with the name. For
this *reason* the construction of the tower became one color, bright like the sun.
⁵ But after they entered ₁together₁ᵈ and became one body, some of them
defiled themselves and were cast out from the family of the righteous, and
again became such as they were previously, but even worse."

9.18 The Purification of the Church

⁹⁵·¹ "How," I said, "sir, did they become worse, having come to know God?"
"The one who does not know," he said, "God and acts wickedly incurs some
punishment for his wickednesses, but the one who has come to know God
ought to do wrong no longer but *ought* to do good. ² Therefore if the one who
ought to do good does wrong, does he not seem to do more wickedness than
the one who does not know God? For this *reason* the ones who do not know
God and who do wrong are condemned to death, but those who know God
and who have seen his mighty power and do wrong, they will be punished
doubly and will die ₁forever₁.ᵉ Therefore in this way the church of God will
be purified. ³ But like you saw the stones taken away from the tower and
handed over to the evil spirits and from there were thrown out, and there
will be one body of those who are cleansed, just as the tower also became as
being made out of one stone, after it was purified. In this way the church

---

a. Literally "different and different"
b. Literally "as also"
c. Literally "and one love"
d. Literally "to the same"
e. Literally "into the age"

of God will also be after it is purified and the evil ones and hypocrites and slanderers and double-minded ones and doers of various wickednesses are thrown out. 4 After these are thrown out the church of God will be one body, one wisdom, one understanding, one faith, one love; and then the Son of God will rejoice greatly and will be made glad in them, having received back his pure people." I said, "Sir, all these things are great and glorious. 5 Still," I said, "sir, explain to me the power and the functions of each one of the mountains, that every soul that has believed in the Lord, upon hearing may glorify his great and wonderful and glorious name." "Listen," he said, "to the diversity of the mountains and the twelve nations."

9.19 The First Two Mountains

96.1 "From the first mountain, the black one, are those who believe such as these: Apostates and blasphemers against the Lord and betrayers of the servants of God. And to these there is no repentance, but there is death, and ₁this is why₁ [a] they are black, for even their descendants are lawless.   2 And from the second mountain, the bare one, are those who believe such as these: Hypocrites and teachers of wickedness. Therefore these also are like the previous, not having the fruit of righteousness, for like their unfruitful mountain, so also the people such as these have the name, but are empty of the faith and have no fruit of truth in them. Therefore repentance is given to these if they repent quickly, but if they hesitate their death will be with the former." 3 "Why," I said, "sir, is repentance for these, but is not for the first, for their deeds are ₁nearly₁ [b] the same." "For this reason," he said, "repentance is given to these, because they did not blaspheme their Lord and did not become betrayers of the servants of God. But because of desire for gain they pretended and taught each according to the desires of sinful people, but they will pay some punishment, yet repentance to them is given because they did not become blasphemers or betrayers."

9.20 The Third Mountain

97.1 "And from the third mountain, the one having thorns and thistles, those who believe are such as these: From them some are rich and others are

---

a. Literally "for this also"
b. Literally "some"

mixed up with many business affairs; the thistles are the rich, and the thorns *are* those who are mixed up in various business affairs. ² Therefore these who are mixed up in many and various kinds of business affairs are not joined with the servants of God but have strayed, being choked by their deeds. And the rich are joined with the servants of God with difficulty, fearing lest they be begged for something by them. Therefore those such as these will enter into the kingdom of God with difficulty. ³ For just as it is difficult to walk on thistles with bare feet, so also for those such as these it is difficult to enter into the kingdom of God. ⁴ But there is repentance for all these, but *it must be* swift, that what they did not do in former times, they may now make amends for the days and do some good. If, then, they repent and do some good, they will live to God, but if they continue in their deeds they will be handed over to those women who will execute them."

9.21 *The Fourth Mountain*

98.1 "And from the fourth mountain, the one having many plants, and the tops of the plants green but withered at the roots, and some also were dried out by the sun; the ones who believe such as these are the double-minded, and the ones who have the Lord on their lips, but do not have him in their heart. ² For this *reason* their foundations are dry and have no power, and only their words are alive, but their deeds are dead. The ones such as this are neither alive nor dead. Therefore they are like the double-minded, for the double-minded are also neither green nor dry, for they are neither alive nor dead. ³ For just as these plants were dried out upon seeing the sun, so also the double-minded, when they hear of affliction, they become idolaters through their cowardice and are ashamed of the name of their Lord. ⁴ Therefore the ones such as these are neither alive nor dead, but even these, if they repent quickly, will be able to live. But if they do not repent, they have already been handed over to the women who take away their life."

9.22 *The Fifth Mountain*

99.1 "And from the fifth mountain, the one having green plants and being rough, the ones who believe such as these are faithful but also slow to learn, arrogant and are pleasers of self, wanting to know all things yet they know nothing at all. ² On account of this stubbornness of theirs, understanding departed from them and a stupid foolishness entered into them. And they praise themselves for having understanding and desire to be self-proclaimed teachers, ₍despite their foolishness₎. [a] [3] Therefore on account of this haughtiness many who exalted themselves were rendered void, for stubbornness and vain confidence is a great demon. Therefore many of these were rejected, but some repented and believed and submitted themselves to those who have understanding, knowing ₍their own foolishness₎. [b] [4] And for the rest of those such as these, repentance also exists, for they were not evil but instead foolish and without understanding. Therefore these, if they repent, they will live to God, but if they do not repent, they will dwell with the women who do harm to them."

9.23 The Sixth Mountain

[100.1] "And those from the sixth mountain, the one ₍with₎ [c] great and small cracks and withered plants in the cracks, are believers such as these: [2] The ones having the small cracks, these are those who have *something* against one another, and are withered in the faith from their own slander, but many repented from these things, and the rest will also repent when they hear my commandments, for the slander of theirs is small and they will repent quickly. [3] And the ones having great cracks, these are constant in their slander and become vengeful, raging against one another. Therefore these were thrown away from the tower and rejected from its construction. Therefore the ones such as these will live with difficulty. [4] If our God and Lord, who is Lord over all and who has authority over all of his creation, does not bear malice against those who confess their sins, but is merciful; does a person, being mortal and full of sin, bear malice against someone as if having the ability to destroy or to save him? [5] But I, the angel of repentance, say to you, however many of you have this heresy, put it away and repent, and the Lord will heal your former sins if you purify yourselves from this demon. But if not, you will be handed over to him for death."

---

a. Literally "being foolish"
b. Literally "the foolishness of themselves"
c. Literally "having"

9.24 The Seventh Mountain

[101.1] "And from the seventh mountain, on which green and cheerful plants *grow* and the whole mountain thrives, and every kind of cattle and the birds of the sky were grazing on the plants from this mountain, and the plants which they were grazing became even more healthy, are believers such as these: [2] They were always sincere and innocent and blessed, holding nothing against one another, but always rejoicing greatly for the servants of God and were clothed with the holy spirit of these virgins, and always having compassion for all people, and they provided to every person from their labors without reproaching and without doubting. [3] Therefore the Lord, upon seeing their simplicity and complete childlikeness, filled them with the labors of their hands and favored them highly in all their deeds. [4] And I say to you who are such as these, I, the angel of repentance: continue in these ways and ⸢your seed will never be obliterated⸣,[a] for the Lord has approved you and recorded you in our number and all your seed will dwell with the Son of God, for you received from his spirit."

9.25 The Eighth Mountain

[102.1] "And from the eighth mountain, where many springs were and all the creation of the Lord drank from the springs, are believers such as these: [2] Apostles and teachers who preached to all the world and who taught the word of the Lord honorably and purely and who kept back nothing at all for evil desire but always walked in righteousness and truth, just as they also received the Holy Spirit. Therefore the passing of those such as these is with the angels."

9.26 The Ninth Mountain

[103.1] "And from the ninth mountain, the desert-like *one*, which had reptiles and wild beasts on it that were destroying people, are believers such as these: [2] Those having spots are deacons who ministered poorly and thoroughly plundered the livelihood of widows and orphans, and made profit for themselves from the ministry which they received to administer. If, then, they continue in the same desires, they are dead and *have* no hope of life in them. But if they turn and fulfill their ministry purely, they will

---

a. Literally "your seed will not be obliterated, even until the age"

be able to live. ³ And the ones with a rough surface, these are the ones who deny and who do not turn to the Lord themselves, but having become barren and having become desert-like by not joining with the servants of God but living alone, they destroy their own souls. ⁴ For like a vine left behind some fence, ₁neglected₁,ᵃ corrupted and ruined by the weeds, and in time becomes wild and is no longer useful to its own master, so also the people such as these have despaired of themselves and become useless to the Lord, themselves being wild. ⁵ For these, then, there is repentance, unless they are found to have denied from the heart. But if someone is found to have denied from the heart, I do not know if he is able to live. ⁶ And I say this not for these days, that someone who denies may receive repentance, for it is impossible to save the one who is about to now deny his own Lord, but for those who denied long ago, repentance seems to exist. Therefore if anyone is about to repent, let it happen quickly before the tower is finished. ₁Otherwise₁,ᵇ they will be destroyed by the women to death. ⁷ And the mutilated ones, these are deceitful and slanderous, and the wild beasts which you saw on the mountain are these. For just as the wild beasts destroy and kill people with their own poison, so also the words of people such as these destroy and kill a person. ⁸ Therefore these are mutilated in their faith because of the conduct which they have in themselves, but some repented and were saved. And the remaining ones who are such as these can be saved if they repent. But if they do not repent, they will be put to death by those women whose power they have."

9.27 The Tenth Mountain

¹⁰⁴·¹ "And from the tenth mountain, where there were trees ₁providing shade for₁ᶜ some sheep, are believers such as these: ² Bishops and hospitable ones who always gladly welcome the servants of God into their own houses without hypocrisy. And the bishops always unceasingly protected the needy ones and the widows by their own ministry and always conducted themselves in purity. ³ Therefore all these will always be sheltered by the Lord. Therefore the ones who have done these things are glorious in the sight

---

a. Literally "experiencing neglect"
b. Literally "But if not"
c. Literally "covering"

of God and their place is already with the angels if they continue serving the Lord until the end."

9.28 The Eleventh Mountain

[105.1] "And from the eleventh mountain, where trees were full of fruit, adorned with many and various fruit are believers such as these: [2] Those who have suffered for the name of the Son of God, who also willingly suffered with all their heart and handed over their souls." [3] "Therefore why," I said, "sir, do all the trees have fruit, but some fruit of theirs is more beautiful than others?" "Listen," he said, "all those who ever suffered for the name are glorious in the sight of God, and the sins of all of them have been taken away because they suffered for the name of the Son of God. But why are their fruits various, and some better than others? Listen. [4] As many," he said, "upon being brought before authority were questioned and did not deny but suffered willingly, these are more glorious in the sight of the Lord; the fruit of these is superior. But as many as were cowardly and in doubt and considered in their hearts whether they should deny or confess, and they suffered, the fruits of these are inferior because this plan entered upon their hearts, for this evil plan, namely, a servant should deny his own Lord. [5] Therefore see to it, you who consider these things, lest this plan remain in your hearts and you die to God. But you who suffer on account of the name ought to glorify God because God considered you worthy, that you bear this name and all of your sins should be healed. [6] So then, you consider yourselves blessed but think you have done a great deed if any of you suffers on account of God. The Lord is graciously giving life to you, and you do not understand, for your sins have burdened you. And if you had not suffered on account of the name of the Lord, you would have died to God on account of your sins. [7] I say these things to you who are wavering about denial or confession. Confess that you have the Lord, lest by denying you be delivered into prison. [8] If the heathen punish their servants when one denies his own master, what do you think the Lord who has all authority will do to you? Put away these plans from your hearts, that you may always live to God."

9.29 The Twelfth Mountain

106.1 "And from the twelfth mountain, the white one, are believers such as these: they are like veritable babes for whom no evil enters in the heart, and they do not know what wickedness is but always remain in childlikeness. 2 Therefore those such as these will dwell in the kingdom of God without doubting, because ₁not with any₁ ᵃ act did they defile the commandments of God, but with childlikeness they remained all the days of their life in the same ₁state of mind,₁. ᵇ 3 Therefore as many as will remain," he said, "will also be like infants, having no evil; you will be more glorious than all who were previously mentioned, for all the infants are glorious in the sight of God, and *are* first in his sight. Therefore you *are* blessed, whoever removes wickedness from himself and puts on innocence. First of all, you will live to God." 4 After he finished the parables of the mountains, I said to him: "Sir, now explain to me about the stones that were taken out of the field and were put into the building instead of the stones that were taken out of the tower, and the round *stones* that were put into the building, and those that are still round."

9.30 The Stones from the Field

107.1 "Listen," he said, "also about all of these. The stones that were taken from the field and were put into the construction of the tower instead of those that were thrown away, they are the roots of the white mountain. 2 Therefore since the believers from the white mountain were all found innocent, the ruler of the tower commanded these to be put from the roots of this mountain into the construction of the tower. For he knew that if these stones go into the construction of the tower they will remain bright and none of them will turn black. 3 But ᶜ if he had added them from the other mountains he would have been obliged to visit the tower again, and to purge it, for all these have been found white, both those who believed ᵈ and those who are about to believe, for they are of the same kind. Blessed *is* this kind because it is innocent. 4 Now also listen about the round and

---

a. Literally "not in any"
b. Literally "wisdom"
c. The beginning of verse 3 is extant only in Latin.
d. The extant Greek is a fragment that picks up in the middle of a sentence.

bright stones. All these are also from the white mountain. [a] Listen then why they have been found round: Their riches have hidden them a little from the truth and darkened them, but they have never departed from God, nor has any evil word proceeded from their mouth, [b] but all equity and virtue of truth. 5 When therefore the Lord saw their minds, that they are able to favor the truth and to remain good, he commanded their wealth to be cut down, yet not to be completely taken away from them, that they may be able to do some good with that which was left them, and they will live to God because they are of a good kind. Therefore they were cut down a little, and placed in the construction of this tower."

9.31 The Round Stones

108.1 "But [c] the others which still remained round and were not fitted into the building, because they had not yet received the seal, were put back in their place, for they were found very round. 2 But this world and the vanities of their riches must be cut away from them, and then they will be fit for the kingdom of God. For it is necessary for them to enter into the kingdom of God for the Lord blessed this innocent kind. Therefore not one of this kind shall perish, for though one of them be tempted by the most wicked devil, and do some wrong, he will quickly return to his Lord. 3 I, the angel of repentance, judge you all happy who are innocent as babes, for your part is good and honorable with God. 4 But I say to you all, as many as have received the seal, keep simplicity and bear no malice, and do not remain in your guilt, or in remembrance of the bitterness of offenses. Be of one spirit and put away these evil schisms, and take them away from yourselves that the master of the sheep may rejoice over them. 5 And [d] he will rejoice if all are found healthy and none of them have fallen away, but if he finds some of them fallen away, woe it will be to the shepherds. 6 But if even the shepherds themselves are found fallen away, what will they say to the master of the flock? That they fell away because of the sheep? They will not be believed, for it is an unbelievable thing *that* a shepherd

---

a. The rest of the material in this section is extant only in Latin.
b. Eph 4:29
c. The first four verses of this section are extant only in Latin.
d. Verses 5 and 6 are extant in Greek.

should suffer something by his sheep; and instead they will be punished because of their lie."

9.32 The Shepherd's Final Exhortation

109.1 "Therefore,[a] amend yourselves while the tower is still being built. 2 The Lord dwells among men who love peace, for of a truth, peace is dear to him, but he is far away from the contentious and those who are destroyed by malice. Give back then to him your spirit whole as you received it. 3 For if you give to the dyer a new garment whole, and wish to receive it back from him whole, but if the dyer gives it back to you torn, will you accept it? Will you not at once grow hot and pursue him with abuse, saying, 'I gave you a whole garment; why have you torn it and given it back to me useless? And because of the tear which you have made in it it cannot be used.' Will you not say all these things to the dyer about the tear which he has made in your garment? 4 If then you are grieved with your garment, and complain that you did not receive it back whole, what do you think the Lord will do to you, who gave you the spirit whole, and you have returned it altogether useless, so that it can be of no use to its Lord, for its use began to be useless when it had been corrupted by you. Therefore will not the Lord of that spirit punish you with death, because of this deed of yours?" 5 "Certainly," I said, "He will punish all those whom he finds keeping the memory of offenses." "Do not then," he said, "trample on his mercy, but rather honor him that he is so patient to your offenses and is not as you are. Repent therefore with the repentance that avails you."

9.33 Explanation of the Marks on the Stones

110.1 "All[b] these things which have been written above I, the shepherd, the angel of repentance, have declared and spoken to the servants of God. If then you believe and listen to my words and walk in them, and correct your ways, you will be able to live. But if you remain in malice and in the memory of offenses, none of such kind will live to God. All these things that I must tell have been told to you." 2 The shepherd himself said to me, "Have you asked me about everything?" And I said: "Yes, sir." "Why then did you not

---

a. This section is extant only in Latin.
b. This section is extant only in Latin.

ask me about the marks of the stones which were placed in the building, why we filled up the marks?" And I said: "I forgot, sir." ³ "Listen now," he said, "about them. These are those who heard my commandments, and repented with all their hearts. And when the Lord saw that their repentance was good and pure, and that they could remain in it, he commanded their former sins to be blotted out. For these marks were their sins, and they were made level that they should not appear."

PARABLE 10

10.1 *The Final Vision*

¹¹¹·¹ After ᵃ I had written this book the angel who had handed me over to the shepherd came to the house in which I was, and sat on the couch, and the shepherd stood on his right hand. Then he called me and said to me: ² "I have handed you over," he said, "and your house to this shepherd, that you may be protected by him." "Yes, sir," I said. "If then," said he, "you wish to be protected from all vexation and all cruelty, and to have success in every good work and word, and every virtue of righteousness, walk in his commandments, which he gave you, and you will be able to overcome all wickedness. ³ For, if you keep his commandments, all the lusts and delight of this world will be subject to you, but success in every good undertaking will follow you. Take his perfection ᵇ and moderation upon you, and say to all that he is in great honor and dignity with the Lord, and that he is set in great power and powerful in his office. To him alone throughout all the world is given the power of repentance. Does he not seem to you to be powerful? But you despise his perfection and the modesty which he has toward you."

10.2 *Keep the Commandments*

¹¹²·¹ I ᶜ said to him: "Ask him himself, sir, whether since he has been in my house I have done anything against his command, to offend against him?" ² "I know myself," he said, "that you have done nothing and will do nothing

---

a. This section is extant only in Latin.
b. Literally "ripeness"
c. This section is extant only in Latin.

against his command, and therefore I am speaking thus with you, that you may persevere; for he has given me a good account of you. But you shall tell these words to others, that they also who have repented, or shall repent, may have the same mind as you, and that he may give a good account to me of them, and I to the Lord." ³ "I myself, sir," I said, "show the mighty acts of the Lord to all men, but I hope that all who have sinned before, if they hear this, will willingly repent, and recover life." ⁴ "Remain then," he said, "in this ministry and carry it out. But all who perform his commandments shall have life, and such a one has great honor with the Lord. But all who do not keep his commands are flying from their own life and against him, and they do not keep his commandments, but are delivering themselves to death, and each one of them is guilty of his own blood. But you I bid to keep these commandments, and you shall have healing for your sins."

10.3 Hermas and the Virgins

¹¹³·¹ "But ᵃ I sent these virgins to you to dwell with you, for I saw that they were courteous to you. You have them therefore to help you, in order to keep his commandments the better, for it is not possible that these commandments be kept without these virgins. I also see that they are with you willingly; but I will enjoin on them not to depart at all from your house. ² Only do you make your house pure, for in a pure house they will willingly dwell, for they are pure and chaste and industrious and all have favor with the Lord. If then they find your house pure they will remain with you. But if ever so little corruption comes to it they will at once depart from your home, for these virgins love no sort of impurity." ³ I ᵇ said to him: "I hope, sir, that I shall please them so that they may ever willingly dwell in my house. And ᶜ just as this one, to whom you handed me over, finds no fault in me, and these will find no fault in me." ⁴ He said to the shepherd, "I know that the servant of God wants to live and will keep these commandments, and will provide for the virgins in purity." ⁵ Upon saying these things, he handed me over again to the shepherd. And calling the virgins he said to

---

a. The first two verses of this section are extant only in Latin.

b. This first sentence is extant only in Latin.

c. The available Greek text runs from here through the middle of verse 5.

them,[a] "Since I see that you willingly dwell in his house I commend him and his house to you, that you depart not at all from his house." But they heard these words willingly.

10.4 *Walk in These Commandments and Live*

[114.1] Then he said to me: "Behave courageously in this ministry, show to every man the mighty acts of the Lord, and you shall have favor in this ministry. Whoever therefore shall walk in these commandments will live, and will be happy in his life; but whoever neglects them will not live, and will be unhappy in his life. [2] Say to all men who are able to do right, that they cease not; the exercise of good deeds is profitable to them. But I say that every man ought to be taken out from distress, for he who is destitute and suffers distress in his daily life is in great anguish and necessity. [3] Whoever therefore rescues the soul of such a man from necessity gains great joy for himself. For he who is vexed by such distress is tortured with such anguish as he suffers who is in chains. For many bring death on themselves by reason of such calamities when they cannot bear them. Whoever therefore knows the distress of such a man, and does not rescue him, incurs great sin and becomes guilty of his blood. [4] Therefore do good deeds, all you who have learned of the Lord, lest the construction of the tower be finished while you delay to do them. For the work of the construction has been broken off for your sake. Unless therefore you hasten to do right the tower will be finished and you will be shut out." [5] Now after he had spoken this he rose from the couch, and took the shepherd and the virgins and departed, but said to me that he would send back the shepherd and the virgins to my house.

---

a. The Greek text ends here.

– *The Martyrdom of Saint Polycarp Bishop of Smyrna*

SALUTATION

The church of God, the one temporarily residing in Smyrna; to the church of God, the one temporarily residing in Philomelium, and to all *gatherings*[a] of the holy and catholic church which reside in every place: mercy, peace, and love of God the Father and our Lord Jesus Christ be multiplied.

POLYCARP'S MARTYRDOM

1.1 We write to you, brothers, ₗthe account of₁[b] those who were martyred, even the blessed Polycarp, who, as if having put a seal *upon it* by his martyrdom, he ended the persecution. For nearly all the things that happened previously happened in order that the Lord might demonstrate to us again[c] a martyrdom in accordance with the gospel. **2** For he waited to be betrayed as also the Lord, in order that we also might be imitators of him not only looking out for ₗour own concerns₁[d] but also ₗthe concerns of our neighbors₁.[e][f] For true and steadfast love is not only to desire oneself to be saved, but all the brothers as well.

THE NOBILITY OF MARTYRDOM

2.1 Blessed and noble, then, *are* all the martyrdoms which, according to the will of God, have taken place. For we, being more reverent, must ascribe

---

a. Here "gatherings" is supplied as the following relative clause requires a referent.

b. Literally "according to"

c. The word ἄνωθεν can have the sense "from above" or "again." Lake and Ehrman use "from above"; Holmes uses "again." BDAG classifies in sense 4, "again."

d. Literally "that with respect to ourselves"

e. Literally "that with respect to those near"

f. Phil 2:4

the ruling power over all things to God. [2] For who would not admire their nobility[a] and patience and love of the Master?[b] When the whips had ripped them to shreds, so that even the inner veins and arteries, the inner work-ings,[c] of the flesh were visible, they endured so that even those standing around had mercy on *them* and wept. But some even attained to such a state of nobility that ₗnoneₗ[d] of them complained or groaned, clearly show-ing to all of us that in that hour, being tortured, the most noble martyrs of Christ were departing the flesh but rather that the Lord was standing beside speaking with them. [3] And paying attention to the grace of Christ they despised the tortures of the world, by one hour purchasing eternal life.[e] And the fire was cold to them, that *fire* of the cruel[f] torturers, for they had set before *their* eyes to escape from *the fire* which is eternal and never quenched, and with the eyes of the heart they looked above to the good things which are preserved for those who have endured, which neither ear has heard, nor eye has seen, nor has it entered into the human heart,[g] but it was shown by the Lord to them who were no longer humans but already angels. [4] Similarly, those who were condemned to the beasts also endured severe punishments, being stretched out on sharp shells[h] and being pun-ished with other various kinds of torture, that if it were possible the tyrant,

---

a. Lightfoot notes: "A favorite epithet as applied to martyrs," also listing *Mart Pol* 3 and 1 *Cl* 5 as further examples.

b. Lightfoot comments: "A not uncommon epithet of faithful slaves in classical writers."

c. Lightfoot describes the sense as "the internal structure and mechanism," pointing to a use by Plutarch "where likewise it is used of the natural processes of 'the house we live in.'"

d. Literally "not any"

e. ζωὴν Lake, Ehrman] κόλασιν Lightfoot, Holmes. Lake and Ehrman read, "by a single hour [of torture] purchasing eternal life" while Lightfoot and Holmes read, "at the cost of an hour exempting themselves from eternal punishment."

f. [6] ἀπηνῶν Lake] ἀπανθρώπων Lightfoot, Holmes, Ehrman. Holmes notes one edition (k, an 11–12th century manuscript) has ἀπηνῶν ἀπανθρώπων. The difference in translation would be from "cruel" (Lake) to "inhuman" (Lightfoot, Holmes, Ehrman).

g. [7] 1 Cor 2:9 (cf. Isa 64:4; 65:16)

h. [8] While κῆρυξ is typically translated "herald," "preacher," or "proclaimer," another well-attested sense, particularly in the context of torture, is that of a sharp sea-shell. BDAG defines a sense of κῆρυξ as "a large, sharp seashell, used in torturing." Lightfoot further notes that "Sea-shells, potsherds, and the like, appear not unfrequently as instruments of torture in the accounts of martyrdoms."

by continuous punishment, might steer them toward denial, for the devil[a] contrived many *schemes*[b] against them.

THE EXAMPLE OF GERMANICUS

3.1 But thanks be to God, for he had no power over any *of them*. For the most noble Germanicus encouraged their fears by the endurance which *was* in him, and he fought impressively with wild beasts. For when the proconsul wished to persuade him and asked *him* to consider his youth, he forcefully dragged himself to the beast, wishing to be released more quickly from their unjust and lawless life. 2 Therefore, because of this, the whole crowd, astonished by the nobility of the God-loving and God-fearing people of the Christians, cried out, "Away with[c] the atheists! Find Polycarp!"

THE EXAMPLE OF QUINTUS

4.1 But one, named Quintus, a Phrygian, recently having come from Phrygia, upon seeing the beasts turned coward. But it was this one who convincingly urged both himself and some others to come forward voluntarily. The proconsul, with much pleading, persuaded this one to take an oath and offer sacrifice. Because of this, therefore, brothers, we do not praise those who hand themselves over because the gospel ₍does not so teach₎.[de]

THE SEARCH FOR POLYCARP

5.1 But the most wonderful Polycarp, ₍when he first heard of it₎,[f] was not disturbed but intended to remain in the city. But the majority persuaded him to go out secretly, and he went out secretly to a small country house not ₍far removed₎[g] from the city, and he stayed with a few *friends*, night and day doing nothing else but praying on behalf of everyone, and the churches throughout the world, which was his custom. 2 And while praying,

---

a. Ehrman includes the last clause in *Mart Pol* 3.1 instead of in 2.4.

b. Here "schemes" is added to the object of the verb "contrive," following up on BDAG's translation of "devise stratagems against." A more generic translation could be Holmes' "many things," though also note Ehrman's "many torments."

c. Luke 23:18; Acts 21:36

d. Literally "does not teach this"

e. Matt 10:23; John 7:1; 8:59; 10:39

f. Literally "when first he heard"

g. Literally "being far distant"

he fell into a trance three days before his arrest. And he saw his pillow being consumed by fire, and turning he said to those with him, "I must be burned alive."

THE PURSUIT OF POLYCARP

6.1 And when those searching for him persisted, he moved to a different country house. And immediately *upon his departure* those searching for him arrived *at the first country house* and not finding *him*, they arrested two young slaves, one of whom being tortured confessed. **2** For indeed it was impossible for him to remain hidden, because those who betrayed him also belonged to his own household. And the captain of the police who by chance was given the same name, being called Herod,[a] was eager to bring him into the stadium so that he might fulfill [his own destiny][b c] becoming a sharer with Christ, and those who betrayed him should undergo the punishment of Judas himself.

THE ARREST OF POLYCARP

7.1 So, taking the young slave on the day of preparation[d] around dinner time, the mounted police and horsemen went out with their usual weapons, as if advancing against a rebel. And closing in on him later in the evening, they found him in a room upstairs, lying down. Now, from there he might have been able to depart for another place,[e] but he did not want to, saying, "The will of God be done."[f] **2** So, having heard that they had arrived, going down he talked with them. Those who were there were astonished at his

---

a. One of the features of *Mart Pol* and most martryology is to note coincidence between the subject (here Polycarp) and the life, betrayal, arrest, and crucifixion of Christ. Noting that the police chief arresting Polycarp was also named "Herod" is one of these coincidences. Whether this was actually true, or contrived to draw a tighter parallel between the arrest and death of Polycarp with that of Christ, cannot be known for sure.

b. Literally "his own lot"

c. There is a connection (cognate word group, κληρόω and κλῆρος) between the destiny/providence of one named "Herod" arresting Polycarp, and Polycarp's destiny/providence of being martyred (following Christ in death).

d. The "day of preparation" was Friday (hence Lake's translation, "Friday"). This is another parallel to the account of Christ's arrest and death.

e. Lightfoot notes this could also be translated "farm" or "estate" instead of the generic "field" or "place."

f. Acts 21:14; Matt 6:10; 26:42 (cf. Luke 22:42)

age and composure, and why there was so much eagerness to arrest an old man such as him. Then immediately he asked that food and drink be given to them at that time, whatever they might want. And he asked them to give him an hour, to pray without disturbance. ³ And when they consented, standing up,[a] he prayed, being so full of the grace of God, that for two hours he was unable to be silent. Those who heard were greatly astounded, and many regretted[b] that they had come against such a godly old man.

POLYCARP BROUGHT TO THE STADIUM

8.1 Now when he had ₍finally₎[c] finished[d] his prayer, having remembered everyone, even those whom he had only met, both important and unimportant, both honored and obscure, and the entire universal church throughout the world, the time came to leave. Sitting him down on a donkey[e] they led *him* to the city, being a great Sabbath.[f] ² And Herod the captain of the police and his father, Niketes,[g] went to meet him. And transferring him to the carriage,[h] they were sitting at his side *and* tried to persuade *him*, and were saying, "But what harm is it to say, 'Lord Caesar' and to offer a sacrifice and ₍so forth₎[i][j] and to be saved?" Now at first he did not answer them, but when they persisted he said, "I am not about to do what you advise me." ³ And they, being unable to persuade him, ₍began to malign him,₎[k][l] and ₍brought

---

a. Matt 6:5; Luke 18:11, 13

b. While μετανοέω typically means "repent" in the New Testament, this usage is more general (not in the context of active repentance from sin), hence the translation "regretted."

c. Literally "at last"

d. BDAG notes that ἐπεί may function as a "marker of time."

e. Matt 21:2; John 12:14. Another parallel with Christ's arrest and crucifixion.

f. John 19:31

g. Both Holmes and Ehrman transliterate the name "Nicetes," as does BDAG; here I follow Lake with "Niketes."

h. Lightfoot notes: "It was a stately, covered carriage, used by high functionaries or by ladies."

i. Literally "this following"

j. On καὶ τὰ τούτοις ἀκόλυθα, Lightfoot specifies "This clause appears not to be given as a forming part of the words of the magistrates," and points to a similar clause in *Mart Pol* 9. The easiest approach in translation, however, is to simply include the clause in the quotation.

k. Literally "began to speak harsh words to him"

l. ₍While translated as a plural ("they began to speak"), this is actually a singular, indicating that Herod (the more prominent of the group Herod and Niketes) was doing the talking. The plural is carried through from the backgrounded statement, "they were unable to persuade him."

him down so roughly, [a] that in coming down from the carriage *he* scraped his shin. And without turning around, as if he had experienced nothing, eagerly with haste he followed *them*, going to the stadium. The turmoil at the stadium was so great that no one could be heard.

"BE STRONG, POLYCARP"

9.1 But as Polycarp entered into the stadium, there was a voice from heaven,[b] "Be strong, Polycarp, and ˌbe a man,! [c] [d] And no one saw who had spoken, [e] but those of ˌour peopleˌ[f] who were present heard the voice. And then, when he was brought forward, there was a great uproar upon hearing that Polycarp had been arrested. 2 Therefore when *he was* brought forward the proconsul asked him if he was Polycarp, and when he admitted *it*, *the proconsul* tried to persuade *him* to recant, saying, "Have respect for your age" and ˌso forthˌ[g] as is their custom to say, "Swear by the fortune[h] of Caesar, repent, say 'Away with[i] the atheists!'" But Polycarp, with a serious face, looked at the whole crowd, those lawless heathens in the stadium, and shook his hand at them, both groaned and looked up to the heaven, *and* said, "Away with[j] the atheists!" 3 But when the proconsul persisted and said, "Take the oath and I will release you. Revile Christ." Polycarp responded, "Eighty-six years[k] I have served him and he has done me no wrong. How could I blaspheme my king who saved me?"

---

a. Literally "with haste brought him down"

b. Josh 1:6–7, 9; John 12:28 (cf. Deut 31:7, 23)

c. Literally "be courageous"

d. 1 Cor 16:13

e. Acts 9:7

f. Literally "us"

g. Literally "other such following"

h. There is some question as to whether the meaning "fortune" or "genius" is best here. Lake and Holmes translate "genius"; Ehrman translates "fortune." BDAG prefers "fortune." Lightfoot has an extensive note, preferring "genius": "This oath was invented under Julius Caesar, and caused some scandal at the time ... Under Augustus days were set apart for the worship of the genius of the emperor."

i. On *Mart Pol* 3.2, Lightfoot notes that both here and in *Mart Pol* 3.2 αἶρε means, essentially, "to take away to execute." The translation, however, follows the traditional translation of this phrase (Lightfoot, Lake, Holmes and Ehrman all agree), "Away with the atheists!"

j. See previous note (i)

k. There are two possible interpretations of the 86 years. These are either the years Polycarp has been alive (he is 86 years old) or they are a reference to how long he has been

POLYCARP STANDS HIS GROUND

¹⁰·¹ But again he persisted, and said, "Swear by the fortune of Caesar." He answered, "If you vainly imagine that I will swear by the fortune of Caesar, as you say, and you pretend to be ignorant of who I am, listen ₍plainly₎:ᵃᵇ I am a Christian. And if you wish to learn the account of Christianity, set a day and listen." ² The proconsul responded, "Persuade the people."ᶜ But Polycarp said, "You, perhaps, I should have considered worthy of an account, for we have been taught to render honor, ₍as is fitting₎,ᵈ to rulers and authorities under God,ᵉ *if* it does not hurt us. But to show *it* to them? I do not consider them worthy that a defense should be made before them."

POLYCARP IS NOT INTIMIDATED

¹¹·¹ And the proconsul said, "I have beasts; I will throw you to them, unless you repent." And he said, "Call for *them*! For repentance *is* impossible for us from better to worse, but *it is* goodᶠ to change from wickedness to righteousness." ² And again he said*ᵍ* to him, "I will cause you to be consumed by fire, since you despise the beasts, unless you repent." But Polycarp replied, "You threaten with fire that burns for a while, and after a little time is extinguished. For you are ignorant of the fire of the coming judgment and eternal punishment, reserved for the ungodly. But why do you wait? Bring about what you wish."

---

a Christian (his age is 86 plus some unknown amount of years). Lightfoot: "It is doubtful whether Polycarp means that he was a Christian from his birth and was now 86 years old, or that it was 86 years since he became a Christian." Lightfoot views Polycarp as being 86 years old as the more likely option.

a. Literally "with plainness"

b. Acts 2:29; 4:29, 31; 28:31

c. Lightfoot notes: "It is not clear with what motive the proconsul says this; whether (1) like Pilate, with a sincere desire to release the prisoner, or (2) as an excuse for his execution, knowing such an appeal to be useless."

d. Literally "according to what is fitting"

e. Rom 13:1; 1 Pet 2:13

f. Of this last clause, Lightfoot notes: "From the choice of words here ... it appears that this clause is intended to refer to the proconsul himself: 'It is you, not I, who have need to repent and to practice justice instead of cruelty.'"

g. Dialogue is implied by the context, so the word "said" is supplied.

POLYCARP TO BE BURNED

12.1 But saying these and many other *words*, he was filled with courage and joy, and his face was full of grace, so that not only did he not collapse,[a] having been disturbed by what was said to him, but instead the proconsul was dumbfounded and sent his own herald into the middle of the stadium to proclaim three times: "Polycarp has confessed himself to be a Christian." **2** Having said this by the herald, the whole crowd, both Gentiles and Jews[b] who were living in Smyrna, cried out with uncontrollable rage and a loud voice, "This is the teacher of Asia, the father of the Christians, the destroyer of our gods, who teaches many to not offer sacrifice or to worship." Saying this, they cried out and asked Philip the Asiarch[c] that he let a lion loose upon Polycarp. But he said it was ₌impossible₌[d] because he had already closed the animal hunts. **3** Then it seemed best to them to cry out with one mind that Polycarp should be burned alive. For the vision which had appeared to him on his pillow, when he saw it burning while praying, must be fulfilled. Turning to those faithful ones with him, he said prophetically, "I must be burned alive."[e]

THE FIRE IS PREPARED

13.1 These things, therefore, happened with such great speed, quicker than it can be said. The crowds immediately gathered together wood and kindling from the workshops and bathhouses, the Jews assisting especially eagerly in this, as is their custom. **2** And when the funeral pyre was prepared, he took off all his own clothes, and having loosed his belt, he tried also to take off shoes by himself, not having done this before, because each of the faithful always was zealous, which might touch his skin more quickly. For he had been adorned with every ₌good thing₌[f] because of *his* way of life, even before his martyrdom. **3** Immediately, therefore, the materials which had

---

a. Gen 4:5, 6

b. The translation "Judean" may actually be more appropriate, but "Jew" is used as the pair "Gentiles and Jews" is more familiar.

c. Lightfoot notes: "The Asiarch was the head of the 'Commune Asiae,' the confederation of the principle cities of the Roman province of Asia. As such he was the 'chief priest' of Asia (see *Mart Pol* 21) and president of the games." (Ed. note: "games" = "animal hunts").

d. Literally "not possible"

e. *Mart Pol* 5.2

f. Literally "fitting good"

been prepared for the fire were placed around him. And they were about to nail *him* as well, *and* he said, "Leave me like this, for he who allows *me* to endure the fire will allow *me* to remain in the fire without moving, *even* without the security from your nails."

POLYCARP'S PRAYER

14.1 And they did not nail *him* but they tied him, and having put his hands behind *him* and having been bound, just like a choice ram from a great flock for a sacrifice, a whole burnt offering, made ready *and* acceptable to God. Looking up to heaven, he said, "O Lord God Almighty, Father of your beloved and blessed child Jesus Christ, through whom we have received knowledge of you, the God of angels and powers and all of creation, and the whole race of the righteous, who live ⌊in your presence⌋.[a] **2** I bless you because you have considered me worthy of this day and hour, that I might receive a share among the number of the martyrs in the cup[b] of your Christ, to the resurrection of life[c] eternal, both soul and body, in the immortality of the Holy Spirit. May I be received among them before you today, in a sacrifice rich and acceptable, just as the truthful and trustworthy God has prepared beforehand, has revealed beforehand, and has fulfilled. **3** Because of this also, for all things, I praise you, I bless you, I glorify you through the eternal and heavenly high priest, your beloved[d] child Jesus Christ, through whom you with him and the Holy Spirit, *be* glory both now and for the ages to come. Amen."

POLYCARP NOT CONSUMED BY FIRE

15.1 And when he sent up[e] the "Amen"[f] and when he finished his prayer, ⌊the men in charge of the fire⌋[g] lit the fire and a great flame blazed out, *and* we beheld a miracle (those permitted to see) who also have been preserved

---

a. Literally "before you"

b. Matt 20:22, 23; Mark 10:38, 39. Also Matt 25:39, 42; Mark 14:36; Luke 22:42; John 18:11.

c. John 5:29

d. Matt 3:17

e. Lightfoot notes this word is used "of the offering up of prayer and speeding to the throne of grace."

f. 1 Cor 14:16

g. Literally "the men of the fire"

to report what happened to the others. ² For the fire, taking on the form of a vaulted room, like the sail of a ship filled by wind, ₍completely sur-rounded₎[a] the body of the martyr. And the body was in the middle, not like flesh burning, but like bread baking, or like gold and silver being refined in a furnace. For we perceived also ₍an intense fragrance₎[b] like the scent of incense[c] or some other precious spice.

POLYCARP KILLED

¹⁶·¹ Finally, then, the lawless ones, seeing his body could not be consumed by the fire, ₍ordered an executioner to go up and stab him₎[d][e] with a dagger. And having done this, a dove came out, and a large amount of blood, so that it quenched the fire, and the whole crowd was astonished that *there was* such a difference between the unbelievers and the elect. ² This one, who also was one *of the elect*,[f] the most wonderful martyr Polycarp, was in ₍our days₎[g] an apostolic and prophetic teacher, bishop of the catholic[h] church in Smyrna. For every word that departed from his mouth both was fulfilled and will be fulfilled.

THE PROBLEM OF POLYCARP'S BODY

¹⁷·¹ But the jealous[i] and envious and evil one who opposes the family of the righteous, having seen both the greatness of his martyrdom and his irre-proachable way of life from the beginning, both that he was now crowned

---

a. Literally "surrounded in a circle"

b. Literally "such a fragrance"

c. The NT only uses λιβανωτός in the sense of "censer," but the word is used in other literature as "incense" (BDAG).

d. Literally "having gone up, ordered an executioner to stab him"

e. Lightfoot helpfully explains: "It was the business of these 'confectores,' as their name implies, to give the 'happy dispatch' to wild beasts which had been hunted in the arena, and sometimes to human beings also. ... In the present instance the 'venationes' had only just ceased, and therefore a 'confector' was at hand. Otherwise he was not a functionary connected with the death by fire."

f. "Of the elect" is supplied based on the context of the previous verse.

g. Literally "the with respect to us days"

h. καθολικῆς Lake, Holmes, Ehrman] ἁγίας Lightfoot. Lightfoot explains his preference of "holy" (against "catholic"): "As a question of external authority, it would be difficult to decide between the two readings; but, as there would be a tendency to substitute καθολικῆς, I have witht hesitation given the preference to ἁγίας."

i. Lev 18:18; Sir 26:7; 37:11

with the crown of immortality and had won ₗa prize nobody could deny₎,[a] he took care that not even his poor body should be taken away by us, although many desired to do this and to have a share in[b] his holy flesh.[c] 2 So he secretly instigated Niketes, the father of Herod and brother of Alce,[d] to appeal to the magistrate not to hand over his body, "Lest," he said, "having abandoned the crucified one, they may begin to worship this man." And they said this, secretly instigating and insistently urging along the Jews, who also watched when we were about to collect it from the fire, not knowing that we will never be able to abandon the Christ, who suffered for the salvation of the whole world of those who are saved, the blameless for the sinful, or to worship anyone else. 3 For we worship this one, who is the Son of God,[e] but we love the martyrs as disciples and imitators of the Lord, and rightly so, because of their unsurpassable affection toward their own king and teacher. May we also become both their partners and be fellow disciples.

POLYCARP'S BODY BURNED

18.1 Therefore the centurion, seeing the dispute raised by the Jews, having placed it[f] in the middle, as is their custom, he burned it. 2 And so we finally took away his bones, more precious than costly stones and honored more than gold. We deposited them ₗin a fitting place₎,[g][h] 3 There, according to our ability, having come together in exultation and joy, the Lord will grant us to commemorate the ₗbirthday₎[i][j] of his martyrdom, both for the memory of

---

a. Literally "an undeniable prize"

b. Lightfoot clarifies with noting the fellowship would be "by gathering together about his grave for the purpose of common worship."

c. Lightfoot explains: "The diminutive is used in pity or tenderness, like σωμάτιον just above."

d. Lightfoot notes she is "A Christian of Smyrna; for she is doubtless to be identified with the Alce mentioned in Ign Smyrn."

e. Mark 3:11

f. Some translations complete the pronoun here with "the body" (Lake) or "Polcarp's body" (Holmes, Ehrman).

g. Literally "where it was also suitable"

h. While most lexicons gloss as "following," the idea is that of the logical next step or the following step; hence the typical translation here of "where it was suitable" or "at a suitable place." Cf. BDAG.

i. Literally "day birthday"

j. In this context, the martyr's birthday is the day of his death.

those who have already competed and of those who are about to *compete*; both *those* in training and *those* in preparation.

POLYCARP'S REWARD

19.1 ₗSuch is the account of₁[a][b] the blessed Polycarp, who, with those from Philadelphia, ₗwas the twelfth one martyred in Smyrna₁;[c] alone by all he is especially remembered, so that even by the heathens, in every place, he is spoken of. He was not only a well-known teacher, but also a distinguished martyr, whose martyrdom all desire to imitate; it happened in accordance with the gospel of Christ. **2** By his endurance he overcame the unjust magistrate and so received the crown of immortality; rejoicing greatly with the apostles and all the righteous ... he glorifies the almighty God and Father and he blesses our Lord Jesus Christ, the Savior of our souls and Shipmaster[d] of our bodies and Shepherd of the catholic church throughout the world.

CLOSING AND GREETINGS

20.1 Therefore you indeed requested[e] the events to be revealed to you at length, but we for the present have explained in summary by our brother Marcion. Therefore, having also heard these things, you send along the letter to the brothers further away,[f] so that those also may glorify the Lord, who appoints his chosen ones from his own slaves. **2** And to him who is able[g] to bring us all in his grace and gift, to his heavenly kingdom, by his one and only child, Jesus Christ, *be* glory, honor, power, *and* majesty ₗforever₁.[h]

---

a. Literally "such [is] that according to"

b. The phrase is idiomatic and translated variously. Lake has "Such was the lot of," Holmes "Such is the story of," and Ehrman "Such are the matters pertaining to."

c. Literally "was martyred twelfth in Smyrna"

d. The word κυβερνήτης is translated several ways. Lake has "Governor," Lightfoot and Holmes have "Helmsman," and Ehrman has "pilot." The sense is that of "captain," or one in charge of a vessel.

e. On the translation "requested," see BDAG 2b "request, ask."

f. Lightfoot notes that these are those "who are farther away," noting similarity with similar phrasing in *Ign Eph* 9.

g. Rom 16:25; Eph 3:20; Jude 24

h. Literally "into the ages"

Greet all the holy ones. Those with us greet you; as does Evarestus, who wrote this,[a] and his whole household.

THE DATE OF POLYCARP'S MARTYRDOM

21.1 And the blessed Polycarp was martyred on the second day of the first part of the month of Xanthicus, the seventh day before the calends[b] of March,[c] a great Sabbath, ₍at around 2:00 in the afternoon₎,[d] And he was arrested by Herod when Philip of Tralles was high priest, when Statius Quadratus was proconsul, but while Jesus Christ was reigning as king ₍forever₎,[e] to whom be glory, honor, majesty, and an eternal throne from generation to generation. Amen.

FAREWELL

22.1 We bid you farewell, brothers, who walk in the word of Jesus Christ, in accordance with the gospel, with whom be glory to God, both Father and Holy Spirit,[f] for salvation, that of his holy elect, just as the blessed Polycarp was martyred. May it be granted to us to be found in his footsteps in the kingdom of Jesus Christ. [2] Gaius copied these things from the papers[g] of Irenaeus, a disciple of Polycarp, who also lived in the same city as Irenaeus. And I, Socrates, wrote it down in Corinth, from the copies of Gaius. Grace be with you all. [3] And I, Pionius, wrote it out again from the copy mentioned above, after searching for it according to a vision, ₍in which the blessed Polycarp showed it to me₎,[h] as I will explain in what follows.[i]

---

a. Rom 16:22, another reference where the scribe sends greetings to those who will read his work.

b. The calends (other translations may have "kalends") are, according to BDAG, "the first day of the month in the Roman calendar."

c. Equivalent with modern-day February 23 (BDAG)

d. Literally "at the eighth hour"

e. Literally "into the ages"

f. The text translated "both Father and Holy Spirit" is omitted by Lightfoot and Holmes.

g. Most translations add "the papers" or "the writings" here as the exemplar of what is copied. Context dictates that something is copied, and that something came from Irenaeus. The plural article attached to Irenaeus shows this is referring to something associated with Irenaeus that is being copied, thus "the papers."

h. Literally "after the blessed Polycarp showed to me"

i. The implication of "what follows" is likely a sequel or further biographical information of Polycarp, and not the immediately following material.

Gathering the pages together, by this time nearly worn out by age, that the Lord Jesus Christ might also gather me together with his elect, into his heavenly kingdom, to whom *be* the glory with the Father and the Holy Spirit ₁forever and ever₁.[a] Amen.

FAREWELL (FROM THE MOSCOW MANUSCRIPT)[b]

23.2 Gaius, who was a disciple of the holy Polycarp, who also lived in the same city as Irenaeus, copied these things from the written work of Irenaeus. 3 For this Irenaeus, at the time of the martyrdom of the bishop Polycarp, was in Rome. He taught many, and many of his most excellent and orthodox writings are still in circulation, in which he remembers Polycarp, because he studied under him. And he ably refuted every heresy, and as he had received the ecclesiastical and catholic rule from the holy one, he also passed it along. 4 And he also says this: that one time the holy Polycarp met Marcion, from whom *come* those who are called Marcionites, and said, "Recognize us, Polycarp!" He said to Marcion, "I recognize you. I recognize the firstborn of Satan." 5 And this is also recorded in the written work of Irenaeus, that on the very day and hour in Smyrna when Polycarp was martyred, Irenaeus, being in the city of the Romans, heard a sound like a trumpet blast, saying, "Polycarp has been martyred." 6 Therefore, from these written works of Irenaeus, as was stated above, Gaius made a transcription. And from the copies of Gaius, Socrates in Corinth, and again I, Pionius, wrote it out from the copies of Socrates, according to a vision of the holy Polycarp, after searching for it. Gathering the pages together, by this time nearly worn out by age, that the Lord Jesus Christ might also gather me together with his elect, into his heavenly kingdom, to whom *be* the glory with the Father and the Son and the Holy Spirit ₁forever and ever₁.[c] Amen.

---

a. Literally "into the ages of the ages"

b. The "Moscow Manuscript" is a 13th-century manuscript of the Martyrdom of Polycarp presently located at the Library of the Holy Synod in Moscow.

c. Literally "into the ages of the ages"

— *Epistle to Diognetus*

INTRODUCTION

1.1 Since I perceive, most excellent[a] Diognetus, that you are very eager to learn the religion[b] of the Christians and are making altogether clear and careful inquiries concerning them, both what God they trust and how they worship him, *so that* they all both disregard the world[c] and despise death,[d] and they consider neither those supposed by the Greeks *to be* gods nor do they observe the superstition[e] of the Jews, and what *is* the deep affection they have for one another, and why then this new race or way of living has come to life now and not before; indeed I welcome[f] this eagerness of yours, and from God, who enables us both to speak and to hear; I ask him[g] to grant me to speak so that above all by your hearing *you* may become better and for you to hear thus, so that *I* may not regret what was said.

PAGAN RELIGIONS

2.1 Come[h] then, purge yourself from all the speculation which preoccupies your mind, and lay aside the habit[i] that deceives you and become a new person, as it were, from the beginning, as if becoming the hearer of a new

---

a. Acts 23:26; 24:3; 26:25

b. Sir 1:25; 1 Tim 2:10

c. 2 Macc 7:11, 23; Acts 17:30

d. Meecham comments: "The Christians' disregard of death would contrast the more strikingly with the wide and deep-seated fear of death which pervaded the ancient world."

e. Acts 25:19

f. Acts 24:3

g. Meecham notes: "The implication of the prayer is that man, apart from divine aid, is unable to speak about God."

h. Jas 4:13; 5:1

i. Meecham comments: "The term may refer to pagan 'custom' in general. But in view of the following polemic it probably relates to the 'habit' of idol worship."

277

statement just as you yourself also admit. Look not only with your eyes but also with your understanding what substance[a] or what form[b] they happen to have[c] whom you call and consider to be gods. ² Now, is not the one a stone, like that which we walk upon, and another is like bronze, no better than the vessels forged for our use, and another *like* a tree ⌊already⌋[d] rotted away,[e] and another *like* silver, having need of a person to guard *it* so that it might not be stolen, and another *like* iron ruined by rust,[f] and another *like* pottery, not looking any better than that which is made ready for the ⌊lowliest⌋[g] service. ³ *Are* not all these of perishable matter? Were they not forged by iron and fire? Did the sculptor not make one of them, and the metalworker one, and the silversmith one and the potter one? Before they were shaped by the skills of these *craftsmen* into their form, were not each of them, each still even now, to have been transformed? Might not the vessels now being made from the same matter, if they would have met the same craftsman, *be* similar to such as these? ⁴ Again, these things which now are being worshiped by you, would it not be possible *for them* to be made by human ⌊hands⌋[h] like the others? Are they not all mute?[i] Blind? Inanimate? Without feeling? Immovable? All of them rotting? All of them decaying? ⁵ These things you call gods, these things you serve, these things you worship,[j] and in the end you become just like them. ⁶ ⌊For this reason⌋[k] you hate Christians, because they do not consider those things to be gods? ⁷ For you, thinking and supposing to praise, do you not despise them even more? Do you not instead mock and insult them more, worshiping the

---

a. Heb 1:3

b. Isa 53:2; John 5:37

c. Tob 5:14

d. Literally "now also"

e. Job 15:7; Jas 5:2

f. Matt 11:7; Jas 5:3

g. Literally "most insignificant"

h. Literally "vessels"

i. Hab 2:18; 1 Cor 12:2 .

j. Meecham notes that this series can be read as either affirmative statements or interrogative statements. The translation above differs from the punctuation of the Greek text of Kirsopp Lake (which this translation generally follows) and treats them as affirmative statements. If translated as interrogatives (questions), the text would be, "These you call gods? These you serve? These you worship? In the end, you become just like them."

k. Literally "Because of this"

unguarded made of stone and clay but locking up those made of silver and gold by night and posting guards by day, so that they might not be stolen? [8] And the honors which you think you offer: if they are able to perceive, you instead punish them, and if they are unable to perceive, you worship them with blood and burnt fat, exposing *them*.[a] [9] These things?[b] One of you should suffer these things! He should endure it being done to himself! But not one person will willingly endure this punishment, for he has discernment and reasoning. But the stone endures,[c] for it has no discernment. Do you not then expose its discernment?[d] [10] And so about Christians not being enslaved to gods such as these, I would have many other things to say, but if anyone does not even think this *to be* adequate, I consider *it* unnecessary to say even more.

JEWISH SACRIFICES

[3.1] And next, about those[e] who do worship God not in the same *way* as the Jews, I think you are especially anxious to hear. [2] The Jews, therefore, because they abstain from this, the previously mentioned worship, may hold the opinion rightly to worship the one[f] God of ⌊the universe⌋[g] and think *him* Master, but if they offer him this worship in the same way as those already mentioned, they miss the mark badly. [3] For by making offerings to those things without feeling or hearing, the Greeks furnish an example of foolishness. So also these,[h] regarding God as having need, ought rather to consider they[i] may show foolishness, not godliness. [4] For the one who

---

a. The thought is that if these gods are not able to perceive or understand, then the very act of worshiping them and offering them blood and animal fat actually exposes them for what they are: inanimate and impotent objects.

b. This refers to the sacrifices (blood and burnt fat) mentioned previously.

c. The point here is that the stone (of which idols and false gods are made) endures because it is an object, not a person or divine being.

d. There is much behind the author's words here. The idea is that by offering sacrifices of blood and burnt fat, and by seeing that the stone idols have no response whatsoever, isn't the lack of response on the part of the stone proof that this is just a stone, and not a god?

e. Here the referent is to "the Christians," which most translations explicity mention.

f. 1 Cor 8:5-6

g. Literally "everything"

h. Here the referent is "the Jews"

i. On this clause, Meecham notes: "Two renderings are possible. ... (a) 'These (the Jews) ought rather to consider it folly maybe, not piety, thinking that they are offering these things to God as though He were in need of them.' (b) 'These (the Jews) ought rather to consider

made heaven and earth and all that is in them,[a] and who provides all to us
for which we have need, he himself would not have need of these things
which he himself grants to those who think to give them. 5 And indeed,
those who think to offer sacrifices to him by blood and burnt fat and whole
burnt offerings, and by these honors honor him; it seems to me to be no different than the one who shows the same generous zeal to the deaf images.
For some offer to those who are not able to have a share in the honor, and
others offer thinking to give to the one having need of nothing.

OTHER JEWISH PRACTICES

4·1 But indeed, the anxiety about their food[b] and the superstition about the
Sabbath and the arrogance[c] of circumcision and the pretense[d] of fasting
and new moon festivals,[e] I do not think you need to learn from me that
they are ridiculous and not worthy of an argument. 2 For then, the things
created by God for the use of people, some of which were created to be
received as good, others of which to be rejected as useless and superfluous,
how is this not forbidden? 3 And to falsely accuse[f] God, as forbidding to do
something good on the Sabbath day, how is this not impious? 4 And even
to boast of the mutilation of the flesh as a proof of election, as if because
of this being especially loved[g] by God, how is this not worthy of ridicule? 5
And attending to their stars and moon, to make observance[h] of months and
days, and making a distinction between the plans[i] of God and the changes
of the seasons, making some of which into feasts, others of which into
times of mourning according to their impulses. Who would consider this
an example of godliness and not of so much more foolishness? 6 Therefore
I think you have learned sufficiently that Christians rightly abstain from

---

that they are showing folly maybe, not piety, by crediting these things to God as though He
were in need of them.'"

a. Exod 20:11; Ps 146:6; Acts 14:15
b. Gen 25:28; John 4:32
c. Meecham notes: "'Excessive self-assertion,' implies both presumption and imposture."
d. Meecham notes this "stands primarily for dissimulation and cunning."
e. Col 2:16
f. Wis 1:11
g. Rom 11:28
h. Gal 4:10
i. Meecham comments: "Here the term relates to the divine 'ordering' of the seasons.".

the general silliness and deception and fussiness and pride of the Jews,
but do not expect to be able to learn from a person the mystery of their[a]
own religion.

CHRISTIAN PRACTICES

5.1 For Christians, neither by country nor language nor customs, are distinguished from the rest of humanity. **2** For they do not dwell somewhere
in their own cities, nor do they use some strange language, nor do they
practice a peculiar way of life. **3** This teaching of theirs has not been found
by any thought or reflection of inquisitive people, nor do they advocate
human doctrine, as some *do*. **4** But while living in both Greek and barbarian
cities, as each have obtained by lot, and while following[b] the local customs
both in clothing and in diet and in the rest of life, they demonstrate the
wonderful and most certainly[c] strange character of their own citizenship.[d]
5 They live in their own countries, but as aliens.[e] They share in everything
as citizens and endure everything as foreigners.[f] Every foreign country is
their country,[g] and every country is foreign. **6** They marry[h] like everyone,
they bear children, but they do not expose[i] their offspring. **7** They set a
common table, but not a *common* bed.[j] **8** They happen to be in the flesh but
do not live according to the flesh.[k] **9** They spend time[l] upon the earth, but
have their citizenship[m] in heaven.[n] **10** They obey the appointed laws, and in
their own lives they surpass the law. **11** They love all people and by all people

---

a. This refers to the Christians; "of the Christians' own religion."

b. 3 Macc 2:26

c. 1 Tim 3:16

d. 2 Macc 11:25; Acts 23:1; Phil 1:27

e. 1 Pet 2:11; Heb 11:13

f. Eph 2:19

g. Literally "theirs"

h. 2 Macc 14:25; 1 Cor 7:28

i. Meecham notes: "... exposure of (female) infants was common enough in the Greco-
Roman world to elicit protests from both Hellenistic Jews and Christian writers." Also note
an interesting parallel found in Deissmann, *Light from the Ancient East*, p. 167.

j. Heb 13:2–4

k. Rom 7:18; 8:4; 2 Cor 10:3; Gal 5:19

l. 2 Macc 14:23; John 3:22

m. The sense "to be a citizen" does not occur in the NT but is frequent in other literature.

n. Phil 3:20

are persecuted. [12] They are unknown[a] and they are condemned. They are put to death and they are made alive.[b] [13] They are poor and make many rich;[c] they lack everything and they have abundance[d] in everything. [14] They are dishonored[e] and in the dishonor glorified; they are slandered and they are vindicated. [15] They are reviled and they give blessing;[f] they are insulted and they give honor. [16] When doing good,[g] they are punished as evildoers; when punished they rejoice as having received life. [17] They are warred upon by the Jews as foreigners and they are persecuted by the Greeks, and those who hate *them* are not able to state the reason for their enmity.[h]

CHRISTIANS ARE THE SOUL OF THE WORLD

[6.1] But to put it simply, what the soul is in the body, this *is what* the Christians are in the world. [2] The soul is dispersed throughout all the limbs of the body, and Christians throughout the cities of the world. [3] The soul dwells in the body but is not of the body; and Christians[i] dwell in the world but are not of the world. [4] The invisible[j2] soul is guarded[k] in the visible body. And Christians are known as being in the world, but their religion remains invisible. [5] The flesh[l] hates the soul and fights against it, having been wronged in no way, because it is forbidden to indulge in its pleasures. The world also hates Christians,[m] having been wronged in no way, because they are opposed to its pleasure. [6] The soul loves the flesh that hates *it*, and its members, and Christians love those who hate *them*. [7] The soul has been locked up in the body, but it holds the body together,[n] and Christians are

---

a. Gal 1:22; Mark 9:32

b. 2 Kgs 5:7; 1 Pet 3:18

c. Gen 14:23; 2 Cor 6:10

d. 1 Cor 8:8; Phil 4:12

e. 1 Cor 6:10; Sir 3:10

f. 1 Cor 6:12; 1 Pet 3:9; Rom 12:14

g. Luke 6:9, 33, 35

h. John 15:25; Ps 34:19; 58:5

i. John 15:19; 17:11, 14, 16; 1 Cor 2:12; Gal 4:14

j. Col 1:16

k. Wis 17:15; Gal 3:23

l. Gal 5:17; 1 Pet 2:2

m. 1 John 3:13

n. The sense "to hold together, to sustain" does not occur in the NT, though it does occur in Wis 1:7. Meecham, following Lake, notes: "The idea that Christians are the preservative

restrained in the world as in prison, but they hold the world together. [8] The soul, *though* immortal, dwells in a mortal tent, and Christians temporarily dwell in corruptibility,[a] waiting for incorruptibility[b] in heaven. [9] When badly treated[c] in food and drink, the soul becomes even better, and Christians, when punished ₗdaily,ₗ[d] increase even more. [10] God has appointed them to so great a position, which is not right for them to reject.

PROOFS OF GOD'S COMING

[7.1] For as I have said this is no earthly discovery handed over to them, nor do they desire to guard a mortal thought so carefully, nor have they been entrusted with[e] the management of human mysteries. [2] But he, truly the Almighty and all-creating[f] and invisible[g] God himself, he established the truth and the holy and incomprehensible word from heaven among people, and fixed it firmly in their hearts, not as some might suppose, sending some servant to people or an angel or a ruler or one of those who manage earthly affairs or one of those entrusted with administration in heaven, but the craftsman and creator of the ₗuniverse,ₗ[h] himself, who created the heavens, who enclosed the sea within its own bounds, whose mysteries all the elements faithfully guard, from whom the sun has received the measure of the daily courses to observe, whose command the moon obeys to shine by night, whom the stars obey following the course of the moon, by whom all things have been ordered and set within limits[i] and put into subjection, the heavens and the things in the heavens, the earth and the things in the earth, the sea and the things in the sea, fire, air, abyss, the

---

of the world is common in early writers, a natural development of the figures used by Jesus of Christians as 'salt' and 'light.'" See BDAG sense 1.

a. 1 Cor 15:53

b. Meecham notes that "ἀφθαρσία is commonly employed by the apologists to denote God's manner of life as free from decay. Applied to Christians it suggests that their destiny was a divine existence of a similar quality."

c. The thought here is probably of voluntary fasting, not of an externally imposed punishment.

d. Literally "according to day"

e. 1 Cor 9:17

f. 2 Macc 1:24; Sir 24:8; 1 Pet 4:19

g. Col 1:15; Heb 11:27; 1 Tim 1:17

h. Literally "whole"

i. Isa 45:18

things in the heights, the things in the depths, the things in between; this one he sent to them. ³ Then indeed, as some people might consider, *did he send him* to rule in[a] tyranny and fear and terror? ⁴ Surely not, therefore, but in gentleness and humility, as a king sending a son *who is* a king, he sent *him* as God, he sent *him* as a human to humans, he sent *him* as one who saves, he sent *him* as one who persuades without force, for violence does not belong to God. ⁵ He sent as one calling, not pursuing; he sent as one loving, not judging. ⁶ For he will send him as judge, and who will endure his coming?[b] *Do you not see them*[c] being thrown to beasts so that they might deny the Lord and they are not overcome? ⁸ Do you not see to the degree that more are punished, the more others increase? ⁹ These things do not seem *to be* the works of people; these things are a miracle of God, these things *are* proofs of his coming.[d]

GOD REVEALED THROUGH HIS SON

8.1 For what person really had knowledge of whatever God is before he came? ² Or do you accept the vain and foolish statements of those pretentious philosophers, some of whom said God is fire (they who are about to go *there*, they give this the name God), and others water, and others some of the elements which were created by God. ³ ⌊Although⌋[e] if any of these reasons are acceptable, it would also be possible for each one of the remaining creatures to likewise be declared God. ⁴ But these things are the illusion and deceit[f] of the swindlers. ⁵ But no people have either seen[g] or known *him*, but he revealed himself. ⁶ And he was revealed through faith, by which alone one is permitted to see God. ⁷ For God, Master and Creator of the universe, who made all things and arranged *them* in order, is not

---

a. Meecham notes ἐπί here is likely either of object or purpose, supplying "to rule in" as a possible translation.

b. The manuscript has a lacuna at this point, with a marginal note from the copyist noting the break was also in his exemplar.

c. Here "Do you not see them" is supplied based on the conjecture (followed by most editions) that the words οὐχ ὁρᾷς, "do you not see," are missing.

d. Matt 24:9

e. Literally "And yet indeed"

f. 2 Tim 3:13

g. Though the verb in Greek is singular in person, the referent ("people") is a collective. In English, it is best to translate using the English plural "have seen."

only benevolent but also even-tempered. [8] Certainly this one indeed was always so, and is, and will be, kind[a] and good and free from anger and true, and he alone is good.[b] [9] And having in mind a great and unspeakably wonderful plan, he communicated it to his child alone. [10] Therefore, ₁so long as₁[c] he kept it in secret and guarded his wise plan, he seemed to neglect us and be unconcerned. [11] But since he was revealed through his beloved child and made known all the things prepared from the beginning, at the same time he gave *everything* to us, both to have a share in his benefits and to see and understand, who of us would ever have expected these things?

THE GOODNESS OF GOD

[9.1] Therefore having already planned everything by himself with his child until the former time, he permitted us to be carried along by disorderly impulses as we willed, being led away by pleasures[d] and lusts. Not at all taking delight in our sins, but being patient, not approving of the previous season of unrighteousness, but creating the present time of righteousness that, in the previous time, being exposed as unworthy of life by our own deeds, now may be considered worthy by the goodness of God, and making it known that by ourselves *it is* impossible to enter into the kingdom of God, we might be able *to enter* by the power of God. [2] But since our unrighteousness was fulfilled and it became perfectly clear that its reward, punishment and death, was waiting, and the time came which God had appointed to make known at last his goodness[e] and power. Oh, the surpassing kindness and love of God! He did not hate or reject or bear a grudge against us but he was patient and bore with *us*, having mercy he himself experienced our sin, he himself gave his own son, a ransom[f] on our behalf, the Holy for the lawless, the innocent for the guilty, the righteous for the unrighteous, [g4] the incorruptible for the corruptible, the immortal

---

a. Mark 8:18

b. Meecham notes: "Not mere repetition. The second statement amplifies the first. 'God is good ... yes, he alone is good' (the sole source of goodness)."

c. Literally "as long as"

d. 4 Macc 5:23; Titus 3:3

e. Titus 3:4–5

f. Mark 10:45; Eph 1:6; 1 Tim 2:6; Titus 2:14

g. 1 Pet 3:18

for the mortal. ³ For what else than that one's righteousness could cover up[a] our sin? ⁴ In who *else* than in the Son of God alone could our lawlessness and ungodliness possibly be justified?[b] ⁵ Oh, the sweet exchange! Oh, the fathomless creation! Oh, the unexpected[c] benefits that the lawlessness of many should be concealed in the one righteous, and righteousness of the one should justify many lawless. ⁶ Therefore, having brought to light in the former time, the inability of our nature to attain life, and now having shown the Savior's ability to save even the powerless,[d] for both *reasons* he wanted us to believe in his goodness to consider him nourisher, Father, teacher, counselor, healer, mind, light, honor, glory, strength, life; not anxious about clothing and food.

BECOMING AN IMITATOR OF GOD

10.1 If you also strive after this faith and first receive knowledge of the Father ...[e] ² For God loved[f] humankind, for whom he made the world, to whom he subjected all things, the things in the earth, to whom he gave reason, to whom *he gave* mind, to whom alone he allowed to look above to him, whom he made in his own image,[g] to whom he sent his one and only[h] son, to whom he promised the kingdom in heaven and will give *it*[i] to those who love him. ³ And having *this* knowledge, what joy do you think will fill *you*, or how will you love the one who so first loved[j] you? ⁴ But by loving *him* you will be an imitator of his goodness. And do not wonder that a person is able to be an imitator of God. He is able, if *God* wills[k] it. ⁵ For in not oppressing[l] one's neighbors, and to not desire to have even more than the weaker ones, and not being rich and compelling those more inferior,

---

a. Jas 5:20
b. Rom 3:26, 30; 4:5; 8:30, 33; Gal 3:8
c. Wis 17:14; 3 Macc 3:8
d. Luke 18:27
e. Lake and Holmes note there is a lacuna in the text here.
f. John 3:16; 1 John 4:9
g. John 3:34; 2 Cor 8:11
h. 1 John 1:9; John 1:14, 19; 3:16, 18
i. Matt 5:3; 1 Pet 1:4; 2 Thess 1:5
j. 1 John 4:19
k. Acts 18:21
l. Wis 15:14; 17:2; Sir 48:12

is being happy, and in these things no one is able to imitate God but these things *are* outside the majesty[a] of that one. [6] But whoever takes up the burden[b] of his neighbor, who wishes to do good to another who is worse off in that he is better off, who having received the things from God, he holds on to these things, providing to those in need. He becomes a god to those who receive *them*; this one is an imitator of God. [7] Then you will see, while being upon the earth, that God lives in heaven; then you will begin to speak of the mysteries[c] of God; then you will both love and admire those being punished because they will not deny God; then you will condemn the deceit and the deception of the world, when you know *what is* the true life in heaven, when you despise the apparent death[d] in this place, when you fear the true death, which is kept for those who will be condemned to the eternal[e] fire, which will punish those handed over to it until the end. [8] Then you will admire those who endure the temporary fire for the sake of righteousness and will consider *them* blessed when you know that[f] fire.[g]

BECOMING PARTNERS

[11.1] I do not say anything strange, nor do I seek information in an unreasonable manner, but being a disciple of apostles, I am becoming a teacher of Gentiles.[h] That which was delivered I worthily administer to those who are becoming disciples[i] of the truth. [2] For who, having been rightly taught and having become pleasing to the Word,[j] does not seek to learn exactly what has been clearly shown by the Word to disciples, to whom the Word appeared,[k] making these things known, speaking with boldness not being

---

a. 2 Pet 1:16

b. Gal 5:2

c. 1 Cor 14:2

d. Wis 3:2

e. 2 Pet 2:9; 4 Macc 12:12; Matt 18:8; 25:41; Jude 7

f. This refers to the eternal fire mentioned in verse 7.

g. The text indicates a lacuna here.

h. 1 Tim 2:7; 2 Tim 1:11

i. 1 Tim 2:4

j. The word λόγος occurs multiple times in this section. In Lake's translation there is a distinction between "word" and "Word"; but it seems unlikely that such a close distinction would be intended by the author in such close proximity. It is better (as with Meecham and Holmes) to understand them all as "Word."

k. John 7:26; 16:29; 18:20

understood by unbelievers, but being explained to disciples who being considered faithful[a] by him learned the mysteries of the Father. [3] For this reason he sent the Word, so that he might be made manifest to the world, who was dishonored by the chosen people, preached by apostles, he was believed in by Gentiles.[b] [4] This one, who from the beginning[c] appeared to be new yet was found to be old, and always is young as he is born in the hearts of saints. [5] This one, the eternal one, who today is considered a Son, through whom the church is made rich and grace being unfolded, is multiplied among the saints, granting understanding, making known mysteries, announcing seasons, rejoicing over the faithful, being given to those who seek, who do not break the oath of faith nor overstep the boundaries of the fathers. [6] Then the fear of the Law is sung and the grace of the Prophets is known and the faith of the Gospels is established and the tradition of the apostles is guarded and the grace of the church exults. [7] If you do not grieve this grace, you will understand what the Word says through whomever he desires, whenever he wishes. [8] For as much as we were caused to express with hard work by the will of the commanding Word, through the love for the things revealed to us we become partners with you.

CONCLUDING THOUGHTS

[12.1] Which *truths*, having read[d] and having heard with eagerness, you will know whatever God grants to those who love *him* rightly, who become "a paradise of delight,"[e] raising up in themselves a flourishing, fruitful tree, who are adorned with various fruits. [2] For in this[f] garden the tree of knowledge and the tree of life[g] have been planted. But the tree of knowledge does not destroy; disobedience destroys. [3] For what is written is not insignificant, that from the beginning God planted the tree of knowledge and the tree

---

a. John 20:27
b. 1 Tim 3:16
c. 1 John 2:13, 14; John 1:1
d. Acts 8:30; 2 Macc 15:39
e. Gen 3:24; 2:15; Joel 2:3; Isa 51:3; *PsSol* 14:2–3
f. This refers back to the "paradise of delight," which is a reference to the Garden of Eden.
g. Gen 2:9

of life in the middle of paradise,[a] showing life through knowledge. Those[b] who did not use it in purity, they were stripped naked from the beginning by deceit of the snake. 4 For life is not without knowledge, and certain knowledge is not without true life; therefore ₍they have been planted next to each other₎.[c] 5 The apostle, seeing the power of this, blaming the exercise of knowledge without the truth of the commandment *which leads* to life, he said "Knowledge puffs up, but love builds up."[d] 6 For he who thinks to know anything without knowledge *which is* true and validated by life knows nothing. He is deceived by the snake, no longer loving life. But he who has knowledge with fear and who seeks after life, he plants in hope,[e] expecting[f] fruit. 7 Let your heart be knowledge and *your* life the true[g] *and* comprehended word.[h] 8 Bearing this tree and picking *its* fruit, you will always harvest the things desired by God, which the snake cannot touch and deceit cannot defile, and Eve is not corrupted but a virgin is trusted.[i] 9 And salvation is made known, and apostles are given insight, and the Lord's Passover advances, and the seasons are brought together and harmonized in order,[j] and teaching the saints, the Word rejoices, through whom the Father is glorified, to whom *be* the glory ₍forever₎,[k] amen.

---

a. Gen 2:9

b. Holmes translates "our first parents."

c. Literally "both have been planted nearby"

d. 1 Cor 8:1

e. 1 Cor 9:10

f. Sir 6:19; Jas 5:7

g. Eph 1:13; Col 1:5; 2 Tim 2:15

h. John 5:24

i. 1 Tim 2:13–15

j. The two clauses here are problematic; the translation above ("and the seasons are brought together and harmonized in order") follows Meecham. See also the extended note in Holmes, who reads "and the congregations" instead of "and the seasons."

k. Literally "for the ages"